For Marta and Elena

Contents

List of figures, images and table   vi
Abbreviations   vii
Acknowledgements   ix
Authors' note   xi

Part One: Democracy, planning and localism

one	Introduction	3
two	Democratic renewal, planning and housing growth in England	9
three	Localism and its antecedents	23
four	Community-based planning and plans	37

Part Two: Capacity building and community-based planning

five	Ashford and its strategic planning context	53
six	Power, capacity and collaborative planning	69
seven	Community dynamics and planning	79
eight	Capacity building and outreach	95

Part Three: The interface with policy actors

nine	Connectivity at the policy–community interface	109
ten	Working with local government	123
eleven	Working through intermediaries	137
twelve	Community-based plans	149
thirteen	Planning's critical interface	163

Part Four: Neighbourhood planning, leadership and democratic renewal

fourteen	Responsibility and responsiveness: lessons from parish planning	181
fifteen	Conclusions	191

References   199
Index   211

List of figures, images and table

Figures

5.1	The County of Kent, and Ashford	58
5.2	Ashford borough	60
5.3	Ashford growth proposals	62
5.4	The principal urban extensions	63
7.1	The case study parishes	81

Images

5.1	New housing at Chilmington Green, July 2010	64
7.1	The village of Great Chart	90
8.1	The picture-postcard village of Woodchurch	97
8.2	Pluckley	103
12.1	The village hall at Appledore	150
13.1	The village of Wye	166
13.2	The Archbishop's Palace at the 'outlying' village of Charing	169

Table

12.1	Parish plan content	153

Abbreviations

ACRE	Action with Communities in Rural England
ACRK	Action with Communities in Rural Kent
AONB	Area of Outstanding Natural Beauty
CASE Kent	Community Action South & East Kent
CPRE	Campaign to Protect Rural England
DEFRA	Department for Environment, Food and Rural Affairs
DPD	Development Plan Document
GADF	Greater Ashford Development Framework
GDP	Gross Domestic Product
GOSE	Government Office for the South East
KALC	Kent Association of Local Councils
LDF	Local Development Framework
LSP	Local Strategic Partnership
RCC	Rural Community Council
RPG	Regional Planning Guidance
RSS	Regional Spatial Strategy
SEEDA	South East England Development Agency
SLA	Service Level Agreement
SPD	Supplementary Planning Document
UK	United Kingdom
UTF	Urban Task Force
VDS	Village Design Statement
WKPS	Weald of Kent Preservation Society

Acknowledgements

First and foremost we are grateful to the parish clerks, chairs, council members and other Ashford borough residents who welcomed us into their homes in 2009 and early 2010. Officers of Ashford Borough Council and many other policy, delivery and support groups also gave their time generously. The maps that appear in Chapters Five and Seven were drawn by Sandra Mather at the University of Liverpool. Interview transcription was undertaken by Eileen Crotty. Detailed comments on an earlier version of this text were provided by both an anonymous reviewer and Professor Stephen Owen, to whom we are extremely indebted, and who we hope are able to detect some improvements in logic and content. Finally, this research would not have been possible without the financial support of the Economic and Social Research Council (RES-062-23-1650) or the patience of friends and family. Claire and Manuela deserve special mention, as do Nick's daughters, Marta and Elena, to whom the book is dedicated. But the usual disclaimer applies: despite all of this help and support, any errors or misrepresentations in this text remain the responsibility of the authors.

Authors' note

Neighbourhood planning is an exploration of planning practice at the critical interface between communities and public sector policy actors, and how the relationships that take root at that interface can contribute to effective planning, widening ownership of the process and helping to broaden agreement around development decisions or forestalling major conflict. The term 'neighbourhood planning' is used in this book as a generic descriptor for the planning activities of community groups, encouraged by the promise of greater policy influence to migrate from parish planning (in the presented case study) to the production of 'neighbourhood development plans' in England. Although the term 'community-based planning' is used, sometimes interchangeably, with the 'neighbourhood' alternative, it is important to note that the former carries the heavy weight of assertion: that planning is genuinely a shared endeavour and undertaken by 'the community', while the latter merely suggests the locating of activity at a particular geographical scale (although the borders of neighbourhoods can be difficult to define, being bound up with the notion of community and its spatial uncertainties). Such debates are not a primary focus of this book. *Neighbourhood planning* is principally concerned with the groups (within wider communities or in neighbourhoods), sometimes self-selecting and sometimes claiming local mandate, who lead on the production of community-based plans. In this book, these groups are represented by parish councils and the general narrative of community-based planning offered deals with the particular experience of parish planning in rural and semi-rural locations within the Ashford Growth Area in Southern England. This experience provides a context for thinking about the neighbourhood development plans that now form part of the United Kingdom (UK) coalition government's localism agenda, and also for investigating the highly questionable contention that community-based planning is itself synonymous with 'participative governance', signalling both a new partnership between 'people and planning' and the prospect of higher-quality, more consensual, development outcomes.

This note serves to clarify the purpose of this book. It is not a 'how to' manual on neighbourhood planning, nor is it a study of community action. Rather, it is an analysis of the way in which groups traditionally *subject to* planning decisions interface with local policy actors and become a more integral part of the planning process. More particularly, *Neighbourhood planning* is concerned with the opportunities created by greater connectivity: connectivity *within* communities, giving claims of community leadership legitimacy; and connectivity *between* actors, establishing the sorts of linkages that suggest a collaborative approach to the policy-making process. An attendant concern is the role of 'professionals' within this same process: the degree to which neighbourhood or community-based planning can be uncoupled from strategy, versus the need for a renegotiated 'meta-governance' arrangement in which local spatial planning retains a clear leadership role. The book emerged from a research project that sought to unpack a range of issues relating to formal and informal planning activity at the community/neighbourhood scale. It tries to attach broader meaning to such activity and is written for those who engage with the practice of planning and also those, including academics and students, who have an interest in the purpose and function of the system, and in future practice.

The structure of the book is explained more fully in Chapter One. Those parts that are predominantly concerned with the Ashford study trace the 'organic' process of community-based planning from inception, through expansion and capacity building, to engagement with policy communities and attempts, ultimately, to connect to formal strategies and influence decision taking (although these later stages are not a feature of the life cycle of all community-based planning). The original purpose of the research on which this book builds was to examine the arrangements for planning at the community scale, looking in particular at the networks through which the community is constituted and which are also used to draw people into planning activity, lending capacity to the aspirations of lead groups. Networks were also conceived as the means by which these groups connect to policy actors, sometimes directly and sometimes indirectly. Moreover, the research sought insights into effective local governance processes, in which public planning might seek reconciliation with private ambition, or achieve greater community buy-in.

But the research, and therefore this book, was fired by a much broader interest in the dynamics of community action, in community governance and in the relationship that neighbourhood groups are able to establish with local government structures. It connects recent and ongoing debates in England to the major themes of meta-governance, power, responsibility and the responsiveness of local state apparatus to community needs. Drawing on theories of communicative action and collaborative planning, on social network theory and the precepts of social capacity building and network power, *Neighbourhood planning* offers a detailed account of planning at a community scale, examining 10 local groups, which, over a period of years, attempted to connect with policy-making structures, make their voices heard and influence the direction of change in their villages and neighbourhoods.

Part One
Democracy, planning and localism

ONE

Introduction

The Conservative–Liberal Democrat coalition government, in power since the UK General Election of 2010, has presented 'localism' as a clear alternative to over-centralised decision making – and as an antidote to dissatisfaction with existing democratic processes – to be delivered partly through a return of responsibility to 'town halls' and partly through a localisation of planning to the community, or 'neighbourhood', level. But localism is not a new concept and 'modern' community-based planning and activism have been around for many decades. Wherever neighbourhoods face the prospect of unsettling or disturbing change, or wish to grasp an opportunity, champions of 'community interest' will emerge, assuming or claiming the right of representation or mobilising support for a local response. In this way, structures of leadership take shape and the foundations for community planning are laid. The established apparatus of national and local government has not always embraced communities' enthusiasm for a greater say in decision making, viewing neighbourhood groups as a hindrance rather than as partners in policy making. But in England in recent years, such groups have received a warmer welcome. Under recent Labour governments, the structures of community representation – especially parish councils – were actively promoted through a series of Local Government Acts, which gave tacit support to new community governance arrangements, and aimed to better connect them to policy making.

But during 13 years of Labour government, the expectations raised were not always matched by delivery. Planning and local government reforms seemed to take divergent paths, with the former centralising powers in regional and national bodies while the latter were laced with the rhetoric of 'communities in control'. There was a perception that too many decisions were taken upstream, leaving local government and neighbourhood groups to squabble over detail while the big strategic decisions descended on communities from above. Government targets, including housing delivery targets, seemed to neutralise the potential of networked community governance, frustrating the ambitions of local people, politicians and professionals. All seemed to be of the view that something insidious was happening in Whitehall and the regional government offices; something that was inherently undemocratic. Such frustrations gave the Conservative Party an opportunity to popularise, again, its advocacy of a 'small state' and eventually bring forward a programme of reforms as the senior partner in the UK coalition government, indecisively elected to power in May 2010. The coalition moved quickly on its promise to dismantle the apparatus of obviously centralised priority setting. Regional planning was effectively scrapped by ministerial decree within a few weeks of the General Election, freeing local authorities from housing and related planning 'targets'. Localism became the mantra of the coalition, a better way to govern, and a new formula for local cooperation. Henceforth, planning would be predicated on this approach, with communities and neighbourhoods being given a bigger role in making the frameworks that would determine future patterns of development, service delivery and land use. neighbourhood development plans, it emerged, would become building blocks for bottom-up planning (DBIS, 2010, p 25).

The robustness of this central plank of the localism agenda is dependent on community groups being able to reconcile their ambitions with local government, connecting their plans with those of paid and trained professional planners and their political leaders. This has never been an easy task, as prior experience demonstrates. And it is the experience of planning at the interface with communities (or 'neighbourhood groups') that provides the critical focus of this book. In 2009, a project began in the Ashford Growth Area in Southern England, which examined the arrangements and challenges for planning at the neighbourhood scale. It had three main aims.

The first related to the community groups themselves, to governance arrangements and to involvement in planning activity. There is an unfortunate assumption that the residents of villages or urban neighbourhoods get together and plan in much the same way as paid professionals, only with less skill and finesse, and with fewer resources. But the objectives of formal planning, to achieve outcomes that balance competing interests, thereby maximising the benefits of development, are seldom shared by community groups, who 'plan' with the intention of raising awareness of local issues and emerging threats. The professionals are assumed to rise above narrow interests, whereas such interests frequently drive community action. So in the first instance, the research was concerned with the objectives of community planning and with the constitution of local groups, especially how these groups form networks of shared interest. In this book, the conceptual basis for thinking about how groups operate and how they extend themselves is set out in Chapter Six – which follows on from four chapters (Chapters Two to Five) dedicated to context (conceptual, mechanical and geographical) – while the discussion of local arrangements begins in Chapter Seven and continues into Chapter Eight. It is important to note that community-based planning is rooted in core groups, who assume the leadership responsibilities described above. But for such planning to flourish, as a shared endeavour, it needs to connect with broader interests. It may even need to seek external support. How all this happens is examined in a series of chapters devoted to communities, community-based planning and capacity building.

The second aim was to gain a detailed view of the interface between local groups, planning authorities and service providers. This had two elements:

- first, how connections are made between parish councils and policy actors, particularly whether these connections are direct (with parishes understanding themselves to be part of a hierarchical system of bottom-up policy making), or whether they are indirect, mediated, links in which the language and aspiration of community action are somehow reconciled with formal policy processes;
- second, how the products of community-based planning are used and what particular modes of use tell us about local aspiration for community action, and also professional perspectives on its value to spatial planning.

The discussion of network dynamics noted above is expanded in Chapter Nine to cover the mechanics of 'interfacing' with community-based planning and plans. Policy actors are initially conceived as existing (with community groups) within potentially shared networks, although cut off or distanced from communities because of poor communication or because of a culture of professional leadership that undervalues local input. It is also the case, and this point is introduced in a broader discussion towards the end of the book, that local policy actors have been locked into a primary relationship with strategic bodies and tasked with delivering outputs specified at higher levels. This has been the traditional meta-governance arrangement in planning policy, with local actors guided by strategic decisions taken above them – an arrangement that has reduced the importance attached to local input, resulting in a system that is largely orientated towards achieving outputs fixed at higher levels. The network perspective on community cohesion is extended into an analysis of interaction with local policy actors, with direct linkages (and how communities work with public officials) investigated in Chapter Ten before indirect, brokered, links are examined in Chapter Eleven. The question in both of these chapters is how community groups work with paid professionals: whether they simply lobby (like as a pressure group) or whether they seek a formal role in the machinery of policy development. This same issue is picked up again in Chapter Twelve, which looks into the use made of community-based plans, internally and externally. But it is also at that point that the purpose of community planning is re-examined: whether its intent is to concentrate local energies around campaigns and projects, or whether a place at the high table of decision making is sought. These are important questions as the analysis moves to reflect on the formalised neighbourhood planning apparatus of the UK coalition government, and they are addressed as our broader analysis of 'communities at the policy interface' is brought to a close.

In the research, a third and final aim tied the first two together, examining the extent to which the processes of community-based planning connect to traditional policy-making structures, suggesting a mode of planning practice that is more alive to aspiration, more locally focused and more likely to deliver reconciliation between neighbourhood projects and broader strategic visions. Using the recent rhetoric of neighbourhood planning, do such processes lead to a new contract between 'people and planning',[1] producing a less combative planning process and delivering broader ownership of final decisions? The research sought evidence, in a sense, of the big prize of collaborative planning: consensus built upon a growing sense of inclusion and empowerment. It failed to deliver this, but highlighted instead an emerging debate on the purpose of planning and especially the place of leadership within a planning process being rescaled to the local and neighbourhood levels. Therefore, the final purpose of this book is to offer reflections on planning at its 'critical interface', between communities and policy actors. The process of reflection begins in Chapter Thirteen, with observations drawn directly from the discussions with local people and professionals in the Ashford Growth Area. It is taken forward in the final two chapters, which pick up the key themes of responsiveness and responsibility in local planning and policy making, and which end by highlighting some of the realities of the 'neighbourhood planning' agenda in England and its orthodox, but not necessarily problematic, attachment to rather standard governmental arrangements in which leadership remains an executive responsibility.

This book is research based and concerned with learning from investigations undertaken in and around Ashford, developing a critical understanding of community-based planning, framed within a broader view of collaborative rationality and its limits. Using research into the recent experience of community-based planning in England, it reflects on the lessons for future planning at the neighbourhood scale. As a research text, this book has tightly drawn boundaries (although these have been pushed out to encompass a broader context) and does not rehearse debates on the nature of community or the difficulties of defining neighbourhood entities. It is not a manual on neighbourhood planning practice, nor does it offer a formula for producing community-based plans. But it emphasises the lessons that can be drawn from recent community planning experiences in England, which is timely given the intention to rescale local planning practice and formalise the role of community actors. It is important to gauge the limits of neighbourhood planning in delivering the participative governance that so many politicians now subscribe to, and to separate investment in new frameworks from effort to realise genuine partnership through establishing close working relationships between 'people and planning'.

Note

[1] The means of 'building a new relationship between people and planning' was the subject of the Town and Country Planning Association Conference in March 2011, although this aim has been set out repeatedly by many bodies since the publication of the Skeffington Report (1969) on people and planning.

TWO

Democratic renewal, planning and housing growth in England

The political and policy framework in which local government operates, and which determines its relationship with key policy actors and with community and interest groups, has been heavily amended over the last 15 years. Successive Labour governments from 1997 drove forward a programme of state modernisation and local government reform that appeared to challenge executive forms of 'top-down' control, by centralised departments and agencies, giving momentum instead to collaborative and participative forms of 'governance', characterised by bottom-up input into decision-making processes by a range of local actors from across the public, private and voluntary sectors. Labour's reform programme, carried forward in several pieces of major legislation, sought to respond to an undercurrent of frustration with the failed politics of the 1980s and 1990s, which seemed locked within a model of executive, centralised power. The New Labour project from 1997 onwards was one of devolution of responsibility for decision making away from the centre, to new political structures in the Home Nations and the English regions and to existing local state apparatus, albeit revamped, modernised and better connected to broader community interests. The passing of responsibility further down the 'chain of command' to community governance structures, later dubbed 'communities in control', was famously claimed as evidence of government's commitment to 'double devolution' (Mulgan and Bury, 2006).

The legislation designed to realise a 'governance shift' in the UK, and specifically in England, is reviewed later in this chapter. But before dealing with the detail of local government reform, and contrasting its objectives with those of systemic changes to planning, it is useful to explore the roots of this process. All British governments, including the current coalition government, have during the period outlined above, appeared to concede power to the local state and to communities. Power has seemingly bled from the public to the private realm, bringing those who were previously governed into the process of government. There is, of course, a broader debate as to whether power has in fact relocated, or whether the emergent apparatus of collaborative governance is designed simply to appease local populations without bringing any genuine change. This question is examined through the lens of neighbourhood planning in England, but here we begin with a focus on the drivers of democratic and functional renewal, rooted in what has been viewed as a 'disaggregation' of state and society, ongoing in Western democracies for at least the past three decades.

Individualisation and 'agencification': drivers of local government reform

Democratic modernisation has been linked to the rise of individualism (Featherstone, 1990; Beck, 1994; Baumann, 1996; Misztal, 1996; Giddens, 1998, 2000; Castells, 2000), which has also given impetus to globalisation in the form of a new interconnectedness that often bypasses, or operates despite of rather than because of, state control. The global flows of objects, information and people, aided by advances in communications, information and transport technologies, have led to an expansion of individual choices, pluralisation of worldviews and liberalisation of lifestyles (Misztal, 1996, p 54). Many observers of these trends (including those cited above) suggest that the global 'diffusion' of culture and identity has been generally incompatible with the traditional, homogenised community structures of the early post-war period, and has led to their replacement by more disaggregated and heterogeneous patterns of sociability.

This has had two important consequences. First, it has served to 'detraditionalise' society, weakening adherence to convention, leading to a questioning of traditional forms of authority. Social behaviour and social trends are increasingly influenced by the ability of individuals to access information and key into global cultures. This has, second, created a highly differentiated society and eroded universal accord with the manifestos and policies of principal political groupings (representing the broad social divisions of the past) and with conventional ideas of citizenship, social contract and allegiance. Within this context, and because of the diversity of needs and agendas expressed by a complex array of community, interest and pressure groups, policy making and the act of government have become increasingly challenging and cross-sectoral endeavours. In the past, good government was thought to be a matter of administering to a relatively stable society, in which aspirations were broadly similar and needs could be easily categorised. In this context, strategies and specific policy options could be set out by experts and decided upon by a privileged political class.

But policy formation, planning and service delivery have since become increasingly complex and cross-sectoral, dependent on collaboration between state and non-state actors (Marsh and Rhodes, 1992). The process of individualisation has generated myriad conflicting interests, articulated through community and interest groups, each with their own priorities and agendas. The initial reaction to this apparent distancing of state from a changing society was to increase the variety and number of centralised state agencies, in the hope that these would be better able to reflect and respond to increased diversity. However, their inability and disinclination to engage directly with a reconfigured society, during the formulation of their strategies and policies, only compounded the emergent difficulties. In order to understand and contend with these challenges, it seemed clear that it was the process of government, and not merely its structure, that needed to be recast, potentially in a more *iterative* mould (Sørensen and Torfing, 2008).

In the UK, the large government departments that once constituted the state were gradually broken down into a bewildering array of autonomous agencies, each with their own political remit (Cloke et al, 2000). This disaggregation process has been referred to as 'agencification' and was initiated in the early 1980s by the first of the Thatcher-led Conservative administrations (Rhodes, 1997, p 54). In a process that Rhodes (1997, pp 17-19) refers to as 'a hollowing out of the state', the New Right sought to confine the role of central government to strategic 'direction', while public policy formulation and implementation were delegated to autonomous agencies. As Jacobsson and Sundström (2007, p 5) observe, 'by hiving off "smaller", recurrent and technical matters into executive agencies, politicians have more time for "big" and "important" matters'. The delegation of power to these agencies was driven by the assumption that public policy is best formulated and implemented in 'zones' away from political influence (Manor, 1999). The process of agencification, however, did not change the basic modus operandi of government: the principles of reliance on professional and scientific expertise, and of limited interaction with interest groups or with wider communities, were retained: it merely resulted in a highly fragmented governance structure and an increase in the number of decision-making state organisations (Pollitt et al, 2004).

The rarity of interaction between decision makers and end users (ie, interest and community groups) meant that outcomes often failed to meet either aspirations or needs (Stoker, 1998). The failure and apparent disinclination of political parties to work with communities at the coalface in any meaningful or open-ended way amplified frustration with the conventions of mainstream politics and heightened general dissatisfaction with the functioning of democracy and of government. 'Democratic renewal' therefore became the goal of those who recognised a need for the state to rebuild contact with citizens and thereby regain lost legitimacy (Giddens, 1998, 2000).

Disaggregation of state and society: the rise of social and political networks

One consequence of this disaggregation of state and society, nationally and locally, has been the increased incidence of network-based interaction between a growing number of diverse actors with a view to addressing mutual and cross-sectoral concerns. However, those operating within the traditional 'public' realm (within government, and in services to the public) and 'non-public' realm (comprising private, voluntary and community actors) have tended to form their own discrete groupings (Newman, 2007), with public realm networks coalescing into 'policy communities' and non-public networks into 'interest groups' (Marsh and Rhodes, 1992), with the latter having only weak connections to the former (Marsh et al, 2009, p 621).

This is because, within policy communities, membership and entry are highly restricted, reserved to civil servants, professionals and sometimes academic advisors. These communities operate in an insular environment, with little external or 'unqualified' input. There is generally predetermined 'consensus' with regard to ideology, values and policy preferences. In contrast, interest groups are less functional and more reactionary in nature, forming as a result of consultation or opposition to particular decisions (emanating from a policy community) or broad concerns – developmental, technological and so on. Membership is often unrestricted and therefore can encompass a diverse range of ideologies, values and preferred actions. Although some level of consensus exists around a particular issue (which is key to the existence of the network, binding individuals together), overall cohesion is frequently weak and the network typically disbands once the issue has been determined. Such networks may form in response to planning and land-use policy, sometimes growing out of established community governance infrastructure, as we will see later in this book.

In the recent past – and in the present – it is this lack of interaction between public and non-public realm actors (expressly, policy communities and interest groups) that can frequently fuel local conflict. The frequency of such conflict, and acceptance of its underlying cause in the failure to deliver an iterative mode of government, was a driving rationale for the state's attempts to modernise and reinvent itself from the 1990s onwards. According to Fung and Wright (2003), the broader societal forces described above found expression in a new era of conflictual politics in which the decision-making arena became a battleground in which opposing groups attempted to impose or overturn decisions, fighting to win rather than seeking consensus or compromise around alternative or innovative solutions. This was seen, in the UK, to have had a negative effect on planning and especially on development decisions affecting housing and infrastructure. Reconnecting different communities, and overcoming the big barriers between public and non-public actors, became a key part of democratic renewal.

Harnessing the power of networks for positive planning and democratic renewal

There is today a large body of analysis and writing (key among which are the works of Forester, 1989, 1999; Innes, 1995, 2004; Healey, 1997, 1999; Innes and Booher, 1999, 2000, 2003; Innes and Gruber, 2001) that contends that collaborative or participatory forms of governance, which break down traditional barriers, can be used to ease conflict and encourage innovative decision making. Collaborative governance, which brings together different actors, has been defined as 'an arrangement where public agencies directly engage non-state stakeholders in a collective decision-making process that is formal, consensus-orientated and deliberative and that aims to make or implement public policy or manage public programs or assets' (Ansell and Gash, 2007, p 544). The collaborative approach is underpinned by (and also advocates) the principles of participation, empowerment, partnership working and networked action. It relies on innovative forms of consultation or dialogue as a way of transforming adversarial relationships into more cooperative ones. This differentiates it from traditional forms of government as it requires 'communities of interest' to be directly included in the decision-making process, rather than decisions being made unilaterally, based solely on the input of advice from experts (Futrell, 2003), and originating therefore in policy communities alone. The approach is said to encourage a 'collective' process, predicated on good communication between policy agencies, service providers and 'stakeholders' (ie, user communities), with the last of these having real responsibility for policy outcomes. Collaborative planning, and its onward linkages into networked governance, is examined in greater detail in Chapter Six.

Democratic renewal appears dependent on increased public political involvement and should, in theory, be achieved through the introduction of more participative forms of government and by making citizens 'stakeholders', as opposed to passive recipients, in the policy-making and service delivery processes (Somerville, 2005, p 135). This perspective is supported by a simple logic: that it is communities themselves who are best placed to inform decision making on matters that directly concern them. They have the clearest understanding of the local context, familiarity with matters of primary concern to community members and knowledge of possible priorities. With regard to functional renewal, increased public political involvement has been considered the most 'natural means' of developing bottom-up solutions, which would impart a sense of shared commitment and joint ownership of issues and resultant policies (Owen et al, 2007, p 51). There are clear advantages attendant on pursuing such 'subsidiarity': community-based planning projects can unite residents, leading to increased participation, better social cohesion and the transformation of individual human capital into shared social capital (Falk and Kilpatrick, 2000), leading to a variety of sometimes unpredictable, but often positive, social innovations. New insights open up, and new knowledge is garnered, which can then be used as the basis of bespoke solutions (policy and programme 'distinctiveness' in recent parlance) to local issues and improve cost-effectiveness in local service delivery (Owen, 2002a, p 81), in part through voluntary action (Moseley, 2000a). Building policy from the bottom up provides a means, moreover, of responding to the major social challenges of our time and of blurring the once-fixed borders between the state and society.

Democratic renewal in the UK

In a 1998 White Paper – *Modern Local Government: In Touch with the People* (DTLR, 1998) – the first Labour government under Tony Blair outlined its objective to devolve power and resources to the level of local political structures and to communities themselves (Doak and Parker, 2005, p 24). The White Paper set out a renewed vision for local authorities, stating that 'community leadership is at the heart of the role of modern local government and councils are the organisations best placed to take a comprehensive overview of the needs and priorities of their local areas and communities and lead the work to meet those needs and priorities' (DTLR, 1998, para 8.1). It also outlined the role that community governance structures – in the form of parish councils – would play in these new governance arrangements: by connecting local authorities with communities in their areas, 'parish councils can work in partnership with their principal council to bring government closer to the people and to establish the decentralised delivery of local government services' (DTLR, 1998, para 2.14). The 2000 Local Government Act enshrined these proposals in law and local authorities were required to produce 'Community Strategies', which were to provide an area-wide integrated strategy, coordinate service delivery and allow local stakeholder interests to shape decision making and policy outcomes (Doak and Parker, 2005, p 24). This was government's answer to the disconnection between policy and interest communities and, in order to facilitate the production of Community Strategies, local authorities were encouraged to establish local strategic partnerships (LSPs) comprising the representatives of local residents, business interests, and public and voluntary organisations. The Community Strategy was also to indicate how the authority and its partners would work together to deliver against key priorities (Owen et al, 2007, p 52). The actions that different partners would need to take, to realise the vision of the Community Strategy, were then to be committed to in a Local Area Agreement. This was Labour's new community framework, with planning providing just one, albeit critical, part of the jigsaw.

A further local government White Paper – *Strong and Prosperous Communities* – eight years later, reiterated the role of local government as leader and as place-shaper (DCLG, 2006, p 52). It also set out a new framework for the strengthening of strategic leadership within local areas, as well as mechanisms to bring together existing, and sometimes disparate, local partners (2006, p 2). The White Paper set out proposals to give local people a greater say in shaping the places in which they live and local public services they receive (2006, p 22). The consequent Local Government and Public Involvement in Health Act 2007 sought to promote empowerment and rejuvenate civic and democratic participation. The empowerment agenda was brought out and reiterated even more explicitly in a 2008 community empowerment White Paper, which sought to introduce a 'duty to promote democracy' for local authorities (DGLG, 2008a, pp 24-6), complementing a 'duty to involve', introduced in the Local Government and Public Involvement in Health Act 2007. A range of actions were triggered by the White Paper, including the provision of publicity lauding the positive benefits of voting, participating in elections and undertaking civic roles. This same community empowerment White Paper envisaged the passing of 'power into the hands of local communities' (DCLG, 2008a, p 1). Government followed up on this vision by issuing 'community power packs' (DCLG, 2008b) and with a detailed response to its White Paper consultation (DCLG, 2009a) and a *Communities Progress Report* (DCLG, 2009b) outlining plans to deliver greater local control through a review of Public Service Agreements. This emphasis on control is important. The Labour administration was operating in a favourable economic context in which expenditure on public services was growing in real terms. Rather than seeking to blur the line between community and public actors, government was looking to identify leaders, pluck them from communities and assign them a place in decision making. The LSPs, with their representatives from community networks, were indicative of this strategy. Individuals were encouraged to cross over into control structures, but services operated in much the same way as they had done in the past. Broader connectivity to whole communities of users remained weak and community governance structures, including the parish councils, gained few additional powers.

Integrated spatial planning and the reform of the planning system

However, the local government reforms introduced by the Labour administrations between 1997 and 2010 ostensibly sought to encourage 'bottom-up' working arrangements and empower place communities in an attempt to promote more inclusive forms of governance and decision making (Moseley, 2002, p 387). The LSPs provided a mechanism with which to take forward this strategy. Concurrently, entire policy areas were presented as being open to community input, not only individual policies and interventions, but also at a strategic level. Government set out its intention to make the planning system work for communities, redirecting it away from its traditional focus on matters of land-use control, to a more widely constituted spatial planning practice (Nadin, 2007). Its future role would be to integrate and coordinate the plans and strategies of service delivery agencies, bringing together strategic perspectives on land development, environmental concerns, resource use, transport, economic development, social infrastructure and so on (Healey, 1997). Planning was presented as occupying a central position in the emergent local government environment: as corporate strategy as much as land-use planning. In order to do so, it needed to be recast and connected to the apparatus of local government reform described above.

The reinvention of planning in the 2000s was seen by some as constituting a fundamental shift, pushing the system to centre stage in government's renewal of local democracy. And even those who viewed the changes as more cosmetic conceded that the idea of 'spatial planning' differed considerably from that of land-use planning in terms of institutional context, content and process. From an institutional perspective, traditional land-use planning was largely undertaken by public actors in isolation from others, and resultant planning documents were 'owned' by councils alone, whereas spatial plans were to be prepared 'collaboratively' by a range of actors, with the plan achieving collective ownership (RTPI, 2001). From a content perspective, the objectives of land-use plans concentrated exclusively on development matters and were required to be in general conformity with higher-level strategies, whereas spatial planning had the scope to encompass social, economic and environmental objectives and although general conformity with higher-level strategies remained a requirement, regard also needed to be given to the objectives of the community strategies (Owen and Moseley, 2003, p 447) produced by the array of different actors forming the LSP. And finally, the process of land-use planning had been guided by top-down prescriptive strategies prepared by planning professionals, whereas spatial planning supposedly embraced 'bottom-up strategy formulation', with the planning system linking in with local governance and community group agendas (Nadin, 2007, p 53). Its intended centrality to the local governance agenda was clear.

At the beginning of the 2000s, reform of statutory planning was initiated by the recommendations of a 2001 planning Green Paper – *Planning: Delivering a Fundamental Change* (ODPM, 2001a) – which asserted that the planning system in England and Wales had become too complex, too slow and failed to engage communities (2001a, pp 3-4). It advocated the need for a planning system that was inclusive and encouraged participation in the preparation of new planning documents and also a more streamlined system, orientated to business needs and better able to promote economic prosperity (2001a, p 6). The Green Paper fleshed out the likely shape of future planning: it indicated that the spatial planning approach would operate at two levels – local and strategic – with the former focused on community planning and engagement and the latter on promoting economic growth and speed (2001a, p 14). After considerable debate, the Planning and Compulsory Purchase Act 2004 brought the vision of the Green Paper to reality: it introduced a two-tiered statutory system comprising Regional Spatial Strategies, to be prepared by regional planning bodies, and local development frameworks (LDFs), prepared by local authorities.

But this legislation strengthened two opposing aspects of the system. On the one hand, it created a clearer strategic focus, switching from advisory regional planning guidance (RPG) to mandatory Regional Spatial Strategies, which would henceforth provide much of the key content of LDFs. This legal status had previously been reserved for

Structure Plans, which were now abolished. These plans had been seen, in some quarters, as too conservative, defending local interests against national targets and exacerbating the nation's housing shortage (outlined in a report for the Treasury and published in the same year as the new Act: Barker, 2004). The Regional Spatial Strategies, with their 15- to 20-year time horizons, provided a critical framework for the scale and distribution of new housing and employment as well as substantial support for forward infrastructure delivery (which could be coordinated by the regional bodies).

But on the other hand, the legislation also sought to bring planning onto the front line of government's efforts to renew local democracy and create clear and constant lines of communication between community actors and policy makers. At the local level, development plans were substituted by LDFs, comprising a suite of documents that, collectively, set out a vision for an area grounded in clear objectives for the development and improvement of the physical environment and a delivery strategy that would, eventually, link into the Community Strategy and the Local Area Agreement. Critical among these documents was the Statement of Community Involvement (see DCLG, 2004). This was to set out how and when planning authorities intend to consult local communities and other stakeholders. It was this component, more than any other, which imported the essence of local government reform and devolution objectives into the statutory planning system (Morphet et al, 2007, p 9). Local planning authorities were now required to 'front load' consultation, so that it began at the earliest stages, allowing communities to participate in the development and formulation of plans, strategies and policies. Later legislation sought to strengthen the governance–planning link. The Sustainable Communities Act 2007, for instance, indicated that strategies and policies contained within LDFs should be 'shaped' directly by Sustainable Community Strategies, as opposed to merely having 'regard' to them, which was the instruction given in the Planning and Compulsory Purchase Act 2004 (Morphet et al, 2007, p 44).

Hence, planning was to be regarded as just one of the means by which a community's wider ambitions could be realised. This shifting context had significant implications. If planning was subservient to wider community interest, and if community networks could define this interest, then a much stronger link between the ambitions of place communities and the actions of policy actors seemed achievable. However, the wider planning context appeared to conspire against this 'new localism' in the policy and governance process. England in the late 1990s and throughout the 2000s lived in the shadow of an ever-present growth agenda, fuelled by a combination of social change, economic prosperity and international migration. Despite the rhetoric of local control, national policy was punctuated by an insistence that bigger objectives needed to be pursued, which would deliver the major infrastructure needed to support growth and bring about a 'step change' in national housing supply. Despite their new role in a process of spatial planning, communities would need to accept a significant degree of top-down control, conceding power to the regions and the centre. This view was most strongly articulated in housing and planning White Papers published in 2007 (DCLG, 2007a, 2007b).

Planning in the 'shadow' of growth

England in the late 1990s faced unprecedented levels of household growth, first highlighted in projections that revealed significant social shifts, specifically shrinkage in average household size, suggesting that more households would form in the decades ahead. This analysis held steady throughout the 2000s, and back in 1997 it helped to set the tone of future political debate. The focus in 1997 was not on how this growth should be managed, but simply where the new homes should go. Labour convinced the electorate that it had a clear strategy for accommodating new growth in the cities and would pursue a renaissance agenda, creating urban areas in which people would want to live. During its first period in office, the focus was on outlining the parameters of this renaissance, and a task force report was commissioned to show how the government might realise its vision (UTF, 1999). It soon became apparent, however, that not all growth could be absorbed within the existing urban footprint. There would need to be planned expansions of some existing centres, and perhaps also growth on hitherto greenfield sites. Taking a cue from RPG, government put together a strategy for planned growth in the South of England that also brought together existing ideas on addressing the needs of 'restructuring' housing markets further north and in the English midlands. But in order to deliver concentrated growth in four major 'Growth Areas' in the south, including Ashford in Kent (and later, a number of strategic growth points and eco-towns), it needed to strengthen the hand of regional planning, creating a system in which it would be possible to direct housing to strategic development sites in support of the 2003 'Communities Plan' (ODPM, 2003). Regional housing targets were, at that time, a feature of the existing planning system. They were fixed in RPG. But as the name suggested, this was merely 'guidance' for local authorities. There was no legal screw that government could turn to oblige authorities to meet the targets. Therefore, government sought to overhaul the system, substituting guidance with strategies that would formally become part of local planning frameworks: not just material considerations but binding elements of a local plan. The reforms instituted in 2004, and outlined above, did just that. The new Regional Spatial Strategies became part of the LDFs. Authorities were obliged to integrate them into local planning. In this way, government had far greater control over compliance with housing targets. For its critics, the system had just become much more top-down.

The targets became a source of frustration in many areas. Growth was a *fait accompli*. The only question was how it would be managed. The 2007 housing White Paper (DCLG, 2007a) reiterated the challenge: the need to deliver 240,000 homes each year for the following 20 or so years. Legislation following on from the 2007 planning White Paper (in the form of the Planning Act 2008) placed power over infrastructure into the hands of an 'independent' commission, tasked with facilitating growth through major projects that could support the expansion of existing centres and also lead development into new areas.

The handling of the growth agenda, through a combination of top-down targets and a transfer of powers to unelected bodies, needs to be viewed against the backdrop of burgeoning enthusiasm for community control, which was itself a response to the big social and political trends highlighted at the beginning of this chapter. The Labour governments appeared to appease this enthusiasm, but they also insisted on creating planning structures that bypassed communities in pursuit of broader and sometimes contested national interests. By 2009/10, frustration with the approach was reaching its zenith. The Conservatives, returning to traditional political territory, were able to argue that this interest should be negotiated for at a neighbourhood level, and that a planning approach predicated on its understanding of genuine 'localism' (see Chapter Three) would renew trust in politics and deliver the homes that 'almost every local community' wants to see (DBIS, 2010, p 25). Echoing the views of Fung and Wright (2003), the incoming coalition government argued that it was Labour's conflictual strategy that communities were frustrated by and not the growth challenge itself or the patent need for additional homes, which the previous government's strategy had clearly failed to deliver. Still, the coalition government faces the same fundamental problem of marrying local aspiration with regional and national priority, set by the context of growth. Its answer, so far, has been to replace the regional planning apparatus and housing targets with an untested system of incentives, designed to encourage communities to accept the case for development.

The politics of social change

Fundamental changes in the fabric of society have given impetus to government reform, gradually broadening support for a departure from a reliance on representative modes of government to more iterative approaches at the local level. In England, Labour administrations after 1997 pursued a strategy of 'subsidiarity', moving some decision-making powers out of the public realm and handing them to strategic partnerships. New life was also breathed into existing community governance structures (see Chapter Four) although with uncertain intent. A key narrative during the 2000s was the increasingly awkward relationship between government's programmes of democratic renewal and planning reform. The Labour governments progressively centralised and strengthened the role of strategic decision making in planning, doing so in a context of unprecedented growth and therefore need for development.

Strategic planning was removed from county control and repositioned at a higher level. The legitimacy with which regional and national bodies directed policy and made interventions (especially around housing and infrastructure), appearing to side-step local representatives, was constantly questioned, becoming a source of brooding resentment in some villages and neighbourhoods. The planning system appeared to challenge the right and the capacity of communities to define local interest and either respond to it themselves or work with local partners towards 'consensus-orientated' interventions (Ansell and Gash, 2007). Moreover, planning appeared to be swimming against a much stronger tide of democratic renewal, ignoring the many interests now staking a claim in the policy process. Both regional planning bodies and Labour's Infrastructure Planning Commission were the targets of sharp criticism in the run-up to the 2010 General Election. Both became early casualties of the subsequent war on 'undemocratic' centralisation, with the incoming coalition government placing apparently greater trust in the capacity of local structures to deliver against the growth agenda.

Means and not ends were the points of political contention in 2010. New planning processes at the neighbourhood and local levels were viewed as the means of delivering additional housing, in full partnership with community groups. Growing local development plans from the bottom up, in the name of 'localism', became the mantra of coalition planning by the end of that year, evolving community planning processes and entering a new world of 'neighbourhood' plans in which growth would be regularly embraced rather than rejected by affected communities.

THREE

Localism and its antecedents

The 'localism' of the UK coalition government is rooted in some of the ideas introduced in the last chapter. It connects with a participatory and collaborative (or 'iterative') understanding of how the structures of governance should function (Corry and Stoker, 2002; Stoker, 2004, 2007) and, like other collaborative approaches that operate at the interface with 'communities of interest', is viewed as an antithesis to centralised control, exerted through executive decision-making structures. With individualisation and globalisation as its backdrop, it is presented as the means to achieve democratic renewal and to rebuild trust between policy communities and communities of interest. Local control over service delivery and community input into policy making seem to have an obvious meaning, and these are not new ideas. In the mid-2000s, Labour's programme of local government modernisation was frequently described as a form of 'new localism' (Davies, 2008, p 3). And during that period, others regularly noted the turn towards localism that appeared inherent in UK public policy (see Morphet, 2004a; Coaffee and Headlam, 2008). Localism is not new, but has deep roots in state theory and particularly in those discourses that focus on the relationship between local and central government and the extent to which the former can be freed from centralised control while still working to secure success in big government initiatives and programmes, in pursuit of a wider public good. However, use of the term is often couched in political rhetoric and conceptual uncertainty. Like other misused terms, 'sustainability' being the most obvious example, it can mean different things to different audiences. The purpose of this chapter is to clarify the origins of localism, to review the part it looks set to play in the coalition's 'Big Society' and then to focus on its 'neighbourhood planning' component and how this, framed by the broader ambition of localism, has become government's chosen mode of iterative governance and democratic renewal.

The centre and the local

Localism seeks a revision of the relationship between central state and governance structures at the local level, with a view to coping with the increasing diversity of individual and community needs and aspirations.

It infers a weighting of power in favour of local interests, challenging the essential nature of centralised control. Liberal democratic views of the state assert that the function of government, at the centre, is to represent and reflect the views of the electorate. The state is a political 'forum' that assimilates a spectrum of opinion, generating policy outcomes that take the form of compromises between contending interests (Dahl, 1989). An alternative view – the social democratic model – is that the state must go beyond mere representation to achieve a more stable society. This is achieved through interventions that pursue social equity, which may not be delivered through electoral compromise alone (Held, 2003). Both of these views treat the state as a political and social fixer, there to deal with the big picture and either force compromise or promote grand welfare programmes in the public interest. But a diametrically opposing view is that a centralised state causes more problems than it solves, because of its inherently oppressive nature. It disrupts and restrains markets (Jessop, 2003) but, just as significant in terms of 'governality', it offers homogenised and centralised authority to an increasingly heterogeneous society (Foucault, 1982).

Much of the thinking on the role and structure of the 'state' has been shaped by post-war trends and experiences, especially the interventions of many European governments into local affairs in order to deliver sweeping welfare reform or expedite reconstruction (Banner, 2002). Until the late 1960s, governments tended to be identified with the social democratic approach described above. Their objective was to stabilise society through welfare programmes. In the UK, powers were regularly removed from local authorities and handed to development agencies that, for example, assembled land and built New Towns. But many planning and development powers were retained by the local state; they were, however, locked into a delivery relationship with the centre (John, 1990). Local authorities were charged with massive clearance and urban renewal programmes, receiving funding from central government. They enjoyed a degree of discretion, however, as to how their statutory duties should be fulfilled. Yet this discretion was wielded within an insular policy environment, with little connection to 'external' communities, which were viewed primarily as the recipients of public policy.

Indeed, by the 1970s, there was growing concern over the 'impermeability of planning' and other areas of public policy, with communities and citizens appearing incapable of getting 'messages through to the institutions which were influencing their lives' (Dennis, 1972, p 237). Part of the problem lay in the operation of local government; but part was tied up in the nature of local–centre relations, particularly in the hiving off of powers and responsibility to agency structures. The means of delivering public policy were seen to be responsive neither to political direction (set by local representatives) nor to communities of interest (Pollitt, 1990). Regarding the latter, the restructuring of primary industries, in urban and in rural areas, had changed the nature of place community – in terms of membership and patterns of sociability (Pahl, 1975; Newby, 1979) – and this was an early driver of the re-patterning of communities noted in the last chapter. Planning for a diversity of needs and interests appeared to require a cross-sectoral and local, rather than a public-led and centralised, approach to the implementation of 'public' policy (Marsh and Rhodes, 1992).

Commitment to reform gathered pace in the 1980s, under the first of the Thatcher administrations, which was formed in 1979. But this was not a commitment to empowering civil society. Rather, it took as its starting point the view that centralised bureaucracy, and planning in pursuit of an obscure public good, ran contrary to the proper functioning of markets and was therefore a threat to efficient government. Efficiency was best served by a neoliberal approach, which introduced market disciplines into the delivery of public services. 'New Public Management', under the Conservatives, sought to: reduce the size and power of local government; reduce public expenditure by growing the private economy; and increase the return on local government spending by making it more responsive to local needs, especially by introducing competitive tendering for local service provision (Williamson, 1995). The privatisation of services was government's response to more varied needs, but in order to push through this programme, it often had to side-step local authorities, essentially removing democracy from service delivery and transferring power to itself (as the enforcer of tendering) and to private providers. After 1979, the centre's relationship with the local state became increasingly antagonistic. It was the Conservatives who responded to the 'detraditionalising' of society, highlighted in Chapter Two, through a programme of 'agencification', and it was the Conservatives who sought a 'hollowing out of the state' (Rhodes, 1997), confining government's role to one of strategic overseer. However, the New Right placed its trust, locally, in agencies and in private actors, not in the local state or in communities.

The democratic deficit in local affairs that deepened in the 1980s and into the 1990s was not immediately addressed by the Labour government elected to power in 1997. In some respects, it kept with the neoliberal approach, pursuing local government efficiencies through target setting and rigid programmes of inspections. However, authorities were given the opportunity to earn trust and a greater degree of autonomy, through improved performance. 'Beacon' authorities were freed from some of the constraints on their activities, and by the 2000s were being called upon to work with communities of interest, and other stakeholders, in order to sensitise their services to local need and aspiration. But the structures put in place to achieve greater connection frequently failed to achieve grassroots buy-in. Rather, they relied on 'representative' community bodies sitting on the 'strategic partnerships', comprising public, private and voluntary sector actors. Community interests often found themselves 'represented' by networks and membership associations with which they had irregular contact and such structures did little to ease general dissatisfaction with local politics and broader political processes (Corry and Stoker, 2002).

Interpreting localism

The outcomes of local government reform during the 2000s – including community strategies, LSPs and the general intention that local authorities should become 'place shapers' (Lyons, 2007) – was touted as the 'new localism' that communities were crying out for. The 1997 Labour government appeared to turn away from the managerialism of the Conservative years, seeing 'local democracy as the normative *raison d'*être for local government' (Lowndes, 2001, p 1966). But it still needed to grapple with 'the strategic dilemmas integral to governing' (Davies, 2008, p 18): in the field of planning, this meant the national political agenda regarding housing and infrastructure, introduced earlier. Distilling the analyses of many other commentators – including Stoker, whose work is returned to below – Davies (2008, p 19) asked: 'if the premise that strong localism is the condition of a vibrant, healthy democracy is right, but present circumstances are unpropitious, what can be done to bring about the long-heralded, never-attained renaissance?' For a start, a challenge to the 'culture and traditions' of centralism would need to be mounted; beyond this, trust would need to be placed in community actors, freed to pursue self-interest so long as 'harm to others' could be prevented.

Building on this foundation, localism is presented as the requisite challenge to centralism: an ethical politics built from the bottom up that treats equally the pursuit of outcomes and the manner by which decisions are reached. It seeks to sustain the legitimacy of those decisions and afford confidence in political institutions. For Stoker (2002), genuine localism pursues three goals:

- the need for a realistic response to the complexity of modern governance;
- the need for more engaging forms of democracy;
- the need to build the social capital and capacity required to foster civic renewal.

Proponents of localism in the past decade have argued that responsibility and accountability should be as localised as feasible and practicable while the central state should be facilitating local solutions rather than directing with a heavy hand. Top-down policy making should be avoided, with government gaining a reflexive understanding of local context and being brave enough to unbind the hands of local actors, giving them the means to address local challenges. Localism is also input-orientated (Corry and Stoker, 2002; Stoker, 2004, 2007; Coaffee and Headlam, 2008). Interaction within the decision-making process is itself a means of building social capital: it is central to the 'iterative' governance required to bring about democratic renewal in a changed and changing society. By bringing together individual rights and responsibilities (ie, the right of democratic participation with collective responsibility for actions), and establishing a clear link from input to outcome, localism becomes a tool for delivering a more engaging form of democracy, and one that generates empathy: for other stakeholders, for constraints and for compromise. This means that it promises to reduce conflicts attributed to the impermeability of public policy processes and frustration with imposed outcomes. Communities are strengthened, democracy is renewed and governance becomes interactive.

This is the case presented for localism, although its effectiveness in answering key 'strategic dilemmas' remains untested in England. Moves to relinquish centralised or strategic control are inevitably accompanied by fears that policy making will descend into myopia, and that planning's role in pursuing a broader public good will be threatened. The localism of the UK coalition government, in power since 2010, has prompted such fears. Its localism takes two forms: first, the return of power to town halls and a strengthening of the role of elected local politicians; and second, the devolution of responsibilities to 'neighbourhoods'. In planning, the first has generally been achieved at the expense of regional structures. During the passage of the relevant legislation through Parliament - in the form of a 'Localism Bill' -there seemed to be broad agreement that by dismantling regional planning, government would be removing the only effective framework for 'bigger than local' cooperation across boundaries without, of course, eliminating the pressures that make strategic planning necessary (Ellis, 2011). However, this form of localism had a strong political motivation, especially in rural Southern England, where there had been considerable opposition to regional housing targets. The other form of localism, sitting beneath the empowerment of town halls, has been the move to 'neighbourhood control'. The rebalancing of regional and local power was a political act that made clear electoral sense in Southern England, and more generally to Conservative-controlled councils. But the attempt to bring together rights and responsibilities at a neighbourhood level, to take some powers from councils and reassign them to community governance structures, appeared to be a bolder move towards genuine democratic renewal, albeit with the important limitations outlined in the next chapter. This form of localism owes much to recent thinking on the wider benefits of 'networked community governance' (Stoker, 2007).

The roots of this form of governance, in theories of communicative and collaborative action, were alluded to in the last chapter but are fully unravelled later in this book. It is sufficient at this point to say that, politically, interactive community governance structures seem to offer the potential for:

• cost savings;
• locally distinctive policy making;
• wider community ownership of outcomes;
• avoidance of the conflicts centred on the closed nature of professional policy making;
• the opportunity for decisions to be taken by, or close to, those who may claim greater understanding of the decision-making context.

This last attribute is critical: networked community governance claims a degree of embeddedness in the social processes that generate shared understanding. It can cope with social complexity, not only within communities of interest but also at the interface with policy actors. By operating across established networks, it delivers broader inclusion; there is a chance that more constant vertical links are formed than those produced through periodic political representation alone (delivering a more permeable relationship with policy communities); citizenship and trust are welcome side-effects; and, finally, the open exchange of views and the debates that communities engage in, result in a more rigorous testing of options, to more acceptable compromises, and to solutions that better fit the context. Hence, the conflicts associated with impermeable, top-down policy making can be reduced.

Stoker (2004, 2007) sees networked community governance not as an invention passed down from the top, but as a natural product of the social changes that have swept through Western democracies, especially the 'new interconnectedness' – noted in Chapter Two – that frequently bypasses state control. Many governments appear to be embracing local social networks as they turn away from managerialism, and accepting that enhancement of democracy is an end in itself, achievable through the assimilation of broader values into the apparatus and processes of governance. Besides the obvious attention given to major policy outcomes, heightened concern for processes has been clear over the past decade. The pace of local government reform under Labour after 2000 was unremitting. Under the coalition, its pace has been blistering, with localism presented as the means by which Labour's 'big state' will be eclipsed by the Conservatives' Big Society.

Localism and the Big Society

Building the Big Society was a key election pledge of the Conservatives in 2009 and 2010. The Coalition Agreement (Cabinet Office, 2010a) made it clear that this vision was broadly shared:

> We share a conviction that the days of big government are over; that centralisation and top-down control have proved a failure. … [W]hen you take Conservative plans to strengthen families and encourage social responsibility, and add to them the Liberal Democrat passion for protecting our civil liberties and stopping the relentless incursion of the state into the lives of individuals, you create a Big Society…. (Cabinet Office, 2010a, pp 7-8)

The rhetoric behind the Big Society – that government cannot do everything on its own, but needs to harness the power of voluntary action and social enterprise – is clearly rooted in the societal changes, and subsequent debate over the function of the state, précised above. In the run-up to the General Election, the idea that society (along with the planning system) was somehow 'broken' was pushed continually. This 'broken society' lacked cohesion, sometimes lacked respect for the law, and was disconnected and disenfranchised from the machinery of government. Great damage had been done by the previous administration's insistence that the state should take the burden of responsibility for a great many things, which should, in fact, have been left to civil society. Personal and collective responsibility had been eroded, and social solidarity had faded away, replaced by 'selfishness and individualism': indeed, 'the once natural bonds that existed between people, of duty and responsibility, [had] been replaced with the synthetic bonds of the state: regulation and bureaucracy' (Cameron, 2009).

The Labour governments were portrayed as a centralising force, responsible for putting too much distance between citizens and centres of power. A 'yawing chasm' had opened up between state and society, fostering indifference towards the political process, and rendering the local state incapable of responding to local needs. This chasm would only be closed if power were handed back to 'citizens, communities and local government' because only when 'people and communities are given more power and take more responsibility can we achieve fairness and opportunity for all' (Cabinet Office, 2010b, p1). Localism became a new label for these ideas, and was said to be about promoting social enterprise and innovation, and giving communities the freedom to try new approaches. The machinery of government would be opened up to an active citizenry, made more accountable and transparent, with politicians unable to hide behind professional advice and undemocratic quangos. On this point, Conservative policy seemed to have broken with the past, especially with the Thatcher years, but a common thread continues to run through Conservative thinking (Oppenheim et al, 2010). While the Big Society seemed to contradict Thatcher's infamous rejection of the idea of society (Thatcher, 1987) – and her insistence that the world comprises 'a living tapestry' of individuals and individual choices – both are rooted in the view that 'big states' undermine the natural human tendency towards self-help.

The quality of life that people experience should be a measure of the responsibility we take for ourselves and our willingness to help others. Both Thatcherism and Cameron's Big Society are grounded in mutualism and a preference for private, non-governmental alternatives to state welfare. In this sense, the latter may be cast as Thatcherism for the 21st century, although such casting is often politically motivated and attempts to link the policies of the coalition government with a broader raft of unpopular Conservative programmes of the 1980s. Thatcher espoused self-reliance without much apparent enthusiasm for filling the voids left by the withdrawal of welfare intervention. The emphasis since 2010 has been on community and voluntary action filling such voids.

Thinking on the Big Society evolved through a number of policy statements and Green Papers. The first – *A Stronger Society* – was published in 2008 and lauded voluntary action while lambasting top-down government (Conservative Party, 2008, p 6). This was followed up in 2009 with the publication of *Control Shift* (Conservative Party, 2009), which clarified how local communities and the local state would operate under a Cameron-led government. Its vision of 'radical decentralisation' had five principal components:

- giving local communities a share in local growth;
- freeing local government from central control;
- giving people more power over local government;
- giving people greater ability to determine spending priorities;
- eliminating regional government.

The control shift envisaged would put power in the hands of citizens, communities and their directly elected representatives. This would, in part, be achieved by revisiting the relationship between the centre and local government, and by removing the regional tier. But it would also involve an idea that was quickly transported into a programme of planning reform: that of creating an 'open source' democracy.

Localism, local government and planning

In the world of information technology, software 'source code' is sometimes made publicly available. Individuals can then adapt that software to meet their own needs, improving it and innovating solutions to encountered problems (Rushkoff, 2009). This principle, applied to local government or to planning, means that processes and tools are opened up, that standardised approaches are adapted to local circumstances and that innovations become possible and probable. A 'radical reboot' of the planning system was promised, and one that would involve localisation and an 'open source' approach, rooted in 'collaborative democracy'. A Conservative Green Paper on the subject – *Open Source Planning* (Conservative Party, 2010a) – set out the need to restore democratic and local control over planning, rebalance the system in favour of sustainable development and produce a simpler, cheaper and less bureaucratic process. The 'over-engineered' planning of the Labour governments received heavy criticism. It was through reform of the planning system that Labour had deprived many communities of genuine democracy. The strengthening of regional planning and imposition of house-building targets were presented as evidence of a creeping democratic denial under the previous governments, and also as an approach that stifled innovation and amplified conflict. In its place, a 'planning system where there is a basic national framework of planning priorities and policies, within which local communities can produce their own distinctive local policies to create communities which are sustainable, attractive and good to live in' (Conservative Party, 2009, p1) was proposed.

The 2010 Localism Bill sought to realise the vision of the Green Papers through planning and local government reform. Aspects of *Control Shift* (Conservative Party, 2009) were expressed in moves to:

- hand local councils a 'general power of competence' and the capacity to act in the interests of communities (unless precluded from doing so by legal impediment);
- give communities the right to call referendums on local issues, which service providers would need to take action in response to;
- hand communities a 'right to challenge', which could ultimately see voluntary groups or social enterprises running local services.

The Bill also set out the intention to revoke regional planning. This same pledge was contained in *Open Source Planning* (Conservative Party, 2010a). In respect to that Green Paper, the Bill sought to replace the 'stick' of regional housing targets with the 'carrot' of a housing delivery incentive scheme: the 'Homes Bonus', payable to local authorities on the delivery of a net increase in new housing. The Localism Bill also outlined the right, to be given to community groups, to draw up neighbourhood development plans for their local area, with a view to shaping development and bringing forward additional housing and economic projects subject to local support, tested by referendum.

Prior to the Bill beginning its journey through Parliament, there were fears that too much power would be conceded to local groups, that planning would become fragmented and that strategic projects would be jeopardised. However, there was some dilution of more radical ideas as these passed from the Green Papers into the Bill. While neighbourhood development plans were to retain their proposed statutory status, they would need to be in conformity with local plans. This meant that principal authorities would retain control over the quantity and the spatial distribution of development between settlements.

The turn away from radical ideas is perhaps a reminder that the current UK government and its predecessors are grappling with the same basic set of relationships, between society and the state, and the same challenges. One key difference, marked out by the way that local government earned 'beacon' status under Labour, is that the coalition has broken with the idea that the local state needs to demonstrate competency and gain trust before its powers are enhanced. Coaffee (2005) distinguishes between a model of 'earned autonomy' under

Labour and the Conservative preference for 'presumed autonomy'. That said, the continuity of thinking is undeniable. The 2001 White Paper – *Strong Local Leadership, Quality Public Services* (ODPM, 2001b) – emphasised a need to revise the relationship between central and local government, freeing the latter from 'unnecessary government controls'. Five years later, *Strong and Prosperous Communities* (DCLG, 2006) sought to move this agenda forward by devolving a broader range of responsibilities to local authorities, and tailoring services to community need, by placing service providers within local fora (strategic partnerships) where they would be answerable to their customers and would need to formulate delivery plans in the context of broader 'sustainable community strategies'. A year later, the Sustainable Communities Act 2007 became the centre-piece of Labour's 'double devolution', enacting key elements of the previous year's White Paper (DCLG, 2006) and enshrining in law the view that local people know best what needs to be done to promote sustainability in their area.

Therefore, much of the rhetoric of the Conservatives after 2008 was well worn. Likewise, its recognition that cynicism and disenchantment with the political process had not dissipated was also acknowledged by Labour. The 2007 *Governance of Britain Green Paper* (Ministry of Justice, 2007) conceded that a growing sense of powerlessness was reflected in falling electoral turnout. The Conservatives responded with *A Stronger Society* (Conservative Society, 2008) and Labour with its *Communities in Control* White Paper (DCLG, 2008a). The latter began by examining who has power, how it is exercised and how communities might access it. It ended by promising to attach greater value to community action and social enterprise, reiterating that government is essentially 'about democracy, and how democratic practices can be applied to our complex, modern society', adding that it is communities and citizens 'who ultimately must hold power in a mature democracy' (DCLG, 2008a, p 12).

But as the party in power, Labour continued to grapple with the 'strategic dilemmas integral to governing' (Davies, 2008, p18). Its Planning Act 2008 appeared to contradict the rhetoric of communities in control, augmenting the powers of regional planning and handing new responsibilities to an unelected quango, in the form of the Infrastructure Planning Commission (see Chapter Fifteen). Without the responsibility of government on their shoulders, the Conservatives were able to present Labour ministers as double dealing, giving power with one hand but taking it away with the other. Their 'empowerment' was tightly restricted, earned rather than presumed, and could not disguise the tendency towards centralism. Yet in power, the coalition finds itself facing the same strategic dilemmas. Localism has already been watered down. Local enterprise partnerships appear to be reconstituted development agencies, with few democratic credentials. And the power of neighbourhood groups will be heavily curtailed by the pursuit of national priorities, reflected in local plans and in a new system of fiscal incentive.

Localism and the rescaling of statutory planning

A combination of strengthened community-based planning, given legal status within the hierarchy of plans and national policy, and the removal of the regional tier clearly constitutes a rescaling of statutory planning in England, albeit with as yet unclear outcomes. The evolution of planning at the neighbourhood and village level is traced in the next chapter, where it is shown that neighbourhood development plans are rooted in a tradition of community-based appraisal and plan making (Owen et al, 2007). These roots run deepest in rural areas, where established community governance structures – in the form of parish councils – are more commonplace and where congregations of middle-class, educated residents are frequently prepared to dedicate time to planning activities, often with a conservation objective in mind (Owen and Moseley, 2003). While government policy is laced with the rhetoric of rights and responsibilities, the propensity to participate and to plan at a neighbourhood level is dependent on a number of key conditions (Stoker, 2004). These include:

- the presence of a sense of community, which provides an incubator for social action;
- acquiring the requisite capacity, within that community;
- providing clear means and apparatus for participation;
- creating a sustained process;
- ensuring obvious traceability from input, through decision, to outcome.

But it cannot be assumed that all communities provide an ideal context. Dominant voices can drown out significant others, resulting in a need for mediation and capacity building (Stoker, 2004). Not all neighbourhood action is genuinely community based, but spurred on by the energy of a few individuals. There is a clear divide between the rhetoric of a collaborative, community-based democracy and the recent reality of some 'community-based' activity in England, which is often driven by a narrow set of interests.

On the one hand, this is a reality that cannot be avoided. Some people have a propensity to participate that is greater than that of their neighbours. If they become the leaders and agenda setters described in Chapter One, and if they take on additional planning powers, then it is still the case that planning has been rescaled. However, on the other hand, enhancements to the means and apparatus of participation suggest a possibility of drawing more people into a participative process. This might mean creating more transparent and accessible community governance structures, an issue that is returned to at the very end of this book. But another means of drawing people in is to convince them that their inputs will lead to clear outcomes. They are not merely participating in order that decisions reached elsewhere are legitimised. This is presented as the point of departure for the coalition's neighbourhood development plans. Unlike previous community-based plans – including parish plans – they appear to have been assigned a definite place within the planning process, suggesting that their content will be influential, even if that influence is constrained by national priority.

FOUR

Community-based planning and plans

The experience of producing and using *parish plans* in England provides the empirical focus of this book. It is this experience, along with the community governance context for parish plans, that is held up as a mirror to the emerging process of neighbourhood development plan production, introduced at the end of this chapter. It is also this experience that exposes some of the frailties of democratic renewal rooted in networked governance, and the realities of community groups struggling to make their voices heard in the shadow of growth and the context of apparently overwhelming strategic priority. Here, we introduce some of the procedural issues that are dissected in later chapters, including the way in which community-based plans may be used to inform local planning policy. The relationship between plans drawn up by community groups and the plans produced by policy actors is an issue dealt with in some detail in Chapter Nine. The basic question of connectivity (to formal policy) has been a major concern for parish plans and will continue to influence thinking on the form, content and production of neighbourhood development plans. There is much that can be carried forward from past experience of community-based planning and plans and some of this is introduced in this chapter, which outlines the evolution of parish planning in England.

Parishes and parish planning

Parishes are the smallest units of government in England, originating from the Local Government Act 1894 (Jones, 2007, p 230). They were given legal recognition and became 'tiers of small-scale local governance separate from the church and ecclesiastical parishes' (2007, p 230). They were originally intended as a form of specifically rural governance. Under the Local Government and Rating Act 1997, 'a community at the village, neighbourhood, town or similar level beneath a district or borough council in England can demand its own elected parish or town council'. Roughly 200 additional parish councils have been created since 1997, although they remain largely a rural phenomenon. The impetus to create more of these councils, extending them to urban areas, was provided by the Local Government and Public Involvement in Health Act 2007, section 94. Prior to the enactment of the Localism Act 2011, parish councils had no *statutory* planning responsibilities or powers, although in recent years they had been encouraged by central government (through initial support from the Countryside Agency and then the Commission for Rural Communities and the Department for Environment, Food and Rural Affairs – DEFRA) to 'connect' with statutory planning by becoming part of the wider process of local evidence gathering and action planning, subsequently used to inform policy development at a more strategic (ie, district-wide) scale. A number of commentators on this subject, including Bishop, Moseley and Owen, charted the growing importance of community-based plans and village design statements (VDSs) in the 1990s and 2000s, in empowering rural communities and shaping – with varying degrees of success – the formulation of strategy and policy at higher tiers (Moseley, 1997, 2002; Owen, 1998, 1999, 2002a, 2002b; Owen and Moseley, 2003; Bishop, 2007; Owen et al, 2007). Bishop (2007, p 343) notes that 'for almost 20 years, there has developed a pattern in which the planning system has given some form of formal "credence" to plans produced at the community level, be they parish plans or village design statements'. The opportunities that these frameworks create, for people to engage with the planning process, has been held up as evidence of a broader 'governance shift' towards a more 'participative' approach to strategising and decision taking (Bailey, 2003). In calling for the creation of additional parish councils, the 2006 local government White Paper – *Strong and Prosperous Communities* (DCLG, 2006, pp 42-3) – argued that:

> Parish Councils are an established and valued form of neighbourhood democracy and management. They are not only important in rural areas, but increasingly have a role to play in urban areas. We propose to build on the existing parish structure, so as to improve its capacity to deliver better services and represent the community's interests ... we will make it clear that there will be a presumption in favour of the setting up of parish councils so that local authorities will be expected to grant communities' requests to set up new parish councils, except where there are good reasons not to, and that existing parish councils are not to be abolished against the wishes of local people.

The White Paper also highlighted the degree to which more fine-grained consultation – concerning the 'shape of local services and policies' – can be achieved through the preparation of parish plans (2006, p 32). In response, Bishop (2007, p 343) argued that although the White Paper was weak on practical detail, 'revivifying community plans would almost certainly be the cheapest, quickest and most cost-effective way of engaging people around the country in the White Paper's agenda'. This view was shared by others, who argued that giving new impetus to community planning would be a means of grounding community strategies (see Chapter Two) and, through these strategies, ensuring that restyled local plans (LDFs after 2004) connected to real preferences. This would add up to a more 'holistic' form of planning and governance (Owen et al, 2007, p 50) and one that was genuinely modernised in the sense that it was better placed to deal with social complexity. Renewed interest in parish planning, although only tentative in the 2000s, became an important, albeit underdeveloped, element of the planning and local government reform package introduced earlier.

Spatial planning at the local level

Most recent conceptions of spatial planning in England share the view that the planning function – especially power over land-use change and capacity to guide and shape development – needs to be seen within the context of holistic governance: not merely as an extraneous 'service' but as a coordinator of different policy areas (Tewdwr-Jones et al, 2006; Morphet et al, 2007). It is also agreed that local government – comprising local authorities and *parish* councils – provides the critical context for the 'spatial approach' to planning. The evolving mechanics of 'local governance' connect directly to planning processes, and to the goals of the planning system.

The Planning and Compulsory Purchase Act 2004 moved planning to the 'centre of the spatial development process, not just as a regulator of land and property uses, but as a proactive and strategic coordinator of all policy and actions' (Nadin, 2007: 46). In the interests of delivering sustainable development – that fitted local context – planning now needed to assign higher priority to the aspirations of its users. The transition away from a more restricted regulatory focus has been driven not only by planning legislation, but also by a number of Local Government Acts, as highlighted in Chapter Two. But the combined effect of planning and local government reform has been to create an uneasy partnership between participative governance and representative democracy (Owen et al, 2007). Specifically, new significance has been attached to participative community-based planning, assigning parish plans (and other community-based plans) a bigger role in England's approach to spatial planning, while strategic dilemmas (particularly concerning the provision of housing and infrastructure) seem to have grown and are sometimes presented as requiring decisive actions from the centre that override community concern. Questions of meta-governance and leadership, which must ultimately frame any discussion of community governance and decision making, were introduced in Chapters Two and Three, and are returned to at the end of this book. The remainder of this chapter focuses on the ongoing development of community-based planning in England, with the most recent developments in the 2000s and 2010s being triggered by critical reforms to the broader planning process.

The evolution of community-based planning and parish plans

Owen and Moseley (2003, p 445) observed at the beginning of the 2000s that 'for the past 50 years village planning in England has been undertaken rather patchily'. For much of the post-war period, the 'very-local community-based planning' (Owen et al, 2007, p 49) represented by the work of parish councils (or voluntary groups linked to these councils) could be reasonably described as a marginal activity, confined to the periodic compilation of 'parish appraisals' and it was these appraisals, initiated in the 1970s, that were the precursor to the recent parish plans examined in later chapters. Parish 'mapping exercises', parish 'appraisals' and eventually VDSs and local housing needs studies formed a matrix of approaches used to understand community needs and priorities.

Parish appraisals, in particular, became a systematic means of gaining an insight into local priorities. A toolkit with this objective in mind was developed by researchers from Gloucestershire College of Art and Technology,[1] who subsequently provided an analytical service to communities using a 'village appraisals approach'. Drawing on local surveys into a variety of issues, these appraisals could be regarded as statistical 'health checks' that aimed to provide an evidence base for subsequent community action (Owen, 2002b, p 47). They were frequently criticised, however, for failing to identify realistic interventions that might be made to address local concerns or catalyse a broader mobilisation of community interests.

There was also some resistance, during the 1970s and 1980s to these systematic tools: parishes felt that appraisals, in particular, were insufficiently flexible, reducing community needs to oversimplified data profiles that obscured the true nature of local challenges. By the 1990s, more open-ended 'parish plans' were seen as an opportunity to break free from the constraints of 'formulaic' appraisals and reflect broader, more aspirational thinking. Parish plans quickly became wishlists, which the parishes expected their local planning authorities to deliver through immediate translation into planning policy. But, unlike the appraisals, their production was neither methodical nor systematic, and there was great disappointment when the vast majority of parish plans were ignored by local authorities.

However, pressure to do more with community-based plans grew during the 1990s. Engagement with community interests, through the planning process and the drawing up of parish and town plans, was encouraged in a 2000 rural White Paper (DETR and MAFF, 2000). Two years after the Labour government's pledge to devolve power and resources to communities, set out in the 1998 local government White Paper (DTLR, 1998) (see Chapter Two), the rural White Paper offered a clear rationale for this devolution, arguing that 'sustainable' rural development was not achievable through centralised state intervention and that 'communities could play a much bigger part in their own affairs and shaping their future development' (DETR and MAFF, 2000, p 145). Within this context, parish plans were viewed, first, as a means of encouraging communities to actively engage in matters of direct local concern (where such encouragement was required) and, second, as a possible feed-in to decisions taken elsewhere that might directly impact on the community (Owen, 2002b, p 45). The interactive production of these plans would deliver social cohesion and capital, thereby increasing the capacity of communities to act in their own interests. The rural White Paper argued that these plans should 'set out a vision of what is important, how new development can be best fitted in, the design and quality standards [they] should meet, how to preserve valued local features and map out the facilities which the community needs to safeguard for the future' (DETR and MAFF, 2000, p 150). Furthermore, they should 'identify key facilities and services, ... set out the problems that need to be tackled and demonstrate how [a place's] distinctive character and features should be preserved' (2000, p 146).

The initial view of government was that parish plans should link with the work of local and county councils and with local plans. With the advent of LSPs, feeding into community strategies and LDFs later in the 2000s, this view adapted to the changing framework of local governance, with parish plans seen as a potential feed-in. But this would only be possible at any meaningful scale if the production of parish plans became the norm rather than the exception. For this reason, the Vital Village initiative was launched under the direction of the Countryside Agency, which was tasked to achieve an initial target of 1,000 communities producing a parish plan by 2004 (Countryside Agency, 2004, p 6). Through a mix of advice and funding (grants were available of up to £5,000 per community), the Countryside Agency was able to achieve this target and subsequently reviewed local experiences of producing parish plans. In 2004, the Agency claimed the following:

- Parish councils had been proactive in engaging local people in the production of parish plans, sometimes being supported in their efforts by regional expertise.
- The parish planning process can become a form of innovative engagement (orchestrated at the 'community' level) and was therefore important in the context of the new planning system, which required local planning authorities to produce an engagement strategy and prepare a statement of community involvement (see Chapter Two).
- Processes of engagement (at local meetings) provide a means of 'invigorating community spirit' (2004, p 9).
- The Agency itself had successfully supported the production of parish plans through expert guidance and grant support. It had organised a 'partnering' support scheme whereby members of parish councils further along the process came to share their experiences with parishes that were still at an early stage.
- The fact that parish plans rarely had the same format was evidence of 'distinctive' local identity and widely differing concerns (rather than any lack of guidance and uncertainty in their production). However, the Agency also alluded to diversity in the level of 'professionalism' with which these plans were put together, pointing out that some parishes had compiled rough documents comprising photographs, descriptions and snippets of local information.
- The format and structure of parish plans would need to be agreed in advance with the local planning authority if there were to be any chance of these local documents being adopted as 'supplementary' planning documents (under the 2004 system; 2004, p 14).

Even in advance of the Planning and Compulsory Purchase Act 2004 (and evolving local government reforms), the Countryside Agency felt that emergent parish plans would play a key role in the planning *process*, and would:

- aid in the process of local engagement;
- help build the evidence base for spatial planning;
- provide opportunities to express 'local distinctiveness' in wider planning frameworks (sometimes through their adoption as Supplementary Planning Guidance and then, after 2004, through translation into Supplementary Planning Documents);
- help create partnerships *at* the very-local level and *with* the parishes;
- increase public understanding (and acceptance) of the planning process (Countryside Agency, 2004, p 16).

More specifically, the parish plans themselves, once they had been produced, would:

- provide a point of reference for LSPs;
- point to and reflect community strategy (and Local Area Agreement) goals;
- aid a coordinated approach to local service delivery, with the local planning authority supporting initiatives emerging from parish plans; likewise
- provide a case for successful funding bids, allowing parish councils to access external sources of funding, or to catalyse support for local initiatives, including Community Land Trusts; and ultimately
- improve local governance, setting a clear agenda that would revive and renew local democracy.

The Countryside Agency was the first to acknowledge that these aspirations for the parish planning process and for parish plans would not be achieved easily. By 2004, 1,200 parish councils had received funding support, but more was needed. Likewise, it was the view of the Agency that additional guidance was required and greater 'professionalism' had to be achieved in the production of plans, so that local authorities would not view them as whimsical, ill-conceived statements that were of little practical value to the planning process. However, from the point of view of the Agency, these difficulties could be overcome with clear leadership and the injection of additional resources. Yet, other commentators pointed to more fundamental barriers preventing reconciliation between formal, established processes of local planning and governance, and the emergent parish plans. Owen et al (2007, p 49) suggested that a 'synergistic relationship between strategic and very local planning' is undermined by key tensions in local governance: between representative and participatory democracy (2007, p 56) and between top-down and bottom-up approaches to (rural) regeneration (2007, p 58), with the former pursuing strategic solutions to what are judged to be strategic dilemmas (Davies, 2008).

But despite these tensions, the drive to ensure that more community groups engage in plan making was still interpreted as a genuine extension of community governance responsibilities (Owen et al, 2007, pp 50-2), and as part of local government modernisation in England (Raco et al, 2006), albeit grounded in a 'different conception of democracy':

> Strategic frameworks are prepared mainly through the processes of representative democracy – by elected bodies working through formal democratic structures as part of their continuous representative responsibilities. Very local community initiatives, on the other hand, are undertaken mainly through participative democracy – by self-identifying groups of articulate residents pursuing their own objectives in the form of one-off projects; albeit some forms of very local community-based activities, notably Parish Plans, have been undertaken, or at least initiated, by elected parish councils. (Owen et al, 2007, p 55)

There is a mismatch between plans, attributable to the mode of production (professional or interest based), but it is also the case that serious questions may be asked of the democratic credentials of 'community-based activities', which claim to grow from the bottom up but which may in fact exclude all but the most articulate individuals and may be driven by a narrow set of interests. Questions of legitimacy in community-based action are returned to in later chapters. Generally, however, collaborative and participative structures have been seen by a great many commentators as an antidote to growing dissatisfaction with representative democracy (Newman, 2007, p 27) and as a means of delivering democratic renewal. Governance, through collaboration and participation, seeks a transfer of responsibility from the public to the personal domain (2007, p 27), and is iterative in the sense used by Sørensen and Torfing (2008).

Reconciliation with higher plans, and between actors

The recent history of parish plans in England confirms that it can be difficult to reconcile the 'sporadic and focused outcomes' of participatory democracy with strategic frameworks, cross-cutting and holistic in scope, that emerge from a 'continuous process' of representative democracy that works through issues over an extended period of time, sometimes reaching compromises, formulating actions and offering solutions built upon majority consensus. This tension has important implications for both the processes and the products of community-based planning – as it relates to higher-level strategy – and raises a fundamental question over the value of community-based plans to formal policy making, if their content has little chance of being genuinely reconciled with broader priorities for housing and infrastructure. This dilemma received some attention in the 2000s: the answer offered was to coordinate and professionalise the production of community-based plans, although little headway was made in this direction.

The UK coalition government faces the same challenge if community plans are to play a significant role in localising the planning process. But rather than launching further investigations into the best means of connecting community ambitions with local priorities, it has given this issue the same irreverent treatment that Alexander gave the Gordian knot. Community groups will draw up plans, following a process set out in statute, and local authorities will incorporate them into local plans: however, their content can be 'flexible' and 'more or less prescriptive' (DCLG, 2011, p 17), so long as they are compliant with national policy. Yet, the potential for mismatch, and conflict, remains unchanged if the processes of local and neighbourhood plan production are entirely separate and there is no meeting of minds around local objectives. However, there appears to be no doubting government's ambition of bringing communities to 'centre stage in the reformed planning system' by giving 'every neighbourhood the chance to shape its own development through the creation of neighbourhood plans, which will give local communities greater flexibility and the freedom to bring forward more development than set out in the local authority plan' (DBIS, 2010, p 24). Not surprisingly, those involved in community-based planning initiatives were quick out of the blocks to laud the benefits of a 'neighbourhood' approach, but also cautioned that working with local groups, with a view to building development strategies from the bottom up, would be a difficult and costly process (Bishop, 2010), with *genuine collaboration* between planners and community groups being the only means of ensuring meaningful compliance between neighbourhood and local plans (Gallent et al, 2011). This theme is picked up again in Chapter Nine and subsequent chapters.

Neighbourhood (development) plans

The UK coalition government sees community-based planning as a practical means of realising its Big Society. The Conservative Party Green Papers, *Control Shift* (2009) and *Open Source Planning* (2010a), both pledged to strengthen the part played by communities in the statutory planning process. To this end, two new neighbourhood-based planning processes were proposed in the 2010 Localism Bill: 'neighbourhood development plans' and 'neighbourhood development orders'. Where the residents of a defined neighbourhood (a rural parish or a self-defining urban neighbourhood) agree that a plan or an order, produced by a mandated local group, is reflective of local aspiration (ie, the plan or order is approved in a referendum), the local authority will be legally bound to adopt it so long as it 'respect[s] the overall national presumption in favour of sustainable development, as well as other local strategic priorities such as the positioning of transport links and meeting housing need' (DBIS, 2010, p 24) set out in the local plan. This presumption in favour of adoption sets the neighbourhood development plan and order apart from previous products of community-based planning: in the past, adoption was the exception rather than the rule, fraught with legal and procedural challenges, especially after 2004 when all development plan documents needed to pass through a rigorous process of sustainability appraisal. This will not apply to the neighbourhood development plan and order, which will be subject to 'light touch' scrutiny (to ensure local plan compliance).

Neighbourhood development plans are likely to be the potential successors of parish plans in many areas and it is the 'plans' produced by community groups that provide the main focus of this book. However, neighbourhood development orders are a potent planning tool in their own right. A series of Neighbourhood Planning Vanguard projects undertaken in 2011 have suggested that these will be drawn up in consultation with planning authorities owing to their highly technical nature. A neighbourhood development order is essentially a modification of the national 'general permitted development order'. This prescribes the uses and, together with the 'use classes order', the changes of use that require planning permission. A neighbourhood group drawing up a neighbourhood development order will be able to tighten or relax the general permitted development order, articulating new regulations specific to the neighbourhood. The intent may be to free the community itself from planning regulation, allowing it to grant outline permission for local needs housing, small business units or community development projects under the rubric of a 'Community Right to Build' (DBIS, 2010, p 25).

The modifications possible will undoubtedly be limited by the need to remain in conformity with the local plan, and to make sure that tighter or more relaxed rules do not impede or contradict plan objectives. Neighbourhood development plans, however, seem less shackled by legal requirement and will, where there are already strong community governance structures, be produced by the same groups that drew up the previous round of community-based plans. The big difference is that they will become part of the development plan system, linking aspiration to policy in a way that hitherto seemed improbable if not impossible. In many rural areas, they will be produced by groups linked to active parish councils. In non-parished areas, there is a hope that 'neighbourhood forums' will emerge, probably evolving from established community groups and networks. In some instances, local authorities may need to work with competing groups to decide who has the right to represent community interests, thereby providing a 'stable basis for neighbourhood planning' (DCLG, 2010). The foundations of this new neighbourhood planning are likely to be differently constituted in different places – and inevitable tussles over legitimacy and right to represent will arise – perhaps generating different models in parished and un-parished areas. During the passage of the Localism Bill through Parliament, a number of groups lauded the advantages of rooting neighbourhood planning in democratically elected parish councils, although the degree to which more established structures of community governance genuinely reflect community interest(s) is examined in later chapters.

Neighbourhood development plans will need to be in compliance with the local plan and local authorities have a duty to support neighbourhood plan production, although they have no additional resources to do so. Compliance will be tested in a light touch examination by an independent assessor, the aim being to ensure that these community-based plans are unable to block developments deemed to be of strategic importance. Clearly, this answers Davies' (2008) concern that moves towards greater localism in decision making need to align with strategic, national priority. However, two worries remain. First, authorities without up-to-date local plans may somehow lose control of development planning or planning committees may become more reticent about making decisions counter to (noncompliant) aspirations articulated forcefully in neighbourhood plans (Gallent et al, 2011). Second, necessary compliance will mean that local plans appear to be an artificial imposition in the 'brave new world of localism', shifting the 'tension inherent in planning from between regional and local to between local and neighbourhood' (Ellis, 2011, p 17).

As well as the duality of models, noted above, there may be other inequities associated with the neighbourhood development planning process. Affluent, educated communities may be more likely to come together to produce convincing neighbourhood development plans, deflecting development away from more vocal neighbourhoods to more acquiescent ones. This problem may be inflated as the latter may be more vulnerable to commercial interests pushing for development or hijacking the neighbourhood planning process. Likewise, the tensions noted by Ellis (2011) may be lessened where development is directed to areas without a neighbourhood development plan, and this may be a tempting strategy for some authorities.

People and planning

The rhetoric of localism is laced with the idea of 'taking power away from officials and putting it into the hands of those who know most about their neighbourhood – local people themselves' (DCLG, 2010). Communities should be able to produce their own plans with minimal interference and intervention from existing policy actors. It is probable in the current fiscal climate (in 2011) that this aim has as much to do with constrained public budgets as a genuine desire not to stifle social innovation or renew local democracy. However, those who have been involved in community-based planning for many years argue that, without external support, it may be difficult to arrive at compliant plans (Bishop, 2011). Local planners will have an interest in ensuring that neighbourhood development plans work with the grain of local priority, and that they are coherent across a wider territory. They will want to work with neighbourhood groups to ensure some common understanding of broader challenges, not least those associated with growth and long-term development trajectories. Compliance is not merely a matter of legal rubber-stamping, but a product of good working relationships between policy professionals and communities of interest at what, later in this book, we refer to as planning's 'critical interface'. A lack of dialogue around parish plans, and their link to local plans, was identified by Owen et al (2007) as a critical failing. Plans produced without regard for other frameworks, and in a communication-free vacuum, are doomed to fail. At worst, they will hinder rather than hasten delivery against community interest, thereby failing to generate greater trust in participative democracy. Bishop (2010, p 379) argues that genuinely 'bottom-up' planning is distinctively different from a 'bottom-only' approach: 'there is a danger that the proposed bottom-up approach would become bottom-only, because a fixation on the truly local could make it difficult, perhaps impossible to address area-wide policy principles about the appropriate distribution of housing, the location of services, sustainable transport and so forth'. The rescaling of planning, now in train, is viewed by some authorities as a potentially costly fragmentation of a trusted service, which risks losing sight of the public good as it pursues narrow local interest (Gallent et al, 2011). This view is undoubtedly a product of the parish planning experience, and in some instances of self-selecting local groups drawing up 'wish-lists', presenting them to local authorities, and getting angry when policy did not fall into line with aspiration. The danger now (from the perspective of some, yet-to-be-convinced, planning professionals) is that some of the wishes may come true, and these may threaten major projects. There is concern that the neighbourhood planning agenda is not grounded in a new relationship or contract between 'people and planning' but on a forced acceptance, by local authorities, of the products of community-based planning, without sufficient questioning of the role that such 'planning' should play, within communities themselves and within the much wider policy-making process.

It is ultimately people and not policies who need to work together in order to deliver effective planning and workable plans. Groups bringing forward community-based plans are motivated by ambitions and by interests that may sit uneasily with local and 'larger than local' planning perspectives and priorities. Communication, and collaboration, between communities of interest and policy communities becomes more, not less, important as the focus of planning shifts downwards. The next chapter introduces the Ashford case study, placing it in its strategic planning context and in the growth context, which inevitably colours community and professional relationships. Subsequent chapters then track the 'life cycle' of community-based planning, culminating in the production and use of community-based plans across a sample of parishes within Ashford borough.

Note

[1] The unit undertaking this work now resides within University of Gloucestershire.

Part Two
Capacity building and community-based planning

FIVE

Ashford and its strategic planning context

There has been an ebb and flow of interest in strategic regional planning in the UK (Tewdwr-Jones, 2004), with the strategic perspective and control at the regional level enjoying notably greater support under some governments than others. Planning at this level has its origins in the 1940 Barlow Report (Barlow, 1940), which gave rise to the post-war New Towns programme and broader attempts to redistribute industry and decant people away from inner-urban locations. Strategic regional planning, together with the public building programmes of the post-war era, share a common root in comprehensive planning and public sector control. After the war, successive waves of New Towns signalled periodic returns to stronger central planning at those times when recurrent concerns over regional economic policy intersected with housing shortages (Aldridge, 1979; Gilg, 2005). Yet, the strategic planning function was slow to evolve from the Town and Country Planning Act 1947. The focus at first was on local plans, with their development control and local policy remit. These co-existed with grander strategies for industry and new settlements but were also quite separate. It was not until the late 1960s, with the arrival of 'structure plans', at the county level, that a broader framework of cross-border coordination was set in place, which, according to Department of the Environment Circular 44/71 (DoE, 1971), was designed to connect national and regional priorities and programmes (including the New Towns) with more local social, economic and environmental goals.

Connectivity between levels of planning – bringing local issues into broader frameworks – was intended as a key feature of the system, although big strategies often fought against powerful ideological positions: for example, with top-down planning in pursuit of prescribed development outcomes being viewed as insensitive and as a threat to enterprise – a view held by Thatcher after 1979 and Cameron in 2011. In the 1970s, this led to a programme of deregulation and, contrary to the views of successive Labour governments, the belief that the concentration of industry and of people in Southern England was no bad thing, but rather just a consequence of market advantage, which regional planning should not seek to undermine (Tewdwr-Jones, 2002).

Such views turned the Conservatives away from planning at the regional level; but towards the end of the 1980s and into the 1990s, it became apparent that a lack of strategic oversight – and poor cooperation between local authorities – often led to the allocation of too little land for housing, employment and new infrastructure: the context for enterprise and for growth could be threatened (Haughton and Counsell, 2004; Tewdwr-Jones and Allmendinger, 2007) and the health of the economy upset by labour undersupply and immobility (Hall, 1999). In order to address these issues, it was proposed that local authorities should convene and prepare regional guidance for submission to the Secretary of State for the Environment (DoE, 1989), which would be agreed and issued by the Department of the Environment as RPG.

From this origin, a process of consolidation was set in train. RPG became a 'material consideration' for local authorities drawing up development plans (as stated in the Planning and Compensation Act 1991), although their tendency to merely repeat national policy threatened to undermine their potentially key role in coordinating the policies of local plans (Baker, 1998) and in providing a genuine strategic steer. However, effort was expended on improving the system almost immediately, with RPG lauded as the means of achieving sustainable development (DoE, 1992) and balancing economic objectives with enhanced quality of life and environmental improvement. Under the Conservatives, however, regional planning remained 'advisory' and did not compel local authorities to either cooperate or accept major development. This changed under the 1997 Labour government, which took the regional planning system and placed it in a new institutional framework, comprising regional assemblies and development agencies, created by the Regional Development Agencies Act 1998. Assemblies were designated the responsible 'regional planning bodies' and charged with the preparation of RPG, to be examined and published by Government Offices created a few years earlier. But still, it was the county structure plans, and not RPG, that provided the principal context for local planning. This changed in 2004, with government transferring power from the counties to the regions. Following the Planning and Compulsory Purchase Act 2004, local plans needed to be in conformity with restyled 'Regional Spatial Strategies', rather than merely 'having regard' to their content: the regional strategies together with the local policies formed the LDF. Other initiatives followed, including a subnational review of the institutional arrangements for regional planning and economic development (DCLG and BERR, 2008), which concluded there that was too much distance between broader planning and infrastructure concerns and economic strategy.

Government's response, through the Local Democracy, Economic Development and Construction Act 2009, was to transfer the planning function of the assemblies to the development agencies, although this change was short-lived as the 2010 General Election precipitated the effective abolition of regional planning in England.

Two apparently contradictory positions emerge from the above narrative. Governments on the Left appear to attach greater importance to more centralised forms of strategic planning, while those on the Right shy away from 'interference' with local democracy, only insisting on a strategic steer where it has a demonstrable economic rationale. But all governments will create structures for dealing with the 'strategic dilemmas integral to governing'. Labour's tendency has been to establish stronger planning frameworks and to impose delivery targets on local government. This was the context for the Ashford Growth Area, introduced below. The Conservatives, on the other hand, have tended to resist regional planning, edging cautiously towards it only where it supports growth. But despite the effective revocation of regional strategies in 2010, history suggests that some future reinvention is probable.

The pre-2010 framework provided the political backdrop for community-based planning in and around the Ashford Growth Area, setting the planning context for dealing with the housing growth dilemma introduced in Chapter Two, and contributing to a local view that 'planning' happens, and key decisions are taken, at a level remote from communities. In the remainder of this chapter, we drill down to the case study communities, placing Ashford and the Growth Area in its regional setting before outlining some of the ways in which villages and neighbourhoods will feel the effects of the growth strategy.

Strategic planning and housing growth in South East England

The South East of England has experienced strong demand for housing over a number of years. This demand – coupled with recurrent under-supply – has resulted in a steep rise in house prices. In 2009, the ratio between average prices and average household incomes was 12:1 (NHF, 2009). This, and other indicators of housing affordability, have led to fears that the region's economic performance will be adversely affected by labour shortages, as people are unable to move south to take up work, or are displaced from the region. In 2007, the South East contributed £187.9 billion to the UK economy: 15.1% of total Gross Domestic Product (GDP) (ONS, 2008). Its importance to the national economy has prompted inevitable concerns over the failure to resolve existing housing shortages and the likely challenge of future growth. In 2006, the South East England Development Agency (SEEDA) projected that the region's population would rise by 64,300 people per annum over the following 20 years, meaning that 1.3 million extra people would live in the South East by 2026 (SEEDA, 2006). These statistics triggered considerable debate over the region's capacity to grow without incurring an intolerable reduction in environmental quality (see CPRE, 2007). Mindful of such capacity concerns, the development agency tried to articulate an economic strategy for the South East predicated on 'smart' growth and what it termed 'sustainable prosperity' (SEEDA, 2006) – shorthand for concentrated investment in areas of existing infrastructural capacity and away from areas of environmental sensitivity; a 'sharper focus' rather than a uniform distribution of development to meet the region's future economic need.

It is essentially through the development of 'Growth Areas', introduced in Chapter Two, that a sharper focus and 'smart' growth will be achieved. The potential of the Growth Areas to meet regional housing demand had been identified in earlier RPG. *RPG9: Regional Planning Guidance for the South East* (DoE, 1994) had proposed a strategy for reducing pressure in the west (from Buckinghamshire, Berkshire and Surrey) and redirecting growth to the east (to Essex and Kent). The same theme was picked up by the Communities Plan (ODPM, 2003), although the content of the two documents differed in terms of their presentation of the solution. While *RPG9* sought to achieve a traditional 'trade-off' between growth and protection, suggesting that precedence would need to be given to one or the other, the Communities Plan touted the possibility of a 'win, win, win' outcome, with concentrated development reducing land take (and therefore environmental impact), and ultimately creating sustainable communities predicated on the co-location of jobs, a mix of homes and good social facilities.

This approach was taken forward in the South East's Regional Spatial Strategy (the 'South East Plan'), which identified a network of 'hubs', some of which were within its Growth Areas. It anticipated that these hubs would provide a focus for more concentrated development, including new and continued investment in regeneration, infrastructure provision and expansion, and further housing and employment growth. The challenge in the region was to:

> recognize that there is a network of cities and towns where most employment, leisure, retail and cultural activity in the region will gravitate, by virtue of their more developed

transport networks and their wide mix of services combined
with demand from accessible populations. As dynamic 'hubs
of activity', they are the logical areas within the South
East within which the various components of growth
will need to be focused and coordinated to help deliver
more sustainable forms of development. A major part of
this approach will be reducing the need to travel through
closer alignment of local labour supply and demand. (GOSE,
2009, p 18)

Across the South East region, there was – and remains – a critical
concern over housing supply, escalating property prices and the social
and economic consequences of low levels of housing affordability. The
aim of consistently raising the level of housing supply, year on year, and
dealing with market disequilibrium became a key part of government's
housing and planning policy in the 2000s. It was originally envisaged
that the Growth Areas, together with Opportunity Areas in London
and Growth Points elsewhere in the country, could deliver an additional
200,000 homes per annum. A housing Green Paper in 2007 (DCLG,
2007a) added eco-towns to the suite of contexts in which new housing
should be built, and suggested additional measures to increase overall
supply. A target of 240,000 homes each year was set, contributing
to an overall total of three million by 2020. The sharp fall in private
house-building output during the downturn and recession seemed to
have put paid to these targets, and ministerial claims that the target
remained credible were met with some scepticism (Smith, 2008). But if
anywhere near this scale of housing growth is to be realised, the Growth
Areas will need to see rapid expansion. Ashford is set to grow at an
unprecedented rate, which seems unlikely to be slowed by the change of
government in 2010. Although the coalition government places no faith
in top-down housing targets, their removal – along with the apparatus
of regional planning – does not signal a retreat from additional house
building. Rather, the government envisages facilitating the delivery of
more homes – through local consensus, through an incentives-based
approach and through the simplification of the planning framework –
than the previous administration, and recognises that its policies will
be judged on their capacity to reduce housing stress and promote new
supply in support of economic growth.

Ashford borough and Growth Area

Ashford is the largest borough in the county of Kent, which forms the eastern tip of the South East Region (see Figure 5.1). The borough is predominantly rural in character and had a population of just over 100,000 in 2001 (102,661: ONS, 2001), which was distributed between the towns of Ashford and Tenterden and the rural hinterlands. More than half of the borough's population (58,936) lived in Ashford, which is by far the dominant service centre. The much smaller market town of Tenterden had a population of 7,565 (ONS, 2001). The remaining 35,000 residents were distributed across the borough's villages and smaller centres. Ashford borough is divided into 39 civil parishes; its northern and western parts lie within the Kent Downs and High Weald Area of Outstanding Natural Beauty (AONB), meaning that the orientation of growth is southward and eastward.

Figure 5.1: The county of Kent, and Ashford

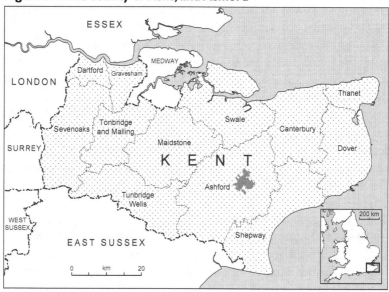

Source: Drawn by Sandra Mather

In 2007, Ashford was one of the top 40% least deprived boroughs or districts in England (ONS, 2007). It is generally affluent, although it suffers some pockets of income and other forms of deprivation. The 2001 Population Census revealed that 65% of the borough's residents were economically active, topping both the regional (64.1%) and national (61.1%) averages (ONS, 2001). Just 1.3% of residents were unemployed and claiming benefit, compared to 1.4% across the region and 2.3% nationally (ONS, 2009). However, on other measures, Ashford appeared less well-to-do than neighbouring areas. While the proportion of residents placed in the highest socioeconomic groups (27.7%) was higher than the national average (27.3%), it was lower than the regional average of 31.9%. The borough's social composition has changed rapidly over recent decades. A combination of high living standards and high-quality rural landscapes has fuelled in-migration and population growth. Between 1991 and 2001, the total population rose from 93,331 to 102,661; by 2011, it was expected to have risen to 119,600 – a 29% increase in just 20 years (ABC, 2008).

Ashford is a market town set within a traditionally agricultural area, but in recent years it has begun to establish itself as an industrial and commercial centre, building on excellent transport links. These include an 'international' rail hub, with fast connections to London (36 minutes), Paris (1 hour, 56 minutes) and Brussels (1 hour, 47 minutes, once a day). The M20 motorway also runs through the borough and there are junctions to the north and south east of Ashford. In 2006, roughly 56,000 people were employed in the borough and roughly the same number commuted to jobs outside of Ashford, many to London. Commuting is an important feature of life within Ashford. In a recent typology tracking economic, political and demographic diversification across rural England, Lowe and Ward (2007) classified the borough as a 'dynamic commuter area':

> In terms of social structure, dynamic commuter areas can be thought of as an extension of the wealthy suburbs of the South East into the surrounding rural areas. They are concentrated in a crescent around the Greater London conurbation.... They are socio-economically dynamic and affluent [and] a young to middle-age, high-income professional class predominates....
>
> Dynamic commuter residents tend to be articulate and well-connected into networks of power and influence, and quite prepared to engage with the politico-administrative system at local, regional and national levels. They would be particularly resistant to further encroachments in terms of land-use and other developments which might undermine the rural idyll into which they have bought. (Lowe and Ward, 2007, unpaginated)

Because residents are articulate and 'well-connected into networks of power and influence', and because they have bought into a rural lifestyle, such areas may be characterised by a propensity towards vocalised concern, even where there are not major housing growth proposals. Major improvements in Ashford's transport infrastructure, especially the opening of the High Speed 1 link to London, is likely to bring more dynamic commuters to the borough in the years ahead, or at least to its rural hinterlands if not to the town of Ashford itself. This may give new impetus to existing debates over development, especially if there are further expansions of the town in the future. Ashford, its major transport links and its key settlements are shown in Figure 5.2.

Figure 5.2: Ashford borough

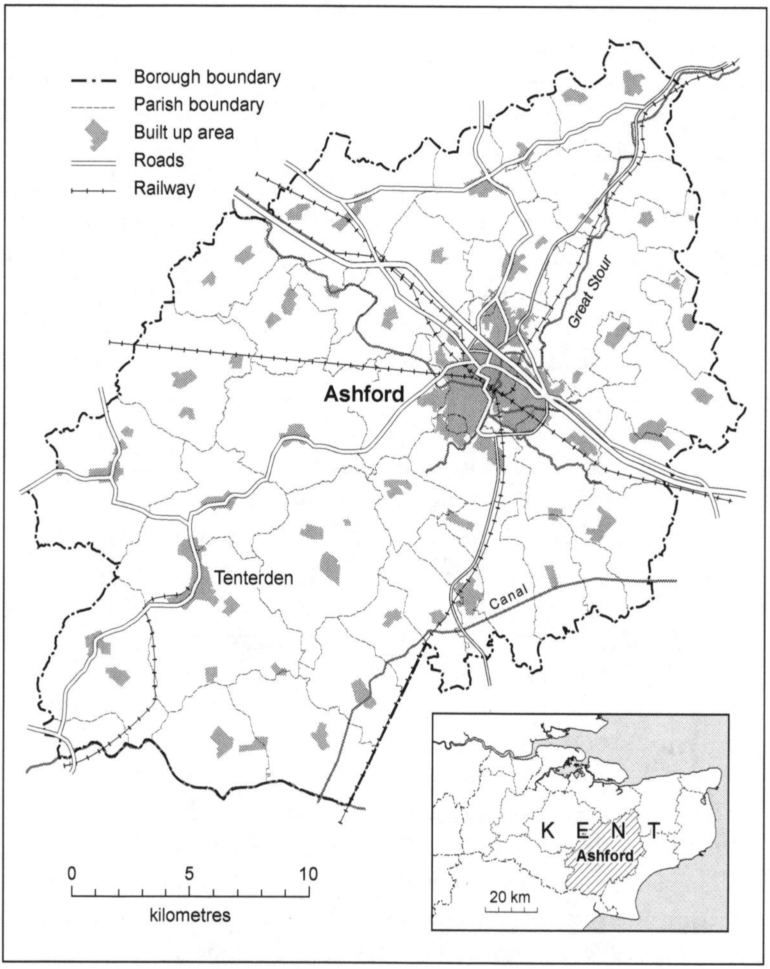

Source: Drawn by Sandra Mather

In 2001, a study on the potential of Ashford to absorb additional growth was commissioned by the regional assembly. This was undertaken by the consultants Halcrow (Halcrow/ABC, 2002) and concluded that employment growth of 18,000 additional jobs and population growth of 35,000 residents would be possible over the following 15 years (2002, p 17). Once Ashford's Growth Area status was confirmed in 2003, a Greater Ashford Development Framework (GADF) was drawn up and published in draft in the following year. The framework, produced by a team of consultants for English Partnerships on behalf of Ashford Borough Council, offered a vision for strategic growth. It evaluated several growth scenarios in light of the requirements of the Office of the Deputy Prime Minister's 2003 Communities Plan (ODPM, 2003), developing a strategic growth model to show how within approximately 16 km^2 of land take, 28,000 new jobs and 31,000 homes could be accommodated between 2001 and 2031. These were the GADF's own revised 'broad-brush' calculations (Urban Initiatives et al, 2005, p 77). Linking to Ashford's Core Strategy, the GADF provided a framework for development and investment by key delivery partners across all sectors.

More broadly, the final iteration of the South East Plan (GOSE, 2009) required that 56,700 additional dwellings be built in the East Kent and Ashford subregion between 2006 and 2026, with 22,700 (47%) concentrated in the Ashford Growth Area (the effective revocation of the Regional Spatial Strategies in May 2010 did not change this 'target'). The borough continues to face a major growth challenge. There is capacity for only 32% of these homes to be built in Ashford itself, with the remainder having to be delivered within urban extensions. The Core Strategy outlines plans to build approximately 15,500 dwellings on greenfield sites.

The growth proposals

The Growth Area agenda is focused on the town of Ashford and its immediate surrounding area (see Figure 5.3). This means that the borough's Core Strategy (ABC, 2008) concentrates planned growth within the town and on its edges, offering a vision of rapid change in terms of large numbers of new homes, new employment sites and new infrastructure. In contrast, the pace of change in some of the borough's more rural and outlying areas will be far slower and incremental, the intention being to preserve environmental quality and maintain the special character of certain villages. The Core Strategy takes forward the broad vision presented in the GADF, accepting that major urban extensions are the most sustainable way of growing the

borough's population and economic base. Two major expansion sites
are identified: the first at Chilmington Green/Discovery Park on the
south-west edge of the town; and the second at Cheeseman's Green/
Waterbrook to the south east (see Figure 5.4). The lack of primary
constraint – either environmental or physical – has made these locations
natural candidates for expansion. There are no landscape designations
(as there are elsewhere in the borough), agricultural land quality is low,
and expansion in these areas has been predicted to be relatively easy to
integrate with existing infrastructure, linking them by public transport
back to Ashford's centre.

Figure 5.3: Ashford growth proposals

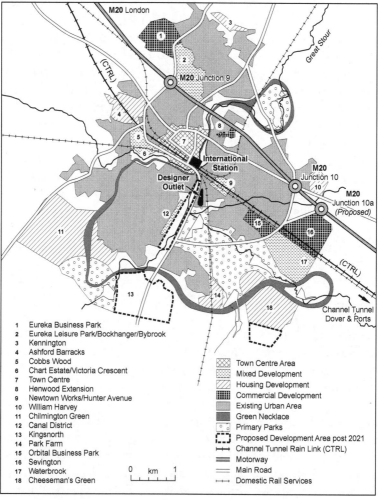

Source: The GADF

Figure 5.4: The principal urban extensions

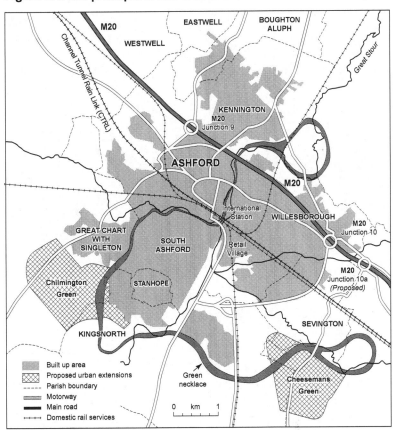

Source: Drawn by Sandra Mather

The Chilmington Green/Discovery Park site lies to the south west of the town and covers part of the parishes of Great Chart with Singleton, Kingsnorth and Shadoxhurst. Core Strategy Policy CS5 states that Chilmington Green will be developed as a 'new mixed-use urban community' and will be designed to maximise the potential use of public transport, walking and cycling with improved links to Ashford town centre and surrounding areas. It will act as a focus for housing, employment and leisure amenity growth. It will be well related to the rural landscape surroundings by the creation of a well-designed and defined edge to the development and a 'sensitive transition' to adjoining areas and the wider countryside. It is intended that the scheme will comprise 3,400 dwellings and provide 600 jobs by 2021, with the potential for a further 3,300 dwellings and 400 jobs by 2031 (ABC, 2008).

Image 5.1: New housing at Chilmington Green, July 2010

The same Core Strategy Policy also details the urban extension at Cheeseman's Green/Waterbrook. Development at Cheeseman's Green will occur to the north west and south east of Captain's Wood (an ancient coppiced hornbeam-oak-ash woodland), which includes parts of Mersham and Sevington parish. The Waterbrook area was previously seen as being suitable mainly for B8 storage and distribution uses, but Policy SC5 suggested suitability for a mix of employment, residential and other uses that would link the area to Ashford town. Although discrete areas, the Core Strategy made it clear that Cheeseman's Green and Waterbrook should be viewed as a single extension with a joint capacity to deliver 4,300 additional homes and 1,475 jobs by 2021, and a further 2,200 homes and 750 jobs by 2031 (ABC, 2008).

Local reaction

Like all growth proposals, those around Ashford provoked a range of responses: concerns and anxieties that inevitably accompany dramatic and unsettling change. The account of reactions here provides a point of entry into the study of communities and neighbourhoods in and around the Growth Area.

Press articles and information from Ashford Borough Council's consultation web portal highlight some of the concerns that the planned growth triggered. Not surprisingly, residents were concerned about the potential impact on their communities and on their homes; and they remained uncertain over the level of impact, and this uncertainty, in itself, was another source of anxiety. Four specific key areas of concern were prevalent:

- impact on areas of rural fringe;
- impact on visual amenity and wildlife habitats;
- housing densities and types and whether these would be 'appropriate';
- the willingness of policy actors to take due notice of community concerns.

Protecting areas of rural fringe from urban encroachment

Some parish councils on the rural fringe vehemently objected to the proposed extensions, arguing a need to protect areas of rural fringe from urban encroachment. In response to the Cheeseman's Green proposal, Mersham and Sevington Parish Council (2006) argued that 'the area covered by the proposal is not part of urban Ashford ... it is completely unacceptable to ignore totally the quality of life and environment of existing residents in the area', adding that if the extension were to go ahead, 'there would be insufficient space left to maintain any extent of rural landscape between Ashford and the communities of rural Sevington and Mersham'. An individual response was that 'these proposals will ruin the pleasant rural surroundings of Ashford: they will create a real risk of flooding in Ashford and cause major traffic congestion'. In 2006, Conservative Member of Parliament for Ashford, Damian Green, came out against the extensions, suggesting that 'Ashford will bear the brunt of the Government's plans and we will lose a significant area of green belt' (*Kent Online*, 2006). The general consensus was that more emphasis should be placed on smaller land releases around the periphery of the town, nearer to existing infrastructure and closer to the urban centre of Ashford. This tends to be the general reaction to urban extension proposals: that authorities should focus more attention on infill sites and seek to increase development density, for the sake of protecting rural land from urban encroachment. However, in Ashford, as in other towns facing the prospect of expansion, this did not appear possible.

Protecting visual amenity and wildlife habitats

Concerns were also raised in relation to the transport infrastructure upgrading that would be needed to serve the urban extensions and the impact they might have both on the visual amenity of the area and on wildlife habitats. One individual response was that:

the provision of a 'SmartLink' [a new 'super-fast' bus link] service to a greatly-enlarged Cheeseman's Green development will be detrimental to the current road network of ancient lanes ... there would also be environmental impacts, possibly on Captain's Wood and on hedgerows, ponds and watercourses ... any connections to the rural road network will also have a detrimental effect on those nearby rural communities. (ABC, no date)

The way in which the urban extensions might 'relate to' the surrounding countryside also triggered concerns, with some parish groups not convinced that the 'transition' from the urban extensions to the wider countryside would be achieved sensitively: 'it is difficult to see how development can be well-related to rural landscape, which is currently open farmland, without drastically changing the character of the area' (Mersham and Sevington Parish Council, 2006, unpaginated). Development, by its very nature, generates significant changes in any landscape, but the concern of communities was that the scale of the proposed development would be entirely out of keeping with rural character.

The appropriateness of housing densities and types

Additional concerns were raised over the density of development within the proposed urban extensions, and also over the associated design of homes. Communities at the rural fringe noted the increasing density of developments on brownfield sites within urban Ashford and were concerned that the requirement to deliver Growth Area housing targets might result in very high densities within the planned urban extensions. Concerns related to whether new development would 'blend in' with the existing pattern of settlement, characterised by low-density clusters of homes interspersed with green space (a typical semi-rural typology). Parishes within the rural fringe pressed for density requirements to be relaxed within the urban extensions, especially at their peripheral extremes: 'landscape which is currently arable and grazing land must be linked sensitively to the proposed housing development that would be adjacent to it' (Mersham and Sevington Parish Council, 2006, unpaginated). However, such moves might contradict the aim of delivering a target number of homes within a specified land-take, and could result in a patchwork of development rather than an integrated extension of the existing town. Replication of the existing typology may not be feasible.

The ability of communities to communicate their concern

Wye with Hinxhill Parish Council (2009) also raised concerns with regards to the LDF process itself and the ability of communities to make detailed objections, as the broad-brush nature of the core strategy document and the accompanying diagrams made this difficult:

> [W]e have considerable concerns about the impact that the Cheeseman's Green / Waterbrook development will have on residents who live within and around the edges of the development site ... our objections can only be made in detail when the Area Action Plan and other development briefs and documents have been prepared ... by this time the proposal for the development of this land will be set in stone. (Wye with Hinxhill Parish Council, 2009)

This particular parish had not always enjoyed the best of relationships with the borough council. In 2005, it faced the prospect of the redevelopment of the former Wye College site by Imperial College London, which signed a development 'concordat' with the council, essentially bypassing the community, and suggesting a rigidly top-down decision-making process. The plans for Wye College were halted by widespread opposition,[1] but the fear that policy actors do not listen to residents appeared to linger.

The Ashford study

The research for this book, partly into how communities responded to development strategies and decisions apparently raining down upon them from government and from regional planning, occurred under a different planning and political regime. But since the election of a new government in 2010, very little has altered in terms of the pace of change and the pressures that development invariably brings for Ashford's communities. Community-based planning groups began preparing their own plans in response to either the wider Growth Area proposals or concerns over smaller, more localised and incremental changes (see Chapter Twelve). The legacy of strategic planning in Southern England – together with Ashford's status as a Growth Area – forms an important context for this study. How communities cope with the pressures that this context generates, how they react to planning decisions and how they interact with policy actors are all questions set within the local and regional environment outlined in this chapter.

But before seeking answers to these questions through local analysis, some expansion of thinking on the benefits of a networked, collaborative planning approach is necessary. Linking back to ideas of iterative governance and democratic renewal, introduced in the opening parts of this book, the aim of the next chapter is to outline the precepts of collaborative rationality, to connect these to thinking on networked approaches to community action and to arrive at some practical ways of understanding how 'place communities', or interests within those communities, organise themselves and communicate with the machinery of public policy. The chapters that follow then explore the life cycle of community-based planning noted at the beginning of this book: a life cycle that moves through inception (Chapter Seven), capacity building (Chapter Eight), connecting with policy actors directly (Chapter Ten) and through intermediaries (Chapter Eleven), sometimes drawing up community-based plans (Chapter Twelve) and achieving a status in the policy and planning process (Chapter Thirteen) that signals either a genuine governance shift or more cosmetic change.

Note

[1] An account of the events at Wye, described as the 'inside story', is offered by Hewson (2007).

SIX

Power, capacity and collaborative planning

> [W]e will create a *new system of collaborative planning* by:
> giving local people the power to engage in genuine local
> planning through collaborative democracy – designing a
> local plan from the 'bottom up', starting with the aspirations
> of neighbourhoods. (Conservative Party, 2009, p 3, emphasis
> added)

The earlier chapters of this book outlined how the established concepts
of 'collaborative governance' and 'spatial planning' were embraced
in the UK as a means of deepening and broadening institutional
capacity by enabling the development of coordinated local responses
to an increasingly complex set of societal and governance challenges.
A decade ago, Allmendinger and Tewdwr-Jones (2002) noted that
these concepts were part of a Third Way in the process of governance,
which itself was short-hand for the idea of a 'new social democracy',
motoring Labour's reform agenda (and now propelling the localism of
the UK coalition government). The principal proponent of the Third
Way and Tony Blair's 'favourite academic' (Carter, 2004, p 54), Anthony
Giddens, joined others in arguing for democratic renewal through a
revival of civil society (Giddens, 1998) that would involve wider and
deeper public participation, building capacity and social capital within
communities, empowering people to have a say in the way decisions are
taken and services delivered, and generally establishing a new contract
and relationship between public, private and community actors. Only
through this mode of collaborative governance – built on the established
idea of communicative action with its links into collaborative planning
– could an attempt be made to address the 'disaggregation' of state and
society noted in Chapter Two.

Collaborative planning and networks

The foundations of the collaborative planning approach are found
in the work of Habermas (1984), who forwarded the concept of
'communicative action' as a way of explaining human rationality.

Habermas was critical of what he considered to be the one-sided process of modernisation, which had been dominated by 'experts' and scientific rationalisation, and which he argued had resulted in society being increasingly 'administered' at a level that was ever-more remote from the lives of ordinary people. Participatory democracy and the ability to openly debate matters of public importance – the fundamental building blocks of a thriving and progressive society – had been nullified through an over-professionalised and closed model of government. This situation was presented as the antithesis of communicative action: a process by which actors in society seek to reach common understanding and to coordinate actions by reasoned argument, consensus and cooperation rather than by strategic action strictly in pursuit of their own goals (Habermas, 1984, p 86).

Habermas provided a theoretical platform for a view of planning that emphasised:

- widespread participation;
- routinely sharing information with the public;
- reaching consensus through dialogue (rather than merely exercising mandated power);
- avoiding the privileging of experts and bureaucrats;
- replacing the model of the exclusive 'technical expert' with one of the inclusive 'reflective planner' (Innes, 1995).

The theory of communicative action was necessarily identified with the accumulation of 'social capital': strategic actions designed to achieve personal goals are individualistic (Habermas, 1984, p 286) whereas communicative action, grounded in dialogue and common understanding, is a shared endeavour that springs from an increased capacity to understand problems and build agreement around particular preventative or remedial actions.

Collaborative planning approaches, built on the principles of communicative action, are premised on *diverse* stakeholders (community members, interest or other local groups in the chapters that follow, but also developers and other business groups) coming together for face-to-face dialogue, each representing differing perspectives on a shared problem or opportunity, and collectively constructing a strategy to remedy that problem or grasp an opportunity. The rationale of collaborative action is that it facilitates a fusion of differing interpretations and perspectives, which can produce innovative solutions that are exclusively possible through interactive cooperation (see Forester; 1989, 1999; Innes, 1995, 2004; Healey, 1997; Innes and

Booher, 1999, 2000, 2003; Innes and Gruber, 2001). Interaction is central to collaborative planning, triggering the formation of networks that evolve and strengthen over time. Through the sharing of skills and knowledge, networks develop greater capacity. The result has been described as 'network power' (Booher and Innes, 2002; Innes and Booher, 2003, 2004), built on the success that previously separate actors achieve in linking together agendas and manifest in their increased capacity to influence decision making. Participants in dialogue also build a lasting sense of shared identity, as part of a larger system, which helps maintain the integrity of collaborative structures.

Together with actor diversity, two further requisite conditions underpin the emergence of network power. First, different actors must find themselves in a situation where their ability to achieve their own goals is dependent on the actions of others, and recognise this *interdependence*. Participants within the network must each have something that others want and need (a skill, an expertise, a contact, a legitimacy and so on) and must recognise their own need for something that only others can provide. A system and process of mutually beneficial exchange needs to take root. This might mean, for example, that one partner brings authority and resources to the table while another brings democratic accountability or the appreciable legitimacy of grassroots support. The concept of *'reciprocity'* captures this idea of mutual exchange, and occurs when actors realise that they can create new opportunities by sharing what each can exclusively offer. According to Booher and Innes (2002, pp 227–8), *interdependence* and *reciprocity* between *diverse* partners are critical to the generation of network power, producing capacities that did not previously exist. The second condition for the emergence of network power is *authenticity* in dialogue and communication. This is the basic requirement for genuine dialogue, grounded in transparency and trust, which is fundamental to the operation of an effective network (Booher and Innes, 2002, pp 229–31).

Social capital as a product of network power

Network power – with its various prerequisites – delivers a greater *capacity* to influence decision making. Enhanced capacity, because of its link to network action and power, infers increased social capital (ie, the human capital that coagulates at the intersections of social networks). Woolcock (1998) links the concept of social capital to the strength of ties between individuals, and to the networks and the norms of reciprocity and trustworthiness built upon these ties. Social capital has been seen as having practical utility, helping communities to mitigate the effects of socioeconomic disadvantage. Putnam (2000, pp 319-25), for example, asserts that where social networks are strong, tangible benefits may be realised for individuals, and for entire communities and neighbourhoods. This is partly because common interest and identity may spawn specific self-help and voluntary initiatives: community groups, for example, may come together to run local services (Moseley, 2000b) that would not otherwise be provided by either the public or private sectors. But more generally, such networks may deliver the solutions and innovations needed to overcome conflicts that inhibit problem resolution without the necessity of direct action: they may 'grease the wheels' of broader processes from which solutions flow (Putnam, 2000). Numerous commentators (including Coleman, 1994; Beem, 1999; Falk and Kilpatrick, 2000; Putnam, 2000; and Field, 2003) have evaluated the importance of building social capital. Falk and Kilpatrick (2000) point to the benefits of collective action in dispute resolution; Putnam (2000) attaches great importance to the trust generated through repeated interaction; and Beem (1999) argues that social capital is merely an acknowledgement of interdependency – the need to work together to get things done.

Social capital is a product of network power and also the raw material that fuels further empowerment. The two – capital and power – share a cyclical relationship. The networks on which capacity is built promote both empowerment (to take or to influence decisions) and the further development of capacity, strengthening and extending networks and so on. *Empowerment* can be viewed as the process of enhancing the capacity of individuals or groups to make choices and to transform those choices into desired actions and outcomes. Social *capacity* at the community level derives from 'the interaction of human capital, organisational resources and social capital existing within a given community that can be leveraged to solve collective problems and improve or maintain the well-being of that community' (Chaskin et al, 2001, p 7).

The underlying concept of *power* – the capacity to implement – is also critical. Empowerment is the process that places power in the hands of people for use in their own lives, their own communities or in society at large, by giving them the capacity to act on issues that they judge important. The idea of empowerment suggests that power is not fixed in any one location; rather, it can move and relocate. But because empowerment also suggests expansion of capacity, the net gains of one individual (or community) need not mean a net loss to another. The reality of groups becoming empowered is that their capacity to influence and implement increases. Furthermore, the capacity of those who previously wielded more exclusive forms of power is also increased by virtue of their connections with new groups, and new alliances. Thus, within a 'new social democracy', power is shared across public and private realms, increasing the capacity of each to jointly implement solutions (assuming the presence of true interdependence, reciprocity and authenticity). This is of course a very positive perspective on power and empowerment, and one which is questioned later in the chapter.

Unequal and uneven power relationships are often viewed as pivotal to conflict, and to the 'adversarialism' that blights local government: one group finds itself in a weak position relative to another, becoming over time frustrated by and alienated from the political process. Some community groups have found themselves in this situation. Yet Parsons (1963) and Foucault (1980) suggest that such a predicament is not inevitable. Parsons' work underpins much contemporary writing on the dynamic nature of power, and also current thinking on how power might be harnessed to address the disparate and often more complex needs of the modern world. His view was that power is not finite and can indeed be expanded and shared, particularly for the purpose of legitimising action or improving 'public administration', and need not be concentrated in a single individual or agency. The idea of 'consensual power' is built on the symmetry of acknowledged common ground (and common interest) and collective strength: with these two conditions met, it is possible to conceive of 'power with' or 'network power' (see above) offering a means of bridging different interests, reducing conflict and establishing a new balance in social relations. Like Parsons before him, Foucault (1980) maintained that power is not inert, and nor is its existence *de facto*, and reducible to institutions or government bodies. Rather, power is *relational*: it is constituted in networks of affiliation. This view, however, reopens the possibility of abuse: that capability is employed by the 'powerful' as a means of imposing a particular outcome or mode of organisation on the *relatively* weak. While this is entirely possible, Foucault argued that there is a more efficient and effective means of wielding power: the sharing and use of undistorted knowledge within a network of independent actors who pursue the common objective of producing and achieving new and improved outcomes is the most powerful *modus operandi*.

The foundations of much of this thinking on collaborative planning were laid in the 1940s and 1950s, with Parsons' work reflecting an undercurrent of concern with social relations and social action. Foucault's view of effective power, built around truth and common goals, and flowing through networks, provides much of the conceptual rationale for reinventing, and therefore reinvigorating, the processes of governance. In the sections that follow, how such networks might be understood (and how the satisfaction of key conditions might be tested) is explored in more detail. This is then followed by a return to the role of power in such networks, and a more detailed examination of whether it is possible to accept that actors will wield power in pursuit of 'optimum' collective outcomes, or whether they will be guided by vested interest.

Network-based planning and social networks

The 'network' concept has contributed a number of important insights into longstanding debates over governance, power, capacity and social capital. It is undoubtedly the case that a decentralisation of capacity in contemporary society owes much to the formation of collaborative networks, through which power flows from the public to the private realm, affording an ever-broader set of actors influence over traditionally institutionalised decision-making processes. Some understanding of the nature and form of these networks can be achieved through 'social network analysis', the characteristics of which have been outlined by Boissenvain (1979), among others. Such analysis focuses systematic attention on the linkages between actors (distinguishing, for example, '*bonding*' relationships between close neighbours from '*bridging*' ties between network subgroups), identifying the relationships between members of a network and revealing their interdependency. It also focuses on the *nature* of relationships, on their strength, and on possible tensions.

In particular, the close analysis of social networks may reveal the position of members relative to traditional loci of power, their access to resources and how their relative capabilities are dependent on their overall position within a network. It is a means of understanding group dynamics, the reciprocity of linkages, and of explaining the flow of power across a network and the degree to which consensual power and action are attainable, given observable network characteristics. Because of its concern with interaction, social network analysis offers more than an institutional perspective: rather than focusing narrowly on institutional capabilities, it can search specifically for capabilities that are relational and have no single owner. The concern with interrelation, interdependency and interaction also makes it possible to identify new forms of social organisation, including coalitions and cliques. The analysis of networks in community-based planning can be used to reveal alliances, of various kinds, and to explore the way in which communities of interest interact with policy communities (perhaps through intermediaries that act as 'bridges') and on what basis. These concerns are elaborated upon in Chapter Nine.

Such analysis is rooted in the work of Moreno (1934) and Warner and Lunt (1941). Following the identification of key relationships between individuals, they set about defining groups (with stronger relational bonds) by mapping the connections and flows of information between them, and then by presenting these 'social networks' diagrammatically. Later, the 'egocentric network analysis' of Barnes (1954), and then Bott (1955, 1957), took a slightly different approach. Barnes and Bott focused on individuals and the nature of their relationships, studying personal networks rather than attempting to deconstruct entire social groups. Individuals were conceived as *egos* and their 'networks' of family, friends and work or recreation associates as *altars*. The critical difference between the *sociometry* of Moreno and the *egocentric* network was that while the former sought to unpack pre-identified groupings (in an organisation of known parameters), the latter let the analysis itself (rooted in an individual) define the social and spatial extent of the network. In the next chapter, an attempt begins to incrementally develop a view of community-based planning networks and relationships, starting with key individuals and extending to local groupings, extra-local alliances and then relationships with policy actors. Thinking on social networks is used to inform discussions of community-based planning arrangements and 'connectivity' actors apparently external to community networks. It provides a perspective rather than a fixed analytical framing and is, again, returned to in Chapter Nine when connectivity between communities and policy actors (and between the products of informal and formal planning activity) is placed under the spotlight.

Critiques of collaborative planning theory

It was only a short jump, from the analysis of social networks, to the idea that while *human capital* is an individual asset, *social capital* is generated through the relationships that individuals share (Coleman, 1990, p 304). There is a rationale for the maintenance of network bonds. While these are sometimes built around emotion or tradition, at other times they will be based on a belief in mutual benefit. The idea that network activity and structure can influence capacity and performance is important, and may explain the level of social capital in an organisation or community, broadly defined. Relational social capital, in Coleman's (1990, p 302) view, is 'productive, making possible the achievement of certain ends that would not be attainable in its absence'. These underpinning ideas are central to a belief in the effectiveness of collaborative planning, but as Burt (2000, p 347) explains, they are grounded in the simple premise that 'people who do better are somehow better connected'.

Great faith in the achievability of optimum shared outcomes underpins the concept of 'consensual power' (i.e. power that is accumulated through networks and through consensus building), and this faith may downplay the effect of vested interest and the pursuit of individual goals. For some commentators, there is something just too perfect and sanitised running through theories of consensual power and collaborative planning. The network conditions of 'network power' – especially diversity – appear easier to satisfy than the power conditions, built on dialogue authenticity, trust and reciprocity. For this reason, critiques of network-based collaborative planning tend to focus on questions of power and the extent to which 'power play' is given due consideration in planning theory (Flyvberg, 1998). Unlike Parsons (1963) and Foucault (1980), many theorists see power not as relational in its construction but only in the way that it creates subordination between the powerful and the weak. Proponents of the idea of 'power over' (Clegg, 1989) place capacity in the hands of competing individuals and agencies who engage in power struggles triggered by conflicts of interest (Lukes, 1974). Power is a means of securing compliance or control and results in relationships of *dependence* and hierarchical structures that are inherently and necessarily unequal. Flyvberg (1998) contends that much collaborative planning theory is 'blind' to prohibiting, restricting and dominating forms of power intended to maintain relationships of super-ordination and subordination. Leadership, for example, is often coercive and concerned with exerting influence over a willing, or an unwilling, follower (McNamara and Trumbull, 2007, p 33). In the UK, government at all levels has sought the compliance of 'partners' by tying funding or resources to particular actions: for example, grant money to housing delivery or to the rapid turnaround of planning applications.

It is in this context that Holman (2008) argues that, in practice, the supposed benefits accruing from collaborative policy formulation and delivery are difficult to achieve, being eroded by powerful forms of coercion and by the concentration of power in a few hands (Holman, 2008, pp 534-53), which leads then to manipulative relationships and to poor communication, as the powerful within a network see little need to listen to relatively weaker interests. In planning, this might mean regulators communicating to local groups but failing to listen to what those groups themselves have to say. This lack of 'authentic dialogue' and 'reciprocity' will hinder the development of a shared context, resulting in a continued divergence in individual perspectives.

For Holman (2008, p 533), the failure to reciprocate causes mistrust, misunderstanding and friction within the network. Well-connected, and often central, nodes dominate communication and 'saturate' the network with their point of view (2008, p535). It is often the case that business interests or public sector actors are more efficient publicists than community groups. Hence, power is determined by the exclusivity of resources, resulting in an imbalanced 'dialogue'.

These criticisms of network-based collaborative planning focus on possible disruptions to the *process*, reducing the likelihood of achieving consensus around particular courses of action, and running contrary to the idea of a genuinely 'collaborative democracy'. But even when key conditions are met, and power appears 'consensual', it is still not certain that agreed outcomes will be achieved. The process of governance may appear more interactive, but interaction remains heavily circumscribed by mechanisms designed to ensure strategic compliance, and one way of ensuring such compliance is to strictly ration the flow of real power from traditional policy actors to communities.

Unpacking 'networked governance' in Ashford

The chapters that now follow are concerned with networked governance expressed through community-based planning. The initial focus is on the informal ways in which communities coalesce around local agendas, reach out to other interest groups and interface with the processes and procedures of 'traditional' planning. These communities are represented in the first instance by the parish planning groups, which have often led on the production of the community-based plans introduced in Chapter Four. These have commonly signalled a desire not only to connect with formal planning frameworks, but also to mobilise community action and generate greater social cohesion around a sense of shared purpose. However, for groups hitherto under-represented in the decision-making process, finding ways to connect to traditional policy actors and shape decisions would seem to be a logical aim of community-based plan production. The ability to achieve this connection, or 'linkage', is a key measure of success in community participation (Holman, 2008, p 526). But while Owen et al (2007) have shown that community plans tend to emerge from increasingly active and vocal networks – with a variety of actors becoming involved in their production – these networks have tended to lack the capacity to solve collective problems, partly because the private realm of community action has appeared, in many instances, incapable of connecting with the public realm of policy making in any meaningful way. The latter has remained closed to local input; interdependency has not been established; and power has remained firmly in the hands of traditional institutions. A number of concepts highlighted in this chapter – including 'group diversity', 'interdependency between members', 'trust', 'reciprocity' and 'authenticity' – offer important guides for understanding how networks operate and how capacity, and connectivity, are achieved. Community dynamics and capacity within Ashford's communities are examined in the next two chapters and this is followed, in Chapter Nine, by an elaboration of how connectivity is achieved between the 'internal' networks of community groups and the 'external' world of policy actors, and the extent to which different interests can be bridged, generating a 'consensual' rather than a coercive form of power.

SEVEN

Community dynamics and planning

Neighbourhood planning is rooted in community dynamics, in the relationships and interactions that bind people together. These interactions may create what Tönnies (1887) described as a 'unity of will' and a sense of shared identity (see also Cohen, 1985), although they can also be a source of division, as fractures form between competing groups and diverse interests (Panelli, 2006). Broadly, communities are constituted of networks of social exchange and it is through these networks that community action is realised, often grounded in the emergence of 'community leaders' and in the coalescence of groupings that play a key role in catalysing interest around planning, development and broader service issues. In this chapter, we examine these groupings and these dynamics within the case study communities, drawing out the context for neighbourhood planning. This chapter also elaborates on the catalysts for, and motivating factors behind, community-based planning: who drives the process and who is co-opted or selected to move things forward. It presents an initial view of 10 communities from the perspective of groups, always including the parish clerk, tied to the parish councils. These are not necessarily viewed as primary nodes within local networks, but as practical entry points into communities, which is what they proved to be for the purposes of the study.

The study parishes

Throughout the chapters that follow, parishes are referred to using a notation that is designed to conceal their identities. Some of the information and views relayed by these 'parish groups' (PGs) was clearly confidential and not for public dissemination. For this reason, the 10 study parishes[1] are referred to as 'PG1' to 'PG10'. Sometimes the identity of parishes is revealed in the narratives and quotations presented. Where this clearly does not infringe on confidentiality, no attempt is made to conceal their identity. The case study parishes are shown in Figure 7.1 How community activism is triggered within different places is inevitably affected by the different experiences of the parishes. This issue is examined later in this chapter. On occasions, community activity gestates slowly as interest in local issues takes root; but sometimes it happens suddenly as passions are inflamed and communities seek to right what they view as great wrongs. In Ashford, some parishes found themselves in the path of planned growth (ie, Great Chart with Singleton, Shadoxhurst, and Mersham with Sevington) or some distance from it (eg, Pluckley); others faced what they saw as considerable threats to the wellbeing of their communities and mobilised in response (eg, Wye with Hinxhill – see Chapter Five). Their capacity to mobilise, or simply to run out a programme of local participation through the parish planning process, was inevitably shaped by their sociodemographic profiles. Some of the communities had a large proportion of retired, professional people within them, ready in many instances to answer the call of community service. They also had a sizeable number of highly articulate, educated people, and also a cross-section of young and old, families and single people. Each of the communities was different, although they were all older (with the exceptions of Mersham with Sevington and Great Chart with Singleton) and apparently more educated/managerial (with the exceptions of Mersham and Pluckley) than Ashford as a whole. The more urban parishes (within the path of the extensions) had more mixed profiles, although the majority of parishes in this study were, broadly speaking, affluent, middle class, older and well educated.

Actual statistical profiles have been omitted from this book as key features are more enlightening than the detail. The modal age group across Ashford was 25 to 44 years and the mean age 39 years. Eight of the 10 parishes were 'older' than Ashford as a whole (using the 2001 Census returns), with the modal age group being 45 to 64 years. There were, as noted above, two exceptions: Great Chart with Singleton and Mersham with Sevington had younger age profiles. The modal group for the former was 25 to 44 years (like Ashford as a whole), and these two parishes had the highest proportions of children under the age of 16 years. Generally, Woodchurch, Wye with Hinxhill, and Charing, at the other end of the spectrum, were the oldest of the selected parishes. Almost 24% of Woodchurch residents were over 65 years of age: the figure for Wye with Hinxhill was 21.6%; and for Charing, nearly 25%. These figures compared to an Ashford mean of just over 16%.

Close to 28% of Ashford residents were in the first socioeconomic class – in 'managerial and professional' occupations. Only Bilsington, Woodchurch and Wye with Hinxhill fell beneath this mean, although, in the cases of Woodchurch and Wye, this appeared to be due to higher levels of retirement. Bilsington had the smallest population of any of the selected parishes and a large proportion of its residents were classed as small employers and own-account workers. This is an agricultural area with many people employed in farming. Generally, the selected parishes mixed commuters engaged in professional occupations with retired households. Despite being generally younger, Great Chart with Singleton along with Mersham with Sevington each had more than a third of their populations in managerial and professional occupations. Pluckley had a similarly 'professional' population.

Figure 7.1: The case study parishes

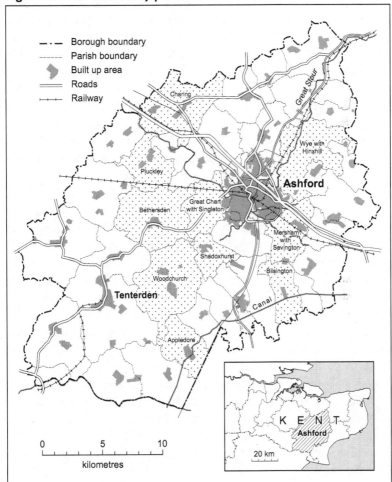

Source: Drawn by Sandra Mather

Communities, parish councils and group dynamics

The vitality of a community is expressed in the connections between its members, and in the bonds that form around common interests, or around conflicts. These are potentially vast in range and in the Ashford communities, a bewildering array of groupings (especially clubs and societies) were present. The majority of these were based around social activities (ie, hobbies and personal interests) such as tennis, bowls and cricket clubs, the Women's Institute (WI) and local garden, drama and historical societies. But some local interest or pressure groups existed with a campaigning function and political face: village design, footpath preservation and flood groups, for instance. High levels of community interaction were alluded to within the selected parishes, alongside the suggestion of ample "community feel" (PG1):

> '[W]e've got a lot of clubs and societies in the village, but they are sports and social, they aren't village planning groups or something like that. So, there's a lot going on and this has always been the case in this village for years and years and years. We're a very lively village.' (PG2)

Levels of awareness within Parish Groups, of other active community groups tended to be high, largely because of a significant degree of 'cross-membership': many parish councillors were themselves members of other groups, and viewed this as evidence of the embeddedness of the parish councils within the social life of the communities they represented. The parish councils were thought, by those interviewed, to occupy a point of intersection between overlapping social networks: councillors were considered to be well connected, which facilitated the sharing of information and local knowledge:

> '[A] lot of it is personal, because of course the parish councillors themselves belong to a lot of these groups, so of course, well, I think they probably all belong to some. Certain things are run by the same people. So obviously there's a lot of cross-membership, information-sharing and liaison.' (PG3)

Because of changes in the composition of parish councils, with new members joining and old ones leaving, it was sometimes difficult for council members to keep track of how many active societies and clubs there were in a parish. This was felt to be significant, as interest groups might have an important role to play in community-based planning, in terms of setting agendas or providing evidence:

> '[I]f we're going to do a community plan, we need to get these people on board with it and involve them because they can actually give us an awful lot of the information and ... spread the net wider, to [those] parts of the community that *can* be contacted. So, we've done a trawl, and it's still growing, but I still don't know how many there are.' (PG4)

The degree of connectivity between parish council members and the wider community – and also the ability to maintain links – will influence capacity, and is indicated here in knowledge of other groups. However, interest networks are not entirely inclusive, giving rise to the suggestion above that some 'parts of the community' remain inaccessible to the parish council, even when that council seems deeply embedded in a wide array of local interests. But still, they regularly provide a stable and constant 'body' within the community and are frequently relied on to act as a central 'hub' for a broader set of community interests:

> '[T]here are some groups of which we are unaware. Several years ago, the village hall did an open day where they generally invited all organisations to come along and we ended up with far more organisations than we expected in the village, so there are almost splinter groups who are possibly involved in the village.' (PG5)

It may be the case that parish councils are unaware of certain groups because of a bias in their own composition, or in their socioeconomic profile, which makes them less likely to come into contact with particular local interests. Some councils had a membership clearly skewed towards an older demographic – 'we only have five councillors: three men and two women. Three of those are retired, I think [and] two of them are in their early eighties' (PG6) – but others seemed more balanced, in terms of age and socioeconomic situations, challenging the often-held view that parish councils are dominated by the retired and the relatively wealthy:

> '[I]'ve got to say, the parish council has got a good continuity to it. We have what I call a healthy movement of people on and off, so it renews itself slowly, one maybe two a year or something like that, it's got a wide coverage and, what I

would say about it is, that everybody contributes positively with the skills they've got. We've got a really good spread.' (PG1)

The degree of direct involvement in the parish council (ie, by non-members through attendance at meetings) was found to be generally low within all of the parishes, unless there was an event of significance or an issue that had prompted particular concern. Only perceived threats to the community, often contentious planning applications, caused the wider community to mobilise and engage with the parish council. Some members lamented the apparent lack of willingness shown by the wider community to get involved in parish council affairs, but others were more circumspect, conceding that it was naive to expect people to attend council meetings unless there was a particular issue that had caught their attention. It is "foolhardy", as one interviewee put it, "to think that people are just going to turn up just to listen to some old locals spouting" (PG6). Moreover:

> 'Parish councils are strange beasts, apart from anything else, you get a strange, eclectic mix of people that sit on them, but unless you actually want to take part and have an interest in it, it sort of goes on around you without you doing much about it. I desperately tried to get more people to our parish council meetings, but it doesn't seem to have any effect ... all the time things are going good, everybody will let you get on with it and take care of it but, as for actually taking part, it's sometimes very difficult for people to come out and put their head above the parapet.' (PG4)

There is sometimes limited interest and participation in parish council meetings, perhaps suggesting an apathy that strikes at the heart of the empowerment and neighbourhood agenda. Parish councils have been widely regarded as 'powerless' and as an 'ineffective' tier of governance, which is a view that may be difficult to challenge especially in less 'accessible' parts of communities. The perceived inability of parish councils to influence strategic decision making, or effect change, often leads to disengagement:

> '[B]asically, everybody leaves the parish council alone, they don't come to meetings, they only get excited when there's something happening on their doorstep ... it is quite demeaning for us, when you give up the time ... to try and

do something and we feel we do a reasonable job but, at the end of the day, when you're in the pub and some of your neighbours say "you lot are a waste of time, aren't you" kind of attitude, you feel like saying "well, you do it then, you come and do something then, you don't want to give up any time do you, but you're very quick to criticise", so you do feel like you've got a double-edged sword. There are those that are really just saying "it's a done deal, so what's the point" and the others that criticise you and say "you're not doing enough".' (PG7)

Despite reference to 'community feel' (PG1 above), a lack of willingness among people to commit their free time to 'community' work was thought to be expressed in low turnout at parish meetings, not only the regular meetings but also special events. There is a difficult balance to be achieved between work and home commitments, and this can limit how much of their time people are able to 'sacrifice'. However, residents sometimes support the parish in other ways, although participation in community-based planning was perceived to be limited to older people:

'[W]e have one problem in this village and that is to involve ... how can I put it ... people in the prime of life, middle-aged people, people with families. You can't get the attention of younger people because they're up to here with their life and their family and their work and their job, anymore than you can get them involved in a planning project. People will give money, that's not the problem, the difficult bit is to get their time and interest and participation.' (PG2)

Participation may also be restricted when the parish council fails to talk with the community at large. Councils may conduct their affairs in an insular fashion, running the risk of being perceived by local residents as closed and 'unavailable', even as cliques with a narrow set of interests. This may lead to the council being regarded as an irrelevance or disconnected from the wider community (PG5). This deters involvement and can make it difficult to recruit new members. The tendency to become protectionist and to close down membership may be attributed to simple clashes of personality, to parochialism and village politics:

'[B]ecause it's such a small village, personalities come into it, and one of the people that is on the steering committee has wanted to be on the parish council for years but, because of problems with somebody else who's on, they couldn't. They wanted to be involved in the village and now they can be [as the blocking member left].' (PG6)

The above discussion gives some indication of the groupings that come together and provide an element of leadership in community-based planning. Members of parish councils tend to be active citizens who want to become involved, who pursue a range of interests and who interact with 'the community' through various social interest networks, 'embedding' themselves in the community. But the community is not merely comprised of those individuals who choose to participate in interest "groups". Those who prefer not to join the Women's Institute or the local golf club should not be seen as necessarily isolated from (and inaccessible to) others. That is not the suggestion being made here. Indeed, it is quite possible that, looking in, and not outwards, parish councils and other community groups appear introverted and disconnected from broader interests: as weak structures of community governance. How they extend their reach and mobilise the community is a topic turned to after an initial review of the catalysts for community action, starting with the urban extensions introduced in Chapter Five.

The urban extensions as a local focus and catalyst

Despite the personal and work-related barriers to broader involvement, community groups recognise that wider participation is a means of strengthening the voice of the community, perhaps through the gathering of evidence to support local campaigning. This is part of the rationale for conducting assessments of housing need among older residents, consultation exercises for new recreation areas, speed limit reviews and open meetings focused on contentious development. Tapping directly into neighbourhood concerns – with councils coordinating working groups or hosting meetings – is a means of expanding the lobbying influence of the council. The urban extensions had become a focus for some of the parishes; a topic that had clearly triggered interest in neighbourhood planning, focusing attention on the apparent impotence of councils in the face of imposed development, but also their power to effect modest change and possibly extract community benefit.

Familiar fears emerged, related to urban encroachment, increased traffic and the loss of rural tranquillity. Groups were also worried that the quality and design of housing within the extensions would be out of keeping with existing development. Instead, it might be 'alien':

> '[W]hat we're seeing being built all round us here are Jerry-built houses. I suppose we've got a conscience, all of us have got this conscience, about seeing this type of development in our village, because we don't want it. And it's not because we're NIMBY [not in my back yard]: we know we've got to have it. We don't want people to look back in the future and say, "who agreed to this awful housing?"' (PG4)

A minority of the groups expressed concerns in relation to issues that transcended parish boundaries. Two of the groups questioned the rationale behind the Communities Plan (ODPM, 2003) and regional planning, suggesting that concentration was not the only sustainable solution to accommodating growth in the South East. An alternative would have been to disperse some of the growth (eg, housing) and help improve the viability of smaller villages within Kent (PG9). Affordability, especially for young people, was also held up as a key challenge:

> '[N]ot one extra house will be built in [parish], as a result of the Ashford development, not one. I think that it's good news, but it may be bad news for [this parish] in the long-run. Not for us, because we're not as young as we used to be *and we don't want any of it*, but I think if you're young in [parish], it might be a mixed blessing because we're not going to get a school, we're not going to get this, we're not going to get that, nothing will ever happen. This could easily be a dormitory village, forever, which is fine for us, but [parish] is getting a bit like that, if you look around, there aren't that many young people here.' (PG8)

Ashford faced the prospect of becoming 'just a big dormitory' for commuters with London jobs, with groups questioning the attractiveness of the town to economic investment. The parish groups knew that Ashford International railway station had been downgraded as a hub station, losing out to Ebbsfleet. Continental services are now more irregular than were originally planned. If fewer investors were to be attracted to the town as a consequence, this could only mean that High Speed 1 is more likely to become an exit route from Ashford (back to London jobs) rather than an access route for people working in the town (PG1) or wishing to invest in the area.

The fear that housing growth will not be matched by investment in jobs is one regularly shared by community groups. Growth is perceived to be housing led. For some parishes, the urban extensions had catalysed interest in parish planning activities, swelling meetings and revitalising the councils. But not all energies had been directed at opposing plans. While a reflective preference for a more dispersed pattern of growth remained evident, the point at which this might have been achieved had long passed. Energies had therefore been redirected at harnessing the maximum community benefit from development, with some communities achieving notable successes. Despite clear limits to the reach of some parish councils, they had managed to bring more residents into a dialogue over potential community gains from development permissions. The extensions had triggered great debate and the parishes had provided an outlet for that debate, with some positive outcomes.

Motivating and mobilising community-based planning

Engagement in community-based planning had been a feature of parish activity in most locations for a number of years, but this did not mean that parish councils had drawn up general plans or produced VDSs (see Chapter Four). Rather, they had concentrated on thematic appraisals (eg, linked to traffic and parking), which they had fed back to Highways or the local police liaison officer. For some, the impetus to produce a broader plan had come from Ashford Borough Council, which was looking to parish evidence to inform the development of its LDF in 2003/04 (ie, the year before legislation requiring production of LDF, but after the Secretary of State had notified chief planning officers of the intention to move to the LDF system). It was the politicians – the local ward members or the Borough Council leader – who had raised the expectation of a tie-in between parish plans and the emergent LDF. Parishes that wanted some strategic input into planning policy – the first motivator – were led to believe that this was entirely possible, and the key purpose of parish plans were as part of the evidence base for the new spatial planning:

> 'Ashford put forward the request that parishes should consider a parish plan. It wasn't the planners asking for it, it was the leader of the Borough Council. I think this was a forerunner because they were having to begin to think about their next ... well what is called the local development

framework, so they wanted to know roughly what the villagers wanted.' (PG5)

But other groups rejected this view of the role of parish plans, arguing instead that plans had a wholly local rationale, with the process leading up to their production offering a means of 'uniting' residents around issues of specifically local concern. One of the parishes – Great Chart with Singleton – identified its community as being physically divided (into rural and suburban parts), and saw community planning as a means of bridging this divide and channelling energies into shared projects. A VDS had previously reinforced the divide. This had focused on the more rustic Great Chart, ignoring the more suburban Singleton. The process, therefore, leading up to the VDS, was itself exclusionary, so moving to a broader parish plan was felt to be a means of rectifying the problem of disunity:

> '[I]t's the only way that you've got any representation for Singleton because you could never do a Village Design Statement because (a) it's not old enough and (b) there's parts of it that you wouldn't necessarily want to protect, and it's growing, so you can't do a Village Design Statement. So, how can we best represent the thoughts and feelings of the people in Singleton?'

Fostering unity or community cohesion, however, is often a secondary consideration. Motivations behind planning exercises tend to be more pragmatic. Often, the drawing up of plans is a means of supporting funding bids for local projects. This was the case in several locations, with groups indicating that the parish plan initiative was started in order to secure funding for the village hall or other key infrastructure. In one example, there had been initial reluctance to undertake the initiative because of concerns that it would involve a considerable amount of effort and might not "produce anything that" the parish council "didn't already know" (PG6). Even the promise of financial support proved an insufficient incentive. A parish plan was only produced when it was realised that the plan itself "was the key to securing money", in this case for the refurbishment of the village hall.

Individual parish councillors tended to be the driving forces behind the production of parish plans, with the councils becoming 'hubs' for the production process: as advocates and initiators of community-based planning. In many communities it was suggested that without the involvement of the parish councils, plans were unlikely to have been produced:

> 'We didn't suddenly as a group of the general public meet up and decide we wanted to do this, no, the parish council chairman, in fact, said "we need this". These were initiatives that sprang from the parish council.' (PG2)

Image 7.1: The village of Great Chart

Generally, parish plans were viewed as a defence mechanism (a way of showing solidarity and warding off unwanted change), a business plan (required for accessing funds) or an opportunity to involve people in a 'project' that has some chance of developing community capacity, although it was not articulated like this. Rather, groups talked about people 'having their say' or 'sharing' their views. The net result, however, was a dialogue within the community that led to a statement of concerns.

Leaders, drivers and co-opted groups

In nearly all instances, the decision to put together a community plan was taken by the parish council, although the idea may have been rooted elsewhere, in the wider community or in another local group that had an interest in a funding bid going forward. But two divergent arrangements for production were then put in place: either the plan stayed with the council, and members took it forward internally, or it was parcelled up as a task for co-opted members or a completely external group who had expressed a desire to lead on plan production. Some parish councils had wanted to 'externalise' the plan, but volunteers had been thin on the ground. Often plans were produced by a very small number of individuals, which called into question the extent to which they were genuinely 'community based' and 'led'. As one PG put it: "in a lot of parishes, it's an individual or a few individuals who feel very strongly about [the plan], rather than the whole body and they carry it through" (PG7). There tended to be narrower support for plan production in instances where the plan itself was not perceived as a response to a broader threat, or where there appeared to be limited vested interest in the plan being drawn up. For example, if the plan lent support to a funding bid for, say, a recreation facility, then it was likely to be driven forward by the group who would directly benefit. But in other instances, a threat on the horizon triggered wider support for plan production, within and beyond the parish council. Sometimes there was an outpouring of enthusiasm, particularly in instances where the plan was viewed as an outlet for frustrations with decisions 'raining down from above', frequently centred on housing development. The core groups used formal (parish newsletters) and informal recruitment mechanisms, drawing in friends and neighbours, to solicit wider support. Those who had been co-opted to parish plan groups expressed a desire to 'make a contribution to the local area', felt that they had been handed an opportunity to express personal concerns or wanted to push agendas linked to their participation in other local groups. A member of the 'local preservation trust' of one village, for example, was looking to ensure that the maintenance of village character was a central theme in the parish plan.

Many people drawn into the community planning process viewed their involvement as a means of social engagement and networking: making friends and building up useful contacts. It was regularly viewed as "a good way to find out about the village and what was going on" (PG9), suggesting again perhaps that not all community plans are fuelled by a desire to shape change. For some participants, they merely provided a focus of local engagement, which may explain why some plans stopped short of articulating development aspirations or the formulation of an action plan (see Chapter Eleven, Table 11.1).

Bringing in expertise

A key feature of 'co-opting' is that it is often perceived to be a means of bringing in additional skills and expertise to the core group: for example, those with architectural, planning or design backgrounds. It is a way of building capacity by extending the network of participants in the planning process. But in the Ashford communities, this had tended not to happen, with the notable exception of a particular village that seemed to have no shortage of skills on which to draw:

> '[W]e've got two prize-winning architects on the group and these are guys who know their way around bricks and mortar and design. So, we're not coming from a point where we're being unreasonable or we don't know what we're talking about.... You've got so much expertise in this village. We're very fortunate.' (PG3)

However, in the majority of communities, enthusiasm and local knowledge were judged to be more important than a particular expertise. There had sometimes been negative experiences of local 'experts' trying to 'hijack' the process, or perhaps core groups felt threatened by those claiming expert knowledge and skills:

> '[W]e had a gentleman who turned up to the first workshop meeting and he stood out the front and he harangued every villager and he pointed out all the defects in architecture in the village. One or two people walked out before we were able to shut him up and he was then not invited to any more of the committee meetings. He thought, or still thinks of himself, as an architectural expert. He had such strong views. He made more of a destructive contribution.' (PG5)

Parish groups tended – again with the exception of the 'very fortunate' village above – to reject contributions that seemed to reduce the scope for creative inputs from a wider range of participants. There was a strong dislike for any form of professionalism in the plan production process that might drown out other voices. A good cross-section of people on the parish plan group was felt to be vitally important. Having representation from different parts of the community was seen as a way of ensuring that different issues received fair hearing:

> '[I]t's more about what people bring from different walks of life, different understandings or perceptions at a way of looking at things. My own view is you want enthusiasm and a willingness to do it, to get involved. You don't need great technical skills or anything like that but it's very useful to have a cross-section of the public.' (PG4)

It is of course possible that members of the core groups felt threatened by the intrusion of experts into the community planning process, and that these individuals would ultimately have brought valuable knowledge to the process, and could have keyed communities into new professional networks. Their exclusion may be a matter of personal choice, on the part of existing members, who choose to co-opt like-minded individuals who help reinforce particular views and agendas, and who fortify the clique without enhancing connectivity to a broader range of opinion and skills.

The 'internal' dynamics of community-based planning

How community-based groups are constituted, and how they connect with their wider community, have huge implications for the types of plan they produce, the purpose of these plans and how they are able to link to broader interests. In this chapter, we have introduced the triggers for community-based plans in contexts where there was already some element of community activity, but which had not always involved itself in the drawing up of actual plans. Plan making is not inevitable: not all communities engage in this process. But in the cases studied, community groups had opted to produce plans. They all had different motivations: for some, plan making was a means of galvanising interest in community issues, and building capacity. For others, it was a pragmatic act, required to access a particular pot of money for a specific project. But for a few communities, parish plan making was a reaction to frustration with the apparent top-down nature of development decision making. What begins as a response to an extraneous threat can quickly become a longer-term strategy for feeding ideas into policy making and attempting to introduce a local counterbalance to the external source of these threats: in the local authority, the regions and among corporations and big business.

A key feature of community-based planning, noted in this chapter, is that it is not a professional activity. Professionalism introduces exclusivity, and may act as a brake on broadening the appeal of neighbourhood planning, which has hitherto been essentially aspirational. This is clearly a point for the future. As neighbourhood plans are rolled out in England, one important question needs asking: is the aim of these plans to introduce professional plan making to neighbourhoods, or is the aim to enhance local participative democracy, where the rules of entry common to 'policy communities' are absent? Both aims are perhaps achievable, with the right support for communities, but this is distinctly different from policy professionals claiming ownership of the process of plan production. How communities build *their own* capacity is a theme picked up in the next chapter.

Note

[1] An initial long list of 22 parishes (affected by Growth Area development indirectly or directly, or apparently 'free' from its effect) was whittled down to just 10 during the early stages of the study. A meeting was held with each of the PGs. These were typically arranged with up to four members of the local community, invariably including the parish council clerk, a member of the parish council. Other participants tended to have been co-opted to the council to assist with a community-based planning exercise, or were actively involved in another parish interest group.

EIGHT

Capacity building and outreach

The degree to which parish councils authentically relay local views and local aspiration has been a key debate for those concerned with community governance issues for a number of years. Parish councils are frequently ridiculed as elitist, out of touch and parochial bodies that lack any real connection to the communities they serve (see Mitchell, 1951; Clark et al, 2007). They have even been called 'feudal', dominated by land and property-owning cliques (Raco, 2007). A question therefore remains as to the extent to which parish councils are either shut off from broader communities or are genuine vehicles for wider participation, and a focal point for building capacity and reaching out to different interests and to their neighbours. This chapter continues the theme of community dynamics, but begins to look at wider communication, within and beyond the immediate neighbourhood. It examines capacity building through the extension of networks: how communities establish lines of communication, how they build alliances and how alliances are maintained. A critical concern, emerging in the last chapter, is whether parish councils – potential hubs for community-based planning – are isolated from wider communities and broader interests, by virtue of how they organise themselves and the priorities they set, or whether they are an authentic focus and outlet for much wider, inclusive, neighbourhood planning processes.

Parish councils: 'communicative' and coordinating neighbourhood hubs?

A reasonable place to start this analysis is at what might be called the 'engagement protocols' of the parish councils: whether electoral mandate and consultation allowed them simply to get on with the task of planning, or whether they sought a more intimate, continual dialogue with local interests and residents. In the Ashford communities, some parish councils distributed regular 'updates' on the progress being made on the parish plan. Following initial consultation on a 'wish-list' of plan content (distributed to all residents), they took the view that they had a 'mandate to just to get on with it'. In this respect, they mimicked the behaviour of the Borough Council. Other groups, however, engaged in a more systematic dialogue with the wider community. Pluckley, Wye and Woodchurch, for example, held public meetings and exhibitions and Bilsington, Great Chart with Singleton and also Pluckley tried to coordinate with wider interests by using networks that linked to other local interest groups:

> '[M]any of the groups that have been mentioned, somebody on the parish council is either a member of one of them or they have close association with members.... When the steering group was set up, everybody from one of those groups was invited to go on the steering group. They helped create the questionnaire, so in that sense they were involved.' (PG5)

Many councils presented themselves as being entirely 'open' to creative input, communicating constantly with residents, but failing ultimately to cultivate interest in the plan-making process:

> '[W]e did write to all the local groups saying we were going to do it and had they got any issues that they wanted to include and then we also, at a later stage, came together and decided the categories that covered some of the issues in each and then we sent that to each group and said: "Have you got any comments or feedback for us?". But we didn't get much response from the local groups. They just left us to get on with it.' (PG7)

An initial view emerges of parish councils operating in much the same way as the Borough Council, and other local authorities, assuming a mandate and playing a traditional leadership role: consulting on possible courses of action, and presenting these as options to be supported or rejected. However, members of these councils are embedded in the communities and neighbourhoods in a way that local authorities are not. They operate through the neighbourhood networks described in the previous chapter, being more intimately bound up with local interest and the 'neighbourly politics' of place. Any outward resemblance to local government structures and protocols breaks down on closer inspection, with parish councils characterised by powerful personalities, a lack of independent capacity, a reluctance to form lasting alliances and relative isolation, which is merely indicative of their place-focus, or their inherent 'parochialism'.

Image 8.1: The picture-postcard village of Woodchurch

Parish clerks as network 'inter-connectors'

The role of parish clerks in council structures is pivotal and is examined again in Chapter Eleven. The clerks, unelected and providing the council with secretarial and administrative support, play a key role in liaising not only with other parish interest groups, but also with service providers. During the preparation of parish plans, clerks are frequently co-opted to the groups taking forward the plan. In the few instances where this is not the case, other council members may act as the go-betweens, providing a conduit between the plan group and the council. Clerks are regularly thought of as 'gatekeepers' and 'ways into' parish councils, and also a way into the wider community. Clerks tend to be the entry point into neighbourhood planning for external groups, including support groups and policy actors.

However, in many parishes, external communication around the parish plan was not viewed as vital. Many local groups viewed their plans as strictly internal documents, while others pondered but were uncertain about the link-up – if one really existed – between neighbourhood or village plans and statements, and the strategies of policy professionals (including LDFs) and service providers. A lack of clarity around such relationships linked back to broader thinking on community-based planning: was its purpose to inform spatial planning strategy, even if just as 'local insight', or was its truer purpose to be merely an outlet for local energies. Some communities had evidently been frustrated and even angered by the Borough Council's apparent lack of interest in their plans. But others were of the view that parish plans were a parish matter, and in terms of production and even in terms of taking forward action against the plan, the community was "completely capable of managing" (PG8) and doing its own thing. But the narrowness of involvement in plan making, with some parish councils making very few attempts to elicit external help, suggested a danger in some instances that plans would reflect the views and priorities of a very small number of individuals. Like the council itself, they might well be 'elitist' or 'feudal' as other commentators have previously suggested. The suspicion that a community plan has highly limited and restricted ownership may undermine external trust in the plan, with potential user groups questioning its utility. This issue is returned to in Chapter Twelve.

Eliciting and receiving external support

One clear measure of a parish plan group's acceptance of broader input into plan making can perhaps be read in the tendency to connect with community planning support groups or with neighbouring councils, for the purpose of learning from wider experience. In Chapters Ten and Eleven, we examine connectivity in a wider sense, looking at how parish groups attempt to key into broader networks as a means of increasing their influence over policy development, or simply as a way of making their voice heard. Here, the concern is simply with expanding capacity through connections to others with different knowledge and skills-sets. In Kent, there are several community network groups, or branches of national community support agencies, operating for the benefit of community groups wishing to engage in neighbourhood planning. Notable among these are the Kent Association of Local Councils (KALC) and Action with Communities in Rural Kent (ACRK).

KALC is a membership body for town and parish councils across the county and provides a range of services, including legal, financial, procedural and general advice to its members. Most of the parish clerks within the studied communities had attended training events run by KALC and most parish councils had received advice, of one sort or another, during the last few years. ACRK, a branch of Action with Communities in Rural England, described itself as a rural community support body providing advice on project funding, affordable rural housing, community facility management and community-based planning initiatives, including the production of parish plans and VDSs.

All of the communities examined had been helped in some way by ACRK.

Active outreach to these groups, and to other parish councils, was, however, rare and where connections had been made, these tended to be more by fortune than by design. Where needs were identified – missing skills, the attainment of which might expedite plan making – these tended to be sought within the community rather than outside of it, unless personal contacts made it easy to identify sources of support in neighbouring parishes or elsewhere:

> 'I think we don't go out to seek contact with lots of other groups: only if we have a specific reason, do we go out and talk to this group or that group. We have very, very little, almost no contact, with our surrounding parishes: we don't have any great interaction with them. People tend to be only interested in their own communities. They're inward looking.' (PG6)

Parish councils seldom pool resources and communication between councils is infrequent. In Ashford, representatives of the parishes met at periodic meetings arranged by either the Borough Council or the Kent Association of Local Councils. The intention was that these would give community groups an opportunity to discuss matters of common interest, to learn from each others' experiences of local projects and to share advice on parish plans. Opinion as to the usefulness of the meetings was divided: while some groups believed that the insights they offered into the workings of other councils and their plan-making processes were interesting, others judged them to be a complete waste of time, being frequently hijacked by a few vocal parish councillors who viewed the meetings as an opportunity to denigrate the borough:

> '[Y]ou can barely stay awake through them. Sometimes, ... somebody from [organisation] gives a presentation with lots of slides, then people usually nod off. You do find that there are a couple of people at those meetings who like the sound of their own voices and they are terribly important and they will bore the pants off everybody else. They don't let anybody else get a word in the whole evening, they've got an opinion on everything and you sit there and you think "I am so bored."' (PG7)

Frustration with existing practices, however, did not necessarily undermine confidence in the potential benefits of working more closely with other communities. But parishes lack the requisite resources. They have neither the time nor the money needed to maintain a dialogue with their neighbours:

> '[P]arish council capacity is very limited because your councillors are volunteers and your clerk is part-time and I haven't met a parish clerk who doesn't feel that there's a host of things that could be done in their parish, but they just haven't got the capacity to do it.' (PG7)

With so many pressing issues within the individual parishes, dialogue with 'non-essential' outside bodies assumes low priority. But it was also felt that meetings with a more 'strategic' focus (that 'transcend local issues') take parish councils away from their core business: it was felt that there was 'nothing in it' for the parishes. Such sentiment appears to confirm that councils have what can be described pejoratively as a parochial outlook. Connections to neighbouring areas and organisations are weak. Such insularity was generally considered inherent in community governance, with councils being constituted with narrow responsibilities and refusing to be distracted from the business of 'fighting the corner' of their neighbourhood or village.

But another perspective on this insularity was offered: that introversion is a product of the particular composition of parish councils. Retired councillors have stunted social networks and have a more limited interest in what is going on beyond the confines of the parish. Working councillors, on the other hand, have wider personal networks that may lead them to display greater interest in other parishes or to hook up with other groups. It was thought that professional or personal ties with people living elsewhere in Ashford (or beyond) encouraged better-connected parish councillors to examine practices in other locations:

> '[A] lot of councillors will be retired because they are the people with the time aren't they? And that's part of the issue about you reaching out, because your "reaching out" is often professional networking and of course if you are working in the fields of planning or whatever, or education, then of course you have that professional network to hand. We don't necessarily have that advantage because of the age profile, just an observation, and it's a common issue.' (PG3)

The community network groups listed above along with a number of conservation groups active in Kent tended to be more proactive in connecting with parish councils and offering support and expertise in various areas of plan and policy making. Such organisations seek a relationship with the councils in order to win support for a particular set of ideas, to influence local thinking or to recruit new members. Within the parishes examined, the Campaign to Protect Rural England (CPRE), which often has a highly visible presence in areas facing the prospect of substantial development, was notable by its absence. Members of the Mersham with Sevington group had encountered CPRE Kent, as had the parish council at Bilsington, but the CPRE was not felt to be measurably active in Ashford. Other groups tended to have a higher-profile presence, including English Heritage and the Weald of Kent Preservation Society (WKPS). The former had helped Bilsington parish undertake a survey of housing needs and had also helped the parish establish better links with the Borough Council's housing department. WKPS lobbies on planning issues across Ashford, Maidstone and Tunbridge Wells, and had advised Bethersden on its representations to Ashford during the consultation stages of the LDF. But these interactions were one-off and rare. More sustained relationships had developed between the parishes and KALC and ACRK.

As noted above, KALC had been a source of training for parish clerks and offered advice to parish councils on more bureaucratic and procedural matters. ACRK had actively assisted the councils, to different degrees, on community-based planning issues, ultimately forming strong relationships with most of the groups examined, who were generally complimentary about the support provided by the body:

> '[T]he organisation that has been immensely helpful, particularly over the parish plan is Action with Communities in Rural Kent. They are all terrific people ... apart from the purse strings; the advice they've given us has been tremendous, not just on getting the plan produced, but how to proceed with some of the issues within the plan. If you're brand new you are given all the information that you think you might need to know and what you shouldn't be doing and everything, which was invaluable.' (PG5)

Other parish groups were similarly enthusiastic. The objective of ACRK's interventions in community-based planning activity is to ensure a better fit between what communities feel that they can deliver in terms of an evidence base and what service providers, including the planning authority, can actually use to inform policy and programmes. ACRK described this as its 'bridging work' and considered itself to be an 'intermediary' between the professional networks of policy making and the raw ambition and enthusiasm of non-professional community groups. The nature of this bridging and intermediary function is examined more closely in Chapter Eleven.

More generally, ACRK aims to play a support role in the production of community-based plans, which nevertheless remain community based, driven by the ambitions of residents, or at least by those who are active on parish councils. In many instances, the interjections of this body were critical, giving new impetus to community planning and helping shape embryonic community plans. ACRK was also able to make crucial connections between the parishes and other actors. But its dynamism contrasts with the apparent inertia of the parish councils themselves, which tended to wait passively for external assistance. However, ACRK is resourced specifically to assist communities and these communities, centred on the parish councils for planning purposes, have themselves extremely limited resources confined largely to goodwill and volunteer time. They are not part of a broader 'system' with neighbouring parishes or external groups because they lack the resources needed for wider collaboration. But admittedly, this resource issue must be viewed in tandem with the understandably parochial view of parish groups: there is a common reluctance to reach out beyond the confines of the parish, to go beyond what they see as their local 'remit'. Few recognise the networking opportunities, and instead view forums that bring neighbourhoods or parishes together as 'tedious' briefing exercises. Parish councils see their responsibilities as being locally anchored, and seldom view their interests as extending beyond their boundaries. There is little sense of unity with neighbouring parishes: they are bound together in a bureaucratic system, but are not always seen to share common concerns. Parishes tend to be passive recipients of support, rarely seeking it out. Such a view of parish councils is not new. Rather, it resonates with previous analyses suggesting that these structures of community governance may have limited interest in connecting with broader concerns, preferring instead to stick to their own patch and narrowly define the local interest. None of this suggests that it would be easy to expand the role of community-based planning: there would be significant obstacles to overcome, in terms of resourcing and outlook, although arguably addressing the first issue would go some distance towards tackling the second. If they were able to take a broader view – if resources permitted – then some community groups would undoubtedly embrace broader responsibilities.

But there needs to be another requisite condition for this broadening of interest: a clear need for a wider view or a show of unity in the face of a shared threat. Community groups must be convinced that such unity is an effective means of achieving shared goals, and that real benefits will flow from bigger-than-local actions.

Alliance building between parishes

Image 8.2: Pluckley

The prospect of certain types of development had resulted in the formation of local alliances. There were numerous examples. A proposal to build an incinerator in the parish of Pluckley, for example, was viewed by the parishes of Bethersden and Charing as a shared threat, as increased traffic and potential nuisance were likely to flow through these neighbouring parishes. A proposal for a lorry park in the parish of Aldington was jointly opposed by the parishes of Bilsington and Mersham with Sevington for similar reasons. This type of collaboration was generally short term, but a common tactic when responding to contentious proposals:

'[W]e sometimes get other parishes, which are subject to these large planning applications, such as the lorry park, or maybe there might be some sort of industrial building or something like that, and they ask for support from the surrounding parishes to object to it.' (PG6)

Most of these 'objector alliances' are dissolved once the threat has passed, and respond to proposals or decisions rather than to ongoing policy development. They are seldom a means of seeking influence over the policy-making process, although this had happened on a few occasions. At the beginning of the LDF process, 12 parishes (Aldington and Bonnington, Bilsington, Brabourne, Great Chart with Singleton, Kingsnorth, Mersham with Sevington, Orlestone, Ruckinge, Shadoxhurst, Smeeth, Warehorne and Woodchurch) formed what became known as the 'South Ashford Parish Partnership'. The partnership hoped that a show of unity would give it greater leverage, with individual representations coordinated and backed up by a collective response:

> '[W]e felt that was important because, obviously, on our own and as individual parishes, we don't have as much clout, or they're not listening to us as much as if half a dozen parishes got together. It's another body to actually make a response because the parish council can make a response and then a joint body can make a response as well. We were just letting them know that we were all "singing from the same hymn sheet".' (PG7)

The South Ashford Parish Partnership was, however, a relatively short-lived collaboration. The alliance between the parishes was strong when the details of the Growth Area were emerging in the LDF, but once they were finalised the alliance began to fragment as all those parishes that were not directly affected began to lose interest. Reflecting on this fragmentation, one member of the group, located in the direct line of growth, reported feeling abandoned and left to 'fight its own corner'. But interestingly, some of the parishes unaffected directly by the growth proposals felt that they had been 'dropped' by the affected parishes. One group explained that after the plans had been agreed, they "went to the meeting [with the partnership] anyway, just the once, but there wasn't anything for us ... we haven't got any development, so they never invited [us] back". Again, it is a shared threat that brings alliances together, and once this dissipates (or only affect a few members) the alliance is viewed as redundant.

However, while the threat was live, mutual support was offered in a number of ways and collaborative working between the parishes assumed a new intensity. For example, the clerks issued jointly signed letters or representations and coordinated the individual parish responses. These were carefully orchestrated, raising the same objections but from different perspectives, thereby building a multifaceted argument. But again, resources become a constraint on the continuation of an alliance beyond the period of threat and few parishes saw any point in maintaining a network in the absence of a strong motivating force. And in the examples cited, these forces were invariably negative. The purpose of the alliance was never to improve an outcome but rather to end or diminish the scale of a problem. To seek improvement or redirection would require parishes to agree a more complex set of parameters against which to judge success (rather than the black-and-white view: development bad, status quo good). To achieve this, the communities would need to jointly agree objectives. They might even need to offer an alternative plan, set within a broader evidence base. They would need to take note of strategic objectives and concern themselves with delivery against these objectives, even if these were disputed. Planning and innovating solutions is a far more complex business than merely opposing ostensibly unpopular top-down proposals. But the rewards are also potentially greater and it is the prospect of community benefit that may well motivate neighbourhood planning in the years ahead.

But in the recent past, opposition – rather than benefits predicated on forward planning – has been the prime catalyst for local action and alliance building and this has given alliances an ephemeral nature: "you respond to threats basically and the threats move around all the time, there's no need to keep on meeting people just to have a chat and a pint". Coming together in this way, and in this context, had delivered few clear benefits, either in terms of outcomes on the ground (which did not appear to change) or in terms of the capacity of parish groups to lobby decision takers or gain influence. In fact, the lack of clear benefit, especially from the South Ashford Parish Partnership, tended to remind councils that such actions are inherently 'alien' to community governance: parish council members got involved to do local things, and not play politics at a borough level. The connection between these two things – acting collectively and strategically, and thereby effecting change locally – was not viewed as particularly strong or as readily achievable. Again, parishes remain parochial: "if it's not actually happening in their parish, they can't seem to see the knock-on effects". Alliances, quite obviously, are built on the expectation of mutual benefit, especially strength in numbers and the lobbying power that this is thought to generate. But these alliances are rarely sustained.

The isolation of parishes?

Within the parishes, groups and individuals readily connect – as we have seen in this chapter and the previous – but connections beyond parish boundaries are far weaker and more fleeting. Parish councils are generally open to external approaches and often welcome the support of other groups. But they are more reticent about reaching out to others, either because of their finite resources, or because those involved on parish councils have a strong focus on *their community*, and may not see the local benefits of alliances that outlast specific threats. It appears that the potential rewards of collaboration – greater understanding of challenges, the development of a shared agenda, an amplification of local voices and increased capacity to act – are seldom realised. Additional resourcing and changes in the perspective of community councils are probably needed if parishes are to change their behaviour. There is also a short-termism in community-based planning, frequently confined to the here and now. Either this is a reality that is difficult to change or it is a product of the perceived powerlessness of neighbourhoods to shape change in the longer term. Effort coalesces around what is perceived to be achievable, but if this perception were to change – and if further resourcing were directed to communities – then a different style of community-based planning might take root. But this presupposes that those involved in neighbourhood planning now, or who might become involved in the future, wish to take on a much broader set of responsibilities, working not only for their community but also for a wider partnership of communities, contributing collectively to the future planning of an area. It is not at all clear whether such responsibilities would be welcomed, or whether communities would simply prefer a more responsive planning system at the district or borough level. This question is picked up again in later chapters.

Part Three
The interface with policy actors

NINE

Connectivity at the policy–community interface

In the last three chapters, we explored, through a review of past studies and also through an initial presentation of local case study material, some of the practical building blocks for collaborative action: the networks that provide the context for consensus building and which give community groups the capacity to work with others in the pursuit of shared outcomes. In Chapter Six, we introduced some of the ways in which dialogue between network members may be problematic, noting a divide between policy and interest communities, which may be expressed in poor communication and a lack of trust, reciprocity and authentic dialogue, and ultimately in coercive power-play rather than in consensual action. This issue provides a key focus for the next series of chapters.

If the possibility of 'consensual power' is accepted, then finding ways to bridge the cultures of policy and community interest seems a worthwhile endeavour. The idea of 'bridging' or 'brokering' between different subsections of a potential more expansive network (bringing together community and policy actors) was introduced within the broader discussion of network mechanics and structure, again in Chapter Six. 'Bridging' has a particular meaning in social network analysis, and is used to refer to sometimes '*weak*', or seemingly incidental ties that can be used to span '*structural holes*', or gaps in what might otherwise be a common network. The concept of 'bridging', taken forward in this analysis, refers to the use of an intermediary or broker who provides a communication link between the private realm of community action and the public realm of traditional policy making – divided by a clear gap – and who has a centrality in a network owing to their occupation of a strategic position between network subgroups. Bridging is viewed both as a general feature of network structure, with intermediaries stepping in to work with community and policy actors, and as a means of dealing with community-based plans: that is, 'bridging' to local plans rather than seeking the direct absorption of community plans into formal policy making. The treatment of community-based plans is given special attention in this discussion, as it is this treatment that expresses different ideas of how best to draw communities into broader democratic processes.

In network analysis, bridging ties are defined as those that link an individual or community to contacts in economic, professional and social circles not otherwise accessible: the bridging tie may be the 'sole means by which two persons ... are joined in a network' (Friedkin, 1980, p 411). Networks that possess such bridges enjoy informational advantages that aid capacity building (Booher and Innes, 2002), a fact that provides the starting point for an expansion of the discussion started in earlier chapters.

A network perspective on 'bridging'

Accessing new information, and enhancing capacity, are often dependent on bridging 'structural holes' (Burt, 1992). Granovetter (1973) suggests that weaker, informal ties sometimes provide a means of communicating with different parts of a network. Strong ties bind together a subgroup (eg, a number of local interests or individuals) but access to another subgroup (eg, comprising policy actors) may be accidental and informal. However, this tie may be absolutely critical to capacity building: hence the idea of the 'strength of weak ties'. Because they serve as bridges, they enable the discovery of new opportunities and may suddenly enhance capacities in a group that had been previously isolated and lacked the resources to achieve its goals. The idea that this tie may be relatively weak, and informal, is used in social network theory to explain why its potential may not have been immediately recognised (it may, for example, take the form of an individual able to connect to decision makers through informal contacts). But it may also be the case that this tie is relatively powerful, not by virtue of its own resources, but simply because of its location in the network. The way it maintains contacts with a diversity of actors (who may have formed cliques) means that it is privy to a diversity of information and may be able to broker deals between these cliques, or act as a forum where shared interests are realised (so rather than being an individual, it may comprise an organisation able to act as an intermediary). Burt (1992) argues that its strength derives in its occupancy of a structural hole within a network, allowing it to become a focal point in broader interactions by virtue of its capacity to span this hole.

The important question here is whether these structural holes exist between territorial communities and extraneous policy actors, and whether bridges can be found to close such holes. These holes may be not only network breaks but also cultural divides between the worlds of policy and community interest, and between formal planning policy making and the aspirations of residents. This point is returned to below.

Bridging ties may be particularly critical in networks with specific characteristics, some of which are significant in the arena of community-based planning. McEvily and Zaheer (1999) argue that bridging ties can be crucial for delivering greater capacity in a network that displays three critical traits. First, it has a low degree of *redundancy*: this means that communication links are simple and often singular, perhaps that the ties that bind actors are centred on named individuals and that without these individuals, these ties would be threatened or fail. Second, the network is characterised by an *infrequency of interaction*: communication is intermittent between most actors, and between some it is a rarity. And third, nodes are *geographically dispersed*, which may also be an impediment to interaction. Under these conditions, bridging ties or brokers take on special significance. They invest time in building stronger linkages and identifying opportunities (Burt, 1992, p 13), and may well be crucial in community-based planning, for instance, where community actors (eg, parish planning groups) are separated from policy actors by distance (see discussion below), place responsibility for communication with a secretary or clerk (see Chapter Eight) and communicate relatively infrequently, and only when pressing matters arise.

Bridging as a means of building capacity and social capital

Bridging has the potential to introduce new capabilities: it has been viewed as central to capacity building, establishing links between diverse partners (with different perspectives or from varied cultures) and therefore helping satisfy the 'diversity' condition on which 'network power', introduced in Chapter Six, is premised. McEvily and Zaheer (1999) argue that in the world of corporate business, companies innovate and build capacity by looking beyond their normal producer-client networks, to see what is happening in other sectors in order to improve their own operation: to achieve desired outcomes with greater efficiency and expediency. Diversity in its network will allow a firm to access novel ideas, to import processes that might be the norm elsewhere, but which have not been tried in its sector. A broader horizon may offer competitive advantage.

In the wider world, Putnam (2000) argues that bridging is fundamental to the capacities of social networks, suggesting that it is only through bridging that capacity is enhanced. Although it is everyday 'bonding' – the direct coming together of equals – between friends and neighbours that generates trust and reciprocity, establishing solidarity *within a community* (2000, p 22), it is through 'bridging' that social and political divides are crossed. Bonding is the means by which communities 'get by', but the sociological 'WD-40' (2000, p 23) provided by bridging extends the reach of networks and allows them to 'get ahead'.

Bridging as a means of reconciling local–strategic tensions

As well as providing some insight into the broader mechanics and potential empowerment of networks, notions of bonding and bridging have a special importance in the context of community planning. Community-based planning, by definition, is rooted in groups of common interest, often with sometimes only weak links to representative bodies and the professionalised policy community. Their separation may be due to the immediacy of their respective concerns, by knowledge of formal policy processes, by their motivations, by what they understand to be their responsibilities and by their priorities. For example, a village or neighbourhood may be within the jurisdiction of a principal authority based in offices some miles away. It may be a focus for groups concerned about a number of local issues, who have limited knowledge of formal policy structures, who are bound and motivated by a desire to conserve certain local features cherished by residents and conservationists alike, who see their responsibility as being to family, friends and neighbours, and their priority as being to shape or prevent local change (see Chapters Seven and Eight). Those in the authority have wider concerns, stretching broadly across the area; they understand the legal parameters of their powers, are motivated by the public good, by private interest or by some 'paradigm' that they feel should guide policy; their responsibility is not to a single place or community and their priorities tend to be strategic. There is significant potential for misunderstanding between these groups. In the past, only limited attempts were made to align local and strategic perspectives, resulting in a brand of policy making often dubbed paternalistic: communities simply did not understand the broader responsibilities of 'parent' authorities, remonstrated constantly, but failed to recognise that these authorities knew best.

The result was a critical tension between neighbourhood groups and policy actors. Local government and planning reforms, as part of a broader democratic renewal, represent the most recent attempt to ease this tension, and more adjustments to policy and practice are likely to follow in the years ahead. These will undoubtedly aim to alter this critical relationship and therefore change the existing balance of power, ostensibly in favour of local interests (see Chapter Three). But a network perspective suggests that different partners might be able to work together more effectively without the need for central government to empower one group at the expense of another: this would involve reconciling different concerns, knowledge bases (local and strategic), motivations, responsibilities and priorities. The idea of bridging has been transported into the community planning field to denote a means of bringing together strategic priorities and frameworks with community ambitions and initiatives.

Owen et al (2007, pp 50-1) argue that with regards to local government and services, 'bridging' offers a means of linking the diametrically opposed concepts of '*governance*' and '*democracy*'. The latter is 'top down', rooted in 'representative authority' and achieves its ends through mandated power. It places great weight on a strategic perspective and its modus operandi is through local authorities, as the principal engines of policy, who work in partnership with other professional agencies. The local authorities provide accountability. The partners bring additional expertise to bear on complex problems that the authority alone is unable to solve, perhaps through the tendency towards 'agencification', examined in Chapter Two. Governance, on the other hand, denotes something that is 'bottom up' and extends beyond the public realm of local government and its expert partners. It begins at a neighbourhood level and involves unleashing local energies. Priorities are defined within affected communities, and local groups are empowered to take actions against them. But the need to build bridges between these concepts, and competing realities, belies an acknowledgement that neither can achieve its goals without reference to the other: the strategic to the local and vice versa. While strategic perspectives frequently promote 'provider-led' approaches to service provision, without giving due consideration to what people or places actually need (Carley et al, 2000), neighbourhood control may degenerate into myopia, focusing on detail, and ultimately lack the coordination needed to deliver service efficiencies. There is a balance to be struck between detail and coordination, or between local and strategic perspectives. The question that follows is whether this can be achieved by a concentration of capacity at one level (in the regions, in the local authorities or in local communities), or whether this capacity should be shared. If it is to be shared – and if achieving consensual power is the goal – then the way that these levels interface becomes critical.

The practicalities of 'bridging' local interests and policy actors

There are two ways this interface can be achieved: directly by way of an inherently unequal *bonding* tie between the local authority and local interests (unequal because of the imbalance in knowledge and capacity to act) or indirectly by way of a bridging or *brokering* tie, with an intermediary providing the link between policy actors and community interests. But why might an intermediary be necessary? Why not develop a direct link between the incumbent authority (with its legally defined responsibilities) and community groups? There are many reasons why this direct dialogue is problematic: the understanding of community issues from a policy perspective is legally bounded, therefore many issues are immediately rejected as *ultra vires*; local authorities are then perceived to be ignoring local concerns, leading to frustration, a lack of trust and a potentially fractious relationship. Communities tend to articulate ambitions while authorities speak in the language of legal possibility. When the two come together directly, there is a tendency to 'instrumentally frame' lay knowledge, diluting or losing the essence of community ambition (because policy actors are professionalised in a way that community actors are not, and the latter reject the need to professionalise and become more 'exclusive': see Chapter Eight). To some extent this is inevitable, but authorities are not viewed as independent arbitrators. Rather, they may be seen as misinterpreting or corrupting community views and this is in itself a threat to consensual planning. It is not uncommon to hear local authorities dismissing community ambitions as 'whimsical' or 'undeliverable' (Gallent et al, 2008) and sometimes this may be true, although this can, in part, be attributed to the disconnection, and misunderstanding, between community aspiration and local government's capacity to deliver. But it is also the case that authorities look for 'facts' from communities, which they as singular critical actor can 'respond' to in some conventional way.

Local interests and the policy community are not bound as equal partners. In a sense, they operate in different worlds or cliques. Authorities may use the mandated power they have to respond to communities in a sometimes formulaic way, and there may be little 'authentic dialogue' in their relationship. Do brokering links (via an intermediary) offer a means of finding common ground between the private realm of community planning and the public realm of local government (Newman, 2007), or are they simply *translators*, bringing greater mutual understanding if not mutual agreement? It might be the case that some brokering links simply perform this latter role and in the case of community planning, it can be imagined that some officials (or even voluntary housing enablers or planning aid workers), embedded in parish planning activity, act as translators but are unable to venture outside the norms of public policy (they simply provide 'friendly faces'). On the other hand, some brokers may have a degree of independent capacity, and may link to a wider array of actors, and may therefore be able to identify new ways of delivering against community goals that break away from standard public sector responses. These debates play out both in the broader relationships that local authorities share with community groups and in the act of plan making. The desire, which grew in the 2000s, to do more with community-based plans and to hang some of the hopes of democratic renewal onto them, has resulted in a debate over the way community plans are brought into the planning process, as a means of empowering communities and strengthening the link between community input and policy outcomes.

Bonding, bridging and plan making

But the linkages between parish plans and higher-level planning frameworks have often been weak (Owen, 2002a, p 86) and it has generally remained unclear as to how local planning policy should respond to, or work with, the planning activities of community groups. The act of plan making is a clear point of reference for understanding the interface between community and policy actors. Plans express different values, priorities and aspirations. Their particular focus and form signal different mindsets and cultures. They are a measure, in a sense, of the width of the structural (and cultural) hole between communities and planning professions – a hole that can be spanned either through controlling community planning or lending it independent support. In the remainder of this chapter, the recent debate on bringing 'conformity' between community and local plans is set out. But in the chapters that follow, it is both the general modes of connection, direct and indirect (through intermediaries), that are examined alongside the particular challenges of tying together plans.

Working with community-based plans: 'controlling' or 'supporting' their production

In the 2000s, community-based parish plans were presented as having a potentially critical influence on statutory plans. In 2003, just before the introduction of the LDF system, the Minister for Rural Affairs at DEFRA, and the Countryside Agency emphasised 'a new opportunity for parish plans to form part of the bedrock of the new Local Development Frameworks' (Countryside Agency, 2003, p 2).[1] Further guidance was provided on the content of parish plans in the following year (Countryside Agency, 2004). It was then suggested that these plans might somehow be incorporated into the portfolio of documents making up the LDF.

The Agency envisaged parish plans as having systematically organised components (Countryside Agency, 2003, p 20), including:

- proposals for development;
- guidance on local character and design;
- proposals on movement and transport;
- economic and community proposals;
- and either proposals or guidance for conservation.

Clearly, putting these in place in a rigorous fashion is dependent on introducing a range of skills into the parish planning process. By and large, the expectations of the Countryside Agency in 2003 were not realised, and parish plans continued to vary in content and quality, reflecting the focus of local concern and the level of support provided to communities (see Chapters Eight, Eleven and Twelve). Integration is dependent on some expert input into parish plan preparation, a fact recognised by the Agency, which envisaged this input coming from a partnership with Rural Community Councils (where these provided a source of planning expertise), with AONB committees (which retain this expertise), with Planning Aid or with individual planning consultants engaged to facilitate the preparation of parish plans (Countryside Agency, 2003, p 20). Hence, integration of the type anticipated by the Countryside Agency was not dependent on direct local authority input, but on parishes building capacity through collaboration with expert bodies, perhaps of the type examined in Chapters Eight and Eleven.

But the Countryside Agency (2003, p 21) also hinted at the possibility of a more direct link with the local planning authority, which might wish to 'employ dedicated "parish planning co-ordinators" to liaise with parish councils and community groups on parish plans and related initiatives', perhaps giving the principal authority more direct control over very-local initiatives, or at least suggesting that parish plans might be framed by more strategic thinking).

Supporting community planning, by helping build independent capacity at the neighbourhood level – and working with and through intermediaries – might be viewed as a means of bridging local aspiration to statutory planning, while local authority control might lead to more complete integration between the two, suggesting the possibility of community plans slotting directly into local plans. These contrasting approaches point to different conceptions of planning in the private realm: as something that needs to be unrestrained and aspirational (serving community development and social innovation) or something that can be controlled, 'sanitised', used directly in policy development and held up as proof of effective democratic renewal.

A 'supportive' approach, grounded in 'bridging'

A study by BDOR[2] nearly a decade ago highlighted the dilemma facing community groups. While some communities wanted to remain 'assertively local' (BDOR, undated, p 3; see also BDOR, 2006) and did not seek the input of outside experts, many were keen to ensure that plans were taken seriously by local planning authorities, and for this reason engaged expert input. However, 'some of the reluctance to engage with others reflected a feeling that "they" will limit control or reduce "our" plan. Sadly, that sometimes appeared to be true because the response from some in local authorities was too often cautious or downright negative' (BDOR, undated, p 3).

A key finding of this work – which drew on case studies in Cornwall, Dorset and Gloucestershire – was that the independent advice coming from the Rural Community Councils tended to be more positive and constructive, while communities needed to be careful about whom they spoke to and sought support from within the local planning authority. The label 'supportive planner' was used to distinguish those within local authorities more amenable to community initiatives (undated, p 3). How community-based plans are linked with district-wide frameworks was regarded as critical by many community groups: remaining independent sometimes jarred against a belief that getting a community plan adopted was the best way to influence planning decisions, as parish councils felt pressured to bring their own plans into line with those of the local authority. This, according to the BDOR study, 'had more of a negative than a positive effect on parish plan scope and ambition'. Moreover, adoption did not always prove possible even where communities tried to produce a document that they thought would sit comfortably with a local plan. Under the 2004 system, adoption became more difficult – because of the project management of development plan documents and other hurdles, including the requirement for sustainability appraisal (which will not apply to neighbourhood development plans) – leading

BDOR to suggest that such direct integration may be less appropriate than identifying other links to a local plan (undated, p 4).

Alongside the building of independent capacity (rather than being directly led by local authority experts), another means of bridging to the statutory framework – as opposed to integrating with that framework – is to link community plans with other strategies that provide a broader template for the local plan. BDOR (undated, p 4) concluded:

> [T]he holistic approach that community groups take to their places and people fits better within the current approaches of Sustainable Community Strategies. The better future link, if support and resources are being sought, is to the Local Strategic Partnership. The next generation of Sustainable Community Strategies, reshaped LSPs and (for funding) Local Area Agreements offer, between them, a far more exciting (if challenging) link between bottom-up community plans and top-down strategies, programmes and funding regimes.

Hence, community strategies and independent experts (including experts drawn from the LSP) were thought to offer a potential bridge between parish and local plans. This bridging tactic is very different from the formal integration of parish plans, perhaps as formalised area action plans, directly into an authority's formal development framework.

An 'integrative' approach, grounded in 'bonding'

While such bridging seemed to offer one way of handling parish plans, government displayed some preference at this time for the idea of a more complete integration of community-based plans into the broader planning system. Research undertaken by SQW Consulting (2007 p 1) for DEFRA suggested that advice and guidance from principal authorities remained a key ingredient in the development of parish plans and would result in documents that were 'more effective at engaging mainstream providers' (that is, those who provide against strategic priorities, in terms of development and services). A capacity for direct integration into the 'wider planning system' was offered as a measure of community plan 'effectiveness' and as a means of ensuring that policy is locally responsive.

The conclusions reached by SQW differed considerably from those of BDOR. While softer 'bridging' was seen as the way forward by the latter, SQW pointed to a need for early and direct involvement of public service providers (including planning authorities) in community-based planning. It also pointed to a need for a much more controlled and structured approach to parish plan preparation, including:

• effective guidance to 'minimise unrealistic objectives';
• a structured process of presenting the plan to the LSP, allowing systematic responses to the plan, and a single official point of contact for those preparing the plan;
• resources to 'build momentum' behind the plan;
• an 'evidence-based' plan that can be used in a 'consistent and meaningful' way;
• clear separation of 'planning priorities' from community objectives within the plan, making it easier for professional planners to 'digest and integrate' the parish plan;
• coordination of objectives across several parishes, so that these can be more easily received by service providers;
• a 'proactive and determined parish plan action group' driving the process and the plan;
• formal endorsement of the plan by the parish council (even 'adoption'), linking to political commitment within the principal authority.

A process of integration through greater control, formalisation and even some form of 'adoption' was envisaged: parish plans would move away from being expressions of community aspiration, and instead become miniature statutory plans. Clearly, this thinking on the future of parish plans strikes a chord with the neighbourhood development plan agenda described in Chapter Four: structured project management of systematised community plans, shaped by professional guidance to ensure compliance with local plans and to prevent these documents from becoming mere 'wish lists' or 'NIMBY statements' (SQW Consulting, 2007, p iv). But this keeps alive the possibility of a permanent tension between communities wishing to think outside the box, and articulate broad aspiration, and policy actors wanting inputs that respect the orthodoxies of statutory planning. Alternatively, future neighbourhood development plans may repeatedly fail the compliance test, or only those emerging from a dialogue between community and policy actors may stand any chance of interfacing successfully with local plans.

Plan making and the relationship between community and policy actors

How to handle parish plans and how to position them within a broader planning process was a key question facing local authorities in the 2000s. The prospect of having to work with neighbourhood development plans brings this issue into even sharper relief. In this changed context, post May 2010, government will encourage the production of plans that can be integrated with broader planning frameworks. These will be predicated on a view that through developing a working relationship with local planning authorities, which are then able to frame expectation (with reference to national policy), community-based plans will become well-reasoned documents with aims and objectives that can be translated and incorporated into local plans. The previous government appeared to share the view that community plans that remained isolated from the planning system had limited or, at best, piecemeal influence over local policy and outcomes (SQW Consulting, 2007, p 45).

However, it has long been apparent that there are real practical challenges when trying to reconcile community-based activities with the products of traditional forms of representative government. What this means in practice is that residents with an interest in influencing local planning or local service outcomes come together in informal settings and take actions (appraisals and assessments, using whatever skills they have available) that will lead to the production of documents that express local concerns and wishes in a variety of ways. However, representative government, with its power mandated at periodic elections, may find it difficult to respond to these informal actions in the private realm and will instead look up the 'hierarchy' for its evidence and reach decisions designed to deliver outcomes not for communities but for actors higher up the 'food chain'. Despite local government reform and the rhetoric of devolution, leading to the introduction of local strategic partnership and Sustainable Community Strategies in the 2000s, statutory planning has remained firmly anchored in the public realm. This reality appears out of step with the rhetoric of decentralising power, and of winning the 'hearts and minds' of communities called upon to accept and support local development (Whitehead, 2009).

A failure to acknowledge the different rationales of different plans, and past attempts to shoehorn parish plans into local planning frameworks, can be viewed as a very crude effort to overcome, or perhaps ignore, the critical differences between community action and professional policy making, and the tensions between participative governance and the exercise of executive power. Arguably, ideas of 'bridging' to and supporting community action articulate the essence of collaborative planning to a far greater extent than the notion that compliance between plans can be legislated for. There seems to be obvious good sense in a strategy of supporting community action and helping community actors understand the constraints in which broader policy must operate. Equally, there is an undeniable logic in working with policy actors to ensure greater understanding of community aspiration. And if these groups are divided by distance and by regularity of contact, or if connectivity is weak – centred on a few individuals – and vulnerable to loss, there is surely a need to build support structures that help foster clear and stronger lines of communication, aimed at achieving shared understanding. Debates over community or neighbourhood planning in England have tended to emphasise the role of plans in expressing the ambitions of communities. But outcomes are unlikely to be positive ones unless residents and policy actors find more effective ways to communicate and work together. This is the major challenge of neighbourhood planning, and one that is examined, using recent experience, in the chapters that follow.

Essential intermediaries

Chapter Six was concerned with how communities harness human capital and transform it into social capital and a potential to influence planning outcomes. In this chapter, the focus has been on brokering or bridging ties and the way in which these same communities may interface with policy actors and turn their own potential into a capacity to shape policy. The tendency of many community groups, which is demonstrated in Chapter Ten, is to establish a direct link to local authorities, and by strengthening that link over time, to seek direct influence over planning outcomes. But where this happens, local interests and local authorities may be bound together in an unequal relationship, in which authorities seek to curtail local aspiration, bringing it into conformity with their own designs and with national priority. The assertion is that communities of interest and policy actors are unequal and non-reciprocal partners, unable to bond in a simple way because they inhabit different worlds and frequently fail to find a common language, or rather one that will not completely extinguish the integrity of community ambition. Likewise, the space between communities and authorities is a barrier to consensual planning, limiting trust and sometimes resulting in mutual suspicion; this space, however, can be closed by intermediaries able to bring together different actors for mutual benefit. These basic ideas are examined in Chapter Thirteen, which builds on a general examination of relationships presented in the next two chapters.

This examination begins at the more direct interface between community and policy actors in the Ashford study area. The relationship between the two is dissected and the act of 'lobbying' is given special attention. Direct links are then contrasted in Chapter Eleven with attempts to mediate more effective relationships through brokers, especially community planning support groups. The focus of these chapters is on process, not product. Community-based plans themselves are examined in Chapter Twelve, before the nature of the interfacial relationship, between residents and planners, suggested by the study, is addressed in a broader synthesis.

Notes

[1] The Parliamentary Under Secretary for Local Government at ODPM – the ministry with responsibility for planning at the time – joined Alun Michael, the Minister for Rural Affairs at the time, in endorsing this guidance on the role of parish plans.

[2] BDOR is a community development consultancy based in Bristol.

TEN

Working with local government

In this chapter and the next, the focus is placed on communication between parish councils, policy actors, service providers and other bodies external to the communities. Reflecting the distinction drawn between bonding and bridging tactics, this analysis has been divided into two chapters. The current chapter considers direct links to the local authority, predicated on a lobbying relationship, with parish councils seeing themselves as part of the hierarchy of local government. The next then looks at a broader range of bridged links through intermediaries, including the support groups introduced in Chapter Seven, the area's LSP and more incidental intermediaries including ward members. The distinction between direct and bridged links is not easy to make. It is sometimes not clear whether a bridge was intended or accidental: parish groups, for example, may have dealings with housing officers regarding a specific development site, but these officers may then bring crucial information (on community feeling) to planning colleagues, potentially influencing policies or decisions. In such instances, there may have been no intention to bridge, but a strong link to housing resulted in an effective, bridged, forward connection. In general, the distinction drawn here is this: *lobbying* tends to be the object of a direct link, predicated on the belief that pressure can be exerted to change a decision; in contrast, *placing* (usually of evidence) is the object of an indirect link, performed in the belief that an intermediary can help transmit this evidence (perhaps a community-based plan), in a translated and useable form, to a decision taker.

To maintain confidentiality, parish groups are referred to using the notation introduced in Chapter Seven. The policy actors, however, are named unless there is a good reason for not doing so.

Lobbying links to the local authority

The majority of parish groups had what they judged to be 'strong ties' into Ashford Borough Council, usually through named officers who had either a parish liaison role or became known to the community during a local project: housing and development control officers had often built up relationships with parishes during and following planning applications. The few parishes who thought that their ties were weak tended to have little direct contact with officers, leaving their ward member to 'represent their interests'. Invariably, it was parish clerks who maintained these links as part of their reporting responsibilities. Such links were considered useful, with officers being called upon to give advice and with communication seen as a means of defusing tensions. Because the clerks were so pivotal at this interface – they were the 'best-connected' individuals, acting as coordinators and communicators for parish councils – they were generally regarded as the 'entry points' into parishes or even as 'gatekeepers'.

But while most communication with public sector services, including the Kent Highways Authority, went through the clerks, political links remained crucial. Lobbying through a ward member was seen as a way of bypassing 'junior' officers and getting to the people with real power, including strategic managers and heads of service. However, the ward members were tarred with the same brush as other politicians, 'filtering information' for political reasons (PG4), and being prone to rhetoric and divided allegiances, working not only for the communities they represented but also for political parties:

> 'I always appreciate [councillor's] contribution to the parish council meetings. He's our borough councillor. He does make sense. When he talks about these things I can understand him. I don't know how he ... talks to people at the Borough Council level, but he does tend to pooh-pooh things the Borough Council are doing because he knows that's what we want to hear. He has tried to keep his feet in both camps and he knows he has to do that.' (PG7)

There were other lobbying tactics, which verged on developing a bridged link. One community sought advantage by asking residents employed by the Borough Council to bring parish concerns to the attention of work colleagues. This strategy was described as 'tunnelling in':

> 'There's a couple of people in the village who actually work in Ashford as well, there's [named individual], so sometimes ... certainly in terms of more the [...] Committee ... there's a number of times when we've tunnelled into Ashford if you like, we've gone in from somebody who works with Ashford Borough Council rather than going through anything formal, we've come into the centre.' (PG8)

Such tactics were incidental and not available to all parish councils. And so for the most part, contact between clerks and named officers provided the strongest and most consistent connection with the local authority. This connection was used for reporting, for signalling disquiet and for soliciting advice on community planning matters. Although clerks had direct access to community liaison officers, it was often the informal links to someone in housing, in leisure services or in development control that were most valued. The potential for disconnection from these personal contacts was viewed as a significant threat to the relationships that had built up between parishes and the Borough Council over a number of years. Disconnection could result from staffing changes or changes in the parish council, or even from the introduction of an automated telephony system that restricted access to officers, directing parishes instead to frontline customer services staff. Because personal rapport was so highly prized, the connection between parishes and the authority appeared extremely fragile and vulnerable to change (see McEvily and Zaheer, 1999).

In some instances, parish groups had become so frustrated with their lack of direct access to officers that they turned increasingly to "a greater exploitation of the links that elected members have with the council". But this tactical shift altered the way they were able to connect with the authority. Previously, the relationship had been multifaceted: discussing proposals and talking through their implications, receiving assistance and engaging in a dialogue that could ultimately persuade one party or the other to shift position. But emphasis on the political link changed this, and the focus was increasingly placed on campaigning. Also, members tried to increase enthusiasm, with parish groups, for community plan production without always spelling out its limitations. Expectations were frequently raised, which ultimately jarred against the bureaucratic realities of planning, increasing frustration with the authority and its policy-making processes. This issue is returned to in Chapter Twelve.

Communication and interaction

The parish perspective – 'fleas on a chimpanzee'

The instrument of communication between parishes and policy actors is the telephone and the focus of this communication is the receipt of planning applications, on which parish councils are invited to provide comment. This simple reality drives a basic spatial dynamic: parishes located further from prospective development – the urban extensions in the case of Ashford – have more irregular but less troublesome relationships with the local authority. And the converse is true of parishes located in the path of growth. This dynamic, however, is altered by the human factor, and by what might appear to be incidental or minor issues occupying the minds of parish councils that appear otherwise free of major threats. Sometimes the ostensibly quiet parishes can occupy an inordinate amount of officer time.

Most interaction with planning teams centres upon planning applications or funding bids. It is this type of contact that establishes personal ties. There is far less interaction of a 'strategic nature': consulting on policy frameworks or the big changes affecting the wider area, for example. An exception to this general pattern was communication around the Core Strategy of the LDF and around a specific planning document framing decisions affecting the parishes: the *Tenterden and Rural Sites Development Plan Document* (DPD) (ABC, 2010). The planning team initiated a formal consultation on this document, running workshops and attending parish meetings to publicise the way parishes could feed into it. They had previously done the same with the Core Strategy. However, some parish groups had not fully understood the relationship between these two documents (see Chapter Five), and had invested the bulk of effort in the DPD, not fully appreciating that its main principles had already been established in the Core Strategy. More generally, parishes are seldom proactive in inputting into these exercises in strategic, larger-scale thinking. Rather, they wait for invitations. Moreover, they rarely view parish plans as an input into borough-wide planning (with connectivity to bigger issues, adjacent areas or the long term) or an opportunity to influence broader thinking. Plans express a distinct view of the role of parish councils: to content themselves with local concerns and, generally, with the here-and-now or immediate challenges.

It is also the case that parish plans do not merely deal with land-use change, but connect to a wider suite of concerns. This reflects the standard practice in parish councils of dealing with a range of public sector services, as 'sectoral issues' arise or projects progress. Clerks have most frequent contact with environmental, leisure and housing services. Parish councils are reactive to residents' concerns: when a blocked drain is reported or there has been an incidence of fly-tipping, it is often the clerk who will call environmental services. There is more of a project focus with leisure services – specifically involving parks and recreation officers – with parishes often looking to upgrade local facilities such as play areas. Contact of this type is intermittent, but where a project is successful, the relationship with the authority can be greatly improved. In relation to a specific project, the group from

Mersham with Sevington recalled the assistance of a particular officer: "she knew that we needed some upgrading and she encouraged us to put in an application and she nursed us all the way through. We couldn't have done it without her".

Such positive experiences helped build trust, making the local authority appear more open to parish councils and, on the whole, friendlier. Many groups reflected on the good relationships they had built up with housing officers. These tended to result from the experience of working on local needs projects, as one group noted:

> 'I've had a very good relationship with the strategic housing manager on a number of projects that I've been working on. She's really good. We can work really well together and we're working on both the local needs and the older person's housing schemes and that's a joint parish scheme actually, the older person's housing, where they are trying to encourage small groups of parishes.' (PG7)

For the most part, housing teams tended to be viewed as a positive force in the parishes, frequently working *with* communities. Perceptions of planning, however, tended to be more varied. While villages sitting outside the path of growth maintained amicable relations with development control (see above), those in the 'firing line' sometimes focused their frustrations on officers. There were exceptions to this. At Great Chart with Singleton, the parish council took the view that a continuous dialogue had exposed the benefits that might accrue from development. This had resulted in a 'sensible conversation' and a series of community benefits, delivered through planning agreements. In this instance, the view at Great Chart with Singleton was that parishes needed to 'do their homework' if they wished to be treated as partners in a process, rather than uniformed belligerents who were perceived merely as obstacles to progress. Parishes have clear responsibilities.

In that particular parish, however, growth was viewed as a fait accompli. The choice faced was to either 'go down fighting' or 'make the best' of the situation. There were perceived to be no clear benefits from the first course of action. Elsewhere, the possible outcomes often appeared less certain and more complex and the behaviour of parish councils – the way they connected to the principal authority – was coloured by perceived bias or by negative experience.

Some of the remoter communities, for example, believed that a clear urban bias in Ashford generally resulted in a lack of interest in the affairs of outlying communities, verging on indifference (PG1). But while the perception of an urban bias had a propensity to taint relationships, it was the loss of trust – owing to negative past experiences – that could turn them decidedly sour. One parish described its relationship with the local authority as a 'struggle': while personal relationships with officers were normal, occasionally edging towards positive, it was the 'entity' of planning that was closeted and could not be trusted. The best they could hope for was "to be a flea on a chimpanzee", irritating it enough to occasionally make it stop and think. All the power rested with the entity, not with the parishes or with any individuals, and this had become a great source of frustration. A view that there were many 'good planners', but that 'planning' – that is, the system – was not fit for purpose was widely shared.

A vague sense of mistrust in the system was replaced in one parish by a firm belief that the local authority simply could not be trusted to take decisions in a transparent way. The experience of a development 'concordat' being signed by the Borough Council and a major landowner in 2005 had placed considerable strain on the parish's relationship with the Borough Council. An agreement to redevelop a major landholding for housing was signed prior to any consultation with residents and then presented as a fait accompli. Vociferous and well-organised opposition eventually 'defeated the proposal', but left a legacy of mistrust that also soured Ashford's relationship with other parishes, which suspected that the same high-handed treatment might one day be in store for them. Yet, despite such difficulties, other parish groups felt that much had been learnt from this experience. From the ashes of that debacle, there was a feeling that all parties were now trying to find common ground. In fact, the experience seemed to have been a wake-up call for many in the council, who now recognised that they had 'got it badly wrong' and needed to engage in a more constant and meaningful dialogue with parishes if they were to secure trust and win support for some of the more challenging development proposals that the borough would inevitably face:

> 'They're certainly trying, and we are too and I would hope they would say the same about us. I think Ashford has come to realise that the parishes probably can contribute far more than they have done in the past and parishes are beginning to realise that they need to contribute more.' (PG5)

But the parish forums organised by the local authority were rarely viewed as interactive. Since the time of the difficulties noted above, parish councils acknowledged a heightened urgency in the authority's efforts to reach out to the communities. However, persuasion seemed to be the objective of this outreach, as opposed to 'authentic' dialogue. Indeed, forums were either one-way briefing sessions or opportunities for the most disgruntled parish councillors to let off steam. In most, "you just end up sitting there and nothing ever gets discussed that you want to discuss: they [the Borough Council] only want to discuss what they want to discuss".

For the most part, parish groups saw little evidence of genuine 'conversation' in the way they connected with the Borough, arguing instead that consultations appeared to be stage-managed means of soothing and placating community interests. Running events at neutral venues, away from village halls, was viewed as evidence that planning officers recognised the controversy of plans and proposals, but wished to avoid a potentially hostile setting. For the same reason, it was claimed, the planners avoid too many meetings in the Growth Area, but are regular attendees at village meetings in outlying communities. Over time, this amplifies the anger and frustration of residents in parishes subject to significant development proposals, and enhances the sense of wellbeing in the quieter villages. Dialogue in the former comes to an end and a 'blockage' forms in the relationship between community and policy maker, with both parties at fault:

> 'I will say that parish councils could possibly make more effort to communicate with the borough and vice-versa, because it's all about communication, and I think there is a blockage somewhere ... but much of life really is about people talking to each other, it has to be two-way and there has to be a fundamental willingness on both sides to talk openly.' (PG10)

Where there are blockages, it is often the case that communities have lost faith in the Borough Council's willingness and capacity to respond to local concerns. The suspicion can quickly arise that policy makers consult merely to demonstrate legitimacy. Not only do they defend their decisions through the process of engagement, they also try to paint these as 'legitimised', undertaking business as usual behind a smokescreen of consultation, which is primarily concerned with "ticking boxes" and "covering their backs" (PG7). One group had strong views on this issue, explaining that consultation is part of a "deciding and defending" process: "it's on the list, 'oh, consult with parish council, tick, done it. Now we can carry on and do what we wanted to do'".

Rather than there being no trust in the dialogue, there is no dialogue to have trust in. This was the view of several groups. Some reserved particular cynicism for the consultations surrounding the Growth Area strategy. Given that the strategy was initiated by central government, as part of the Communities Plan (ODPM, 2003), groups felt that any attempts by local communities to either oppose it or make recommendations that would ultimately delay it would naturally be resisted by the Borough Council. In reality, there was nothing that parish councils or local community groups could do to 'shape' the strategy – which was entirely top down – and therefore the consultations were 'empty'. Central diktat cannot be challenged:

> 'I sometimes wonder if these councillors are naive or something when they talk about consulting with the public. Do they actually believe it? Are you saying "yes, if you object to this, we're really going to take it on board and odds are we'll agree with you and scrap the plans"? I can't see that.' (PG8)

But all of this cynicism and frustration could not entirely extinguish the good interpersonal relationships between some clerks and some officers. What many parishes valued was the willingness of officers to listen to community groups and do 'as much as they could' within the parameters of decisions that had been imposed upon them as much as upon the parishes. It was also acknowledged that within the framework of these big strategic decisions, officers were often willing to concede as much as they could in terms of detail. Under these circumstances, trust in individuals could be maintained even when trust in the process (or in the 'entity') was lost.

Personal dynamics are critically important at the interface between parishes and local authorities, and seem to improve in areas afflicted by fewer challenges and in those instances where the limited power of local policy actors to make concessions is acknowledged. Good interpersonal relationships, built on a dialogue that delivers mutual understanding, have a propensity to entirely change the experience of policy making. But all too often, these relationships stand in the way of this dialogue, either because planning professionals focus on the 'education and persuasion' of local residents or because the expectations of parishes far exceed what officers are able to deliver.

The local authority perspective

From an officer perspective, the parish councils provide the critical entry point into communities. They are the 'practical community' for planning purposes although that is not to say that the existence of other voices is not acknowledged. Occasionally, effort is expended on building links with community interest groups, but these usually lack a capacity to engage with policy makers in a consistent way and, for this reason, emphasis is placed on connecting with the parish councils, building "pretty good linkages" and engaging in "proactive" discussions (planning policy team). The relationship with parishes was framed by the adopted Statement of Community Involvement (part of the LDF), which set out how planners in the Borough Council would involve communities in planning matters. One officer noted that "we've done more than our formal requirement to engage ... particularly with parish councils", emphasising the claim that ties were strong. Again, these strong links with parishes were thought to compensate for the paucity of connections with other groups, which were difficult to identify and which may not have had a "window of opportunity to get involved".

Parish councils have been the principal, if not sole, framework for neighbourhood planning in rural and semi-rural areas. In instances where a parish has both 'urban' and 'rural' parts, there is a clear tendency for the rural part to be better represented. Development control officers have a statutory duty to notify parishes, where they exist, of planning applications received. For development control, parishes provide a procedural interface. Where they are absent, or where interests appear to overlap, notifications may be sent to other groups. Listed residents' associations (eg, the Sandyhurst Lane Residents' Association on the edge of Ashford) sometimes substitute for parish councils, or documents are sent to conservation or preservation societies (including the Weald of Kent Protection Society). Other urban forums will receive application notifications where there are no parish councils, but the distribution of planning documents to non-elected bodies is not a statutory requirement: rather, it is a means of forging better relationships and trying to avoid difficulties further along the planning process.

Whether parish councils or urban community forums were the point of contact for development control officers (the former being easier to deal with), the objective of this contact tended to be 'notification' rather than 'consultation'. Statutory duty required information to be dispatched. For smaller applications, the strategy tended to be one of 'wait and see'. Documents were posted and no further action was taken unless a response was received. For bigger applications, perhaps more contentious ones, officers tended to engage in more personal contact with the objective being to 'push things along'. It was often necessary to take particular care when dealing with Ashford's rural communities, many of which were thought to contain significant numbers of articulate, educated, middle-class residents with a vested interest in development issues. From a development control perspective, this could make the interface with rural communities more challenging. But from the perspective of most officers, relations with communities in rural Ashford had been defined by a great many positive experiences, especially around the delivery of rural housing projects. Strong 'member support' for such projects within the Borough Council meant that the housing department had a high-profile presence in rural Ashford, which was built, at a parish level, upon regular contact between residents and project officers. But the delivery of affordable homes for local need had not only cast housing officers in a positive light, it had also improved relations with other parts of the local authority.

Improving connectivity to 'communities'

The good interpersonal relationships highlighted in the parishes were confirmed in the local authority. However, many officers took the view that better connectivity with communities had also been achieved through systemic changes in local government and in planning, a view generally refuted by parish councils, which viewed the system as increasingly complex, remote and inaccessible (see Chapter Eleven). Notably, the secretariat of the LSP argued that a once-remote and high-level structure had been brought closer to residents, and stronger community links had been achieved by rebalancing the membership of the LSP towards County and Borough Council members, alongside representatives of voluntary and community network groups. These provided a counterbalance to 'agency representatives' from the Government Office, SEEDA and The Housing Corporation (now the Homes and Communities Agency), and brought a realignment with the interests of communities. But while additional political representation from within Ashford may well bring advantages, the extent to which it will strengthen community connection is unclear. The claim that having additional 'voluntary and community' sector representation brought the LSP closer to communities was rejected by the parish councils who argued that 'community networks' were in fact distant membership associations who, while advancing the need for a local perspective, were themselves detached from any *particular* local view.

Hence, the LSP sought representation of the local, but had no direct connection to the parishes.

The Borough's planning policy team was clear that planning reform in the 2000s, like the new local governance structures, had also brought policy makers closer to communities. In particular, it was suggested that its Statement of Community Involvement had "focused people's minds" on the processes and benefits of engagement. Planning policy was no longer going "out with an advert to consult on a document" but instead engaging communities in the "way they want to be engaged". Indeed, officers thought of themselves as highly proactive in the gauging of local interest, contrasting this to an unspecified period of apparent reluctance to talk to communities. This new enthusiasm to work with and for parish groups was highlighted by development control officers who, like the parish groups, referred to the "development of the Tenterden and Rural Sites DPD", which had "built a lot of bridges" and strengthened local ties. For their part, parish groups had an entirely different take on the Tenterden and Rural Sites DPD consultation. While they valued the opportunity to input, many were frustrated that issues of principle had been previously agreed in the Core Strategy. Many had not realised that this would be the case, had waited for the 'rural' document to be issued and had then found that the opportunity to challenge issues of *principle* had passed (see Chapter Thirteen).

The 'parochialism' of parish interests

From a policy-making perspective, any improvements in the mechanics of interfacing with community interests may ultimately be offset by the inevitable frictions focused upon key personalities. A familiar picture was painted of vested interest and conflict in Ashford's affluent rural areas, where there are large numbers of 'politically active' professional residents, who constantly confront planning proposals with "unreasonable expectations". "Parochial" and "closeted" attitudes make it difficult to work with some parish councils. However, relationships were said to vary from one parish to another, and also from individual to individual within parishes, but the relationship with *parish councillors*, who tended to be "retired, professional people wandering the streets ... looking for something to do" was considered especially problematic.

More generally significant was the rejection of expert opinion as being out of touch with the realities of daily life. Highways officers felt accused of not having a real 'feel' for places, with residents assuming that "all traffic engineers live in cul-de-sacs" and so cannot understand the concerns of communities blighted by heavy traffic along arterial roads. There was felt to be a 'dehumanising' of professionals across the board: an aversion to professional opinion and a lack of trust in it. While some officers were undoubtedly resilient to interpersonal tensions, others lamented the lack of empathy between residents and officers of the council, arguing that officials were commonly seen as 'the enemy' and out of touch.

Such personal experiences are important in shaping relationships, for better or worse, but it is also the case that attitudes, regularly expressed in rural areas that have received significant levels of middle-class migration, place an added strain on otherwise good relations. Planners pointed to what they saw as a proliferation of anti-development sentiment in some communities, underpinned by a vested interest – in maintaining the character of villages – which they nevertheless conceded to be totally understandable. The policy team avoided the pejorative use of the term 'NIMBY', asserting that their relationship with parishes had been generally good, accepting that there are many "communities who want to have a say in the future of their settlements". It was conceded that events such as the aborted housing development discussed earlier, had soured relationships with some communities, bred mistrust, and that there were certainly "lessons to be learnt". Because of their regular contact with parish clerks – being on "first-name terms with most" – development control officers claimed a particular insight into the local authority's relationship with its parishes. Frustration is greatest, and tensions at their deepest, where parish councils lack a general understanding of their role and position in broader local government structures, where they are uninitiated in the art of lobbying and unable to find their way around the apparatus of local service provision. Parishes need resources to get the best out of these structures and apparatus. This means that some larger, more affluent parishes find that the system appears to work for them, while their smaller neighbours may feel alienated by the same system.

Communication is critical, both communication (and the 'open channels') between the parishes and the local authority, and communication within communities, which develops proper understanding of what parish structures can genuinely achieve. Friction with parishes can be worst at community meetings attended by service providers. These events sometimes reveal parish councils to be disconnected from the wider community: officers become the focus of frustration for some residents. But the reality is that the parish council has failed to connect with local people and with higher structures. Rather, they are isolated and do not provide the necessary conduit through which people on the ground communicate with those providing them with services:

> 'I think the problem here is about communication more than anything else ... the local residents or the constituents have no real understanding of what parish councils do and they probably have no understanding of what Ashford Borough Council does. I think it's trying to disseminate who does what and when and I think that's the problem: people don't really understand who is responsible for the roads, who does this and who does that and then, how does that impact upon the decision makers?'

But if communities are bewildered and challenged by the policy environment and its constraints, attempts to open it up by chipping away at it may ultimately prove fruitless. Their tactics may need to change, and they may only achieve influence with the right support.

The 'reactive' community

In some areas, parish councils are an established feature of local governance, representing the interests of residents and playing an important role in securing quality services for communities. But they are generally a 'representative structure' with a mandate to connect with external bodies on behalf of their constituents. Here, we have examined the conventional processes of upward connection to service providers through the parish clerks and council members. Parishes have traditionally lobbied providers with the aim of securing a specific outcome. The pattern of observe–respond is present in the relationship with Highways, which is regularly viewed as a 'fixer' and contacted whenever anything goes awry with roads and pavements. It is also present with development control, which notifies parishes of planning applications and then waits for (but does not necessarily seek) a response. Planning policy's relationship is different as it is not triggered by daily events, but rather a cycle of strategizing, which requires a relationship that is synchronous with the preparation and review of statutory planning documents as they are issued and consulted upon. But, the direct connectivity of parish councils to broader structures has several common features:

- It is predicated upon, and favours, personal relationships with parishes invariably preferring to work with named officers.

- The relationship is largely a lobbying one, with parishes reacting to events (usually local but occasionally relating to broader planning policy) and seeking to bring about change by demonstrating anger with a decision or outcome.
- It is strongly reliant on the clerk as a key juncture in the link between the parish council and service providers. The degree to which information flows freely through the clerk is unclear, but they are critical players, connecting external agencies to the 'community'.
- But the community is not the parish, and parishes may have weak connectivity themselves to the people they serve. It is certainly wrong to assume that where a policy actor connects to a parish or neighbourhood group that 'participatory' processes are in play. The extent of participation may remain limited to a few, highly specific interests.

Finally, what prevents a reactive parish or neighbourhood group, with weak connectivity to the apparatus of local government, become proactive and better connected? There is a certainly a case for establishing a greater range of connections – for building in greater 'redundancy' – and for bridging over the undercurrent of mistrust that may exist between 'planning and people'. This is examined in the next chapter. But the proactive community is also a well-resourced one, which has the means to develop new relationships, engage positively in community-based planning and become more than merely reactive.

ELEVEN

Working through intermediaries

In Chapter Nine, 'intermediaries' were characterised as 'brokers', negotiating a relationship between the community and policy actors. It was suggested that such intermediaries bridge the potential divide between community groups looking to put together plans, and either the planning authority – that might be looking to use the neighbourhood perspective in some way – or service providers, which might be steered by the content of a community-based plan. Given the thrust of local government reform in the 2000s – delivering Labour's own brand of 'new localism' – and the creation of structures designed to open up policy processes to a broader array of local actors, it has been hypothesised that the LSP, or some future equivalent, might play this type of role (Bishop, 2007; Owen et al, 2007). On the other hand, there may well be incidental 'weak ties' acting as go-betweens, and that these might include ward members sometimes pushing particular community agendas or residents with informal connections to one or more stakeholders. Some evidence of the latter was highlighted in the last chapter, with employees of the local authority bringing issues of community concern to the attention of colleagues. But overall, only very weak evidence of such ties was found. And while some stakeholders view the LSP, with its corporate connections, as a potentially important 'broker' between policy actors and communities, this did not appear to be the prevailing state of affairs. This issue, and the apparent failure of this local governance apparatus, is examined in the first part of this chapter. The second part then looks at support groups in neighbourhood planning and the part they play in easing communication between key parties. These are the expected 'intermediaries' but it is perhaps the unexpected case that parish clerks may also be considered intermediaries, although perhaps in a more pejorative sense. Some stakeholders described them as 'gate-keepers' who control the flow of information to and from the community. They are part of the parish council but in a sense separate from it, forming bonds with support groups and developing their own special relationships with local officials. On some occasions, they have a powerful influence on what communities know about policy actors and vice versa.

Linking through others

The local strategic partnership

Local government reform during the 2000s pointed to the possibility of a more networked approach to local governance with LSPs occupying a central position, mediating between community interests and stakeholders, and contributing to a more connected and participatory form of spatial planning expressed through the drawing up of Community Strategies. It was implied that communities and neighbourhoods able to connect with the LSP would have a direct hand in 'place shaping' (see Lyons, 2007) and would be far more likely to receive the services they needed.

The reality in Ashford seemed a world apart from this rhetoric. None of the parish councils recalled any dialogue with the LSP (or at least not any that they were aware of) and few were certain of its function, suggesting instead that their own vagueness 'spoke volumes'. Those in the parishes who had come across the LSP believed that its purpose was to distribute information on services via email or that it was a 'high-level talking shop' with little direct relevance to the borough's residents. It came as news to many groups that the partnership was in the business of drawing up a Community Strategy, which seemed to some to be oddly named and without any clear link to Ashford's 'real communities'. The community component, according to the LSP itself, came from the partnership's mix of membership, comprising service providers and a number of 'community networks' (eg, the vice chairman of the Ashford Community Network, claiming to represent 800 community groups and eight black and minority ethnic groups, sat on the LSP). The latter meant that the LSP was 'heavily weighted towards community representation', with the networks providing a good functional 'interface' with communities. On the back of a community engagement exercise completed by the Borough Council in Spring 2010 (which had involved surveying residents' views, and which had achieved a response rate of under 1%), it was argued that by 2011, community network representation – combined with the survey's lessons on what communities needed – would mean the alignment of service provision and a 'mandate from all of the communities'. This was a claim that communities were more than ready to dispute, arguing that second-hand representation from networks did not constitute engagement let alone a mandate of any kind. It also painted an aggregate view of communities, ignoring difference: community was being conceived at the wrong scale.

Furthermore, while the network members of the LSP appeared to give the partnership a route (albeit a questionable one) into neighbourhoods, the parishes tended to be of the view that these networks were more active in urban wards where they substituted for parish councils. The lack of parish representation or connection meant that anything the LSP produced would have a strongly urban bias, centred upon the Growth Area and urban extensions. This line of argument converged around the view that LSPs might be synthetic substitutes (constituted at the wrong level) for 'real' participation.

The net result, from a parish group perspective, was that the LSP, as a body, failed to connect with residents and therefore was not expected to add anything to the connectivity between neighbourhood governance structures – the parishes – and higher-level actors. Generally, the structures that had emerged in the 2000s were poorly understood and parish councils maintained a more traditional view of how they might work with decision makers, based largely around lobbying and around the few strong relationships (with key officers) that appeared to offer inroads into the Borough Council (see last chapter).

This analysis of the failure of LSPs to connect to place communities is repeated elsewhere. Given the shared community focus of partnerships and parish councils, albeit at different spatial scales, Owen et al (2007) argued that a fit should be sought between Community Strategies produced by the LSP and the content of community-based plans, adding that this could be realised through the appointment of liaison officers, tasked to work with communities (Owen et al, 2007, p 69). Referring to a number of local studies across England, these authors perceived 'an acceptance that the community strategy could help broker the policies and decisions required by many bodies to address very local problems' (2007, p 70). But despite this perception, Owen et al observed 'very little traffic' on these 'bridges' between community and policy actors and these same findings emerge from Ashford.

'Special relationships' and lobbying

It is sometimes the case that officers developing a 'special relationship' with the parishes (see Chapter Ten) may come to view themselves, in a sense, as intermediaries: friends of the parishes who sympathise with their concerns and are able to bring these to the attention of colleagues. Such special relationships, as noted in the last chapter, often form around positive experiences with a measureable outcome. They have a propensity to alter the standard 'lobbying' relationship that parish councils regularly share with authorities. Officers involved in affordable housing schemes tended to be popular with parish groups, who regarded them as people able to get things done. Housing officers, in general, maintained good relations with the parishes.[1] This was recognised by other authority officers who often looked to housing to provide a steer on, or at least an insight into, parish issues. In Ashford, this tended to happen at a 'Rural Round Table' – a forum bringing together the rural housing enabler, officers (with a rural remit) of the housing and planning departments, representatives of the council's legal department, Kent Highways and registered social landlords currently progressing rural schemes in Ashford. At these meetings, usually frequented by more junior officers but occasionally with more senior managers in attendance, housing officers were often viewed, and viewed themselves, as having a line to the parishes. They tended to know what was happening at any point in time and what actions appeared to placate or make parishes happy. Hence, an opportunity was recognised to develop policies that better reflected the concerns of community groups: to turn local developmental work into a broader view of the needs of Ashford's communities.

But this opportunity was not easy to grasp. Even the officers with the best relationships with the parishes struggled to transform passion for local projects, or against development proposals, into sustained engagement around strategic issues. The dialogue with parishes centred on projects was viewed as distinctly different from the 'consultations' surrounding housing strategies or development plan documents. There was no institutional learning from the experience of working with communities. Strategies could only legally be informed by consultation, which was kept separate from participatory processes. Officers were understandably frustrated by this, questioning the value of 'consultation' as a process and edging towards the idea that, through dialogue, it might be easier to identify issues of key concern rather than 'wasting time' on issues that 'communities don't see as important'.

Ultimately, the various public sector-led strategies being produced were not alive to the subtle signals that emerged through the special relationships that project collaboration gave rise to. It suggests flaws in a consultation process around policy, or around officer-led options, which might only be remedied by more direct and constant input into plan development. The 'decide and defend' (ie, consult) approach seemed to generate only fleeting glimpses of community perspective, but not a deeper understanding of residents' concerns. The community-based plans were thought to be potential resources for institutional learning. However, this learning could only occur if the resources were available to work more closely with parish councils. Some officers viewed better understanding of the content of these plans as a means of sidestepping potential conflicts (hence, planning officers were keen to hear as much as possible from housing colleagues about the 'feeling within the parishes', again using them as a bridge to residents) but there was also some consideration of the benefits that a more systematic partnership with community-based planning might bring. 'Dipping into parish plans' was viewed as a means of augmenting the evidence base for the LDF, although this was thought to be a potentially large task, with some plans being 'difficult to make sense of' and, collectively, it would be difficult to construct policy on the complex 'common threads' of community planning. But partnership – working *with* communities to develop evidence – was considered a much more fundamental step that would require a significant shift in the culture of local authority planning and policy making. In April 2010, as the last interviews were being conducted, the prospect of far-reaching changes to the planning system loomed large. Some communities, and some officers, had begun to reflect on the implication of these changes although the transformation of parish plans into 'neighbourhood' plans, linked into local plans, had not been countenanced. The relationship between parishes and officers, however convivial in some instances, remained based on the view that planners plan and communities live with the consequences (rather than pursuing agendas in a collaborative manner). In order to change things, communities engage in lobbying: seeking to influence the views not only of elected members but also of the officials who have delegated power over the small changes that are important to the residents of a village or neighbourhood. Although much of the discussion above has focused on working through the most approachable officials, communities are still essentially engaged in lobbying, partly because they do not have the capacities or knowledge to become more embedded in the local policy process.

It was conceded, in the communities themselves, that lobbying – the continual communication of issues arising – was not necessarily the most effective means of securing long-term influence, or shaping change. What was needed instead was a means of understanding 'which buttons' to push with policy makers in order to bring about some lasting change, and help – when needed – with pushing those buttons.

Support groups in neighbourhood planning

From the point of view of support groups, either communities had a tendency to supply service providers with the wrong information (which could not be acted on) or the right information was not getting to the providers simply because they were unaware of its existence. Supporting community activity is often simply about making the connections between what one party is offering and what another needs. This brokering function appeared to be included in the remits of several of the voluntary sector representatives with seats on the LSP, including the Ashford Community Network, the Kent Association of Local Councils (KALC), Community Action South & East Kent (CASE Kent), Ashford's Citizens' Advice Bureau and Ashford Churches. However, returning to the point made earlier, these groups tended to focus on representing community interest and it was left to one very specific broker – Action with Communities in Rural Kent (ACRK) – to actively work with community and policy actors on the type of brokerage outlined above.

The planning team highlighted the role played by ACRK in helping instigate community-based planning and working with officers to translate residents' aspiration into action plans. Housing officers lauded its role – along with that of the English Rural Housing Association – in 'democratising' community planning by helping broaden engagement on local needs projects. It was sometimes felt – and this appears to be common to parish planning – that decisions were taken by too few people and that there was a risk of insufficient outreach to all sections of the community or all parts of a neighbourhood (see Chapters Seven and Eight). ACRK and a few other bodies were instrumental in popularising the process and raising awareness. This was part of their remit and they also brought the resources for such outreach into the planning process.

Like similar groups across the country, ACRK aims to develop a direct working relationship with the parish councils, the clerks and the elected and co-opted members. It embeds itself within the democratic structure of the community, attempting to add capacity. But this is a resource-intensive approach. The rationale is that communities seldom have the capacity and the knowledge to fully engage in the planning process and that external assistance is often crucial. In Kent, ACRK and its partners have become spread increasingly thinly. They are viewed as a conduit into parishes and one of the best ways to work with policy actors. This popularity has put the organisation under considerable pressure. The response has been to move to a briefing and training role, with ACRK working with KALC to provide 'how to' templates: how to connect with policy, how to translate aspiration into action and how to influence. The problem, however, is that briefings do not allow the support groups to add capacity, embed themselves in the process or guarantee that knowledge will get to where it is needed. Overburdened clerks attend the briefings, often alone, and new information may not necessarily result in new ways of working in the parishes. A conversation is had between the clerks and the support groups, but this is not a conversation with the community.

This is a critical issue. Connections to the 'community', in planning terms, are often simply connections to a small self-selecting body: that is, the parish council. Notions of 'community-based planning' or 'neighbourhood planning' suggest an inclusive, participatory approach to decision making. But this is not guaranteed. There is some hope that a support agency, working closely with a community, will be onsite to democratise the process (as asserted by ACRK), but there are great risks associated with brief, intermittent contact with a clique or with one individual. There are particular concerns with the role of clerks and the danger that by seeking a clear line of communication, community aspiration is simply boiled down to one set of views. Clerks may become gatekeepers to the community.

Gatekeepers

Parish clerks have traditionally performed a vital role at the interface between parish councils and external bodies. They are often the 'face' of the community from the point of view of local council officials, who will have more regular contact with clerks than with the parish council chair or other elected or co-opted members. It is the clerks who are instrumental in forming the 'special' relationships noted earlier. One of the Ashford officers had previously been involved in the enabling of rural housing projects. This had brought her into close and regular contact with the parish council clerks, who she came to view as potential obstacles to community access:

> 'When you've got a good clerk, then they're fantastic. They respond to you; they make sure the information goes to the right [parish] councillors and everything. But you can get clerks who, for whatever reason, are perhaps not very responsive or they are protecting either their own interests or those of the members of the parish council and sometimes you have to find a way of bypassing them, diplomatically.'

Clerks may become hugely powerful within the community-based (and broader) planning process, but they may also become 'weak' links in the chain of communication, curtailing the flow of information into and out of the parish. For some, clerks were viewed as being outside the collective (parish) view, brokering deals, persuading or dissuading depending on their own perspective. Such actions are simply part of the political process within communities, but it is the ability of clerks to influence opinion through the presentation of facts, when those facts first become available, that makes them so critical at the interface with communities:

> 'For me, one of the big issues is the 'clerk run' [distribution of briefings to members]. She's there to act as the *secretary*, or in an *administrative* role, for the parish council and I feel that they're sometimes gatekeepers.... Four of five areas you've been trying to get into sometimes share the same clerk: that's quite powerful if that individual is making decisions about what goes to the parish council and what doesn't and ... what's put on the agenda.'

Parish council clerks have power in the process, whether this is wielded cynically or accidentally. Limited capacity means that clerks may filter information as they see fit, or are simply not able to respond to everything they receive. Suggestions of cynical influence tended to be based on anecdotal evidence, or simply on suspicion born of frustration.

But these discussions raise further questions over community capacity, particularly if parishes start to take more responsibility for 'planning' and for working with traditional policy actors in the broader planning process. Clerks, it appears, are already filtering and prioritising information (as agenda setters) in what might seem to be quite arbitrary ways, simply to make their roles more manageable. They are prioritising established relationships, focusing on information from 'trusted partners'. Email messages, especially circular ones, are sometimes ignored. This is partly why the parishes in the study knew so little about the LSP or indeed about Ashford's Future (the Special Delivery Vehicle for the Growth Area). These bodies sent out newsletters and engaged in activities that might be described broadly as 'publicity'. Their contact with the parishes was certainly not targeted or personal, and therefore not viewed, by the parish groups, as significant. Organisations that wanted a relationship with parish councils needed to invest time in building that relationship, but for many this was either not a priority or clearly unnecessary. The regional development agency's view on this matter was that a significant minority of people simply want 'agencies' that operate at a strategic level to 'get on with it' and that those who desire information 'will seek it out'. But this belief appeared contrary to that of the clerks, who lacked the time and energy to turn detective, and who prioritised information that was communicated personally. Parish groups already felt disconnected from many of the area's strategic bodies, labelling the regional agencies 'remote' and 'secretive'. Of course, their major concern was with the functioning of these agencies, especially their role in strategic planning for housing, but their apparent unwillingness to engage (along with the failure of the LSP to connect with people, at least in a way judged appropriate by parishes) added to the air of mistrust and resulted in clear support for a more local, connected approach to 'strategic' policy formulation.

Communication

Lines of communication may be populated by numerous 'translators': officers enjoying special relationships with parishes, the parish council clerks, or support groups that aim to improve the volume and quality of dialogue between traditional policy users and producers. Modes of communication are critically important: some are a turn-off for parishes and serve only the efficiency objectives of policy actors, but do not achieve the effective engagement they ostensibly seek. While the Highways Authority has embraced new technology and maintained a web portal – My Kent Highways Online – it maintains telephone contact with clerks and holds regular parish meetings. It liaises with Partners and Communities Together (PACT), a network of 'community wardens' who provide a link to the parishes and feed back on highways matters. Show case events run by planning policy officers, including rural conferences, provide a more direct interface, but it is still the contact with named officers that is most highly prized among parish councils. As well as the resource concerns affecting parishes, it is also the case that key local authority departments find it difficult to resource the kind of interpersonal engagement that seems to do most to ease tensions and give parishes the confidence and capacity to engage in community-based planning aligned to public sector policy development. It is often clerks who raise concerns about the move from personal to electronic communication, viewing this as evidence of a new aloofness among officials. Similarly, less proactivity in dealing with parishes is sometimes viewed as disengagement, an unwillingness to work with communities on equal terms, and also a transfer of responsibility to planning's private realm without a commensurate transfer of resources.

The 'supported' community

Bridging, in the sense used by other commentators on the state of community-based planning in England, tended – in this study – to be confined to the work of specialist support groups (although it can also apply to placement of community plans for maximum impact, an issue that is picked up in the next chapter). These recognise that there is a gap to be bridged, between community aspiration and policy development, and ascribe the label 'bridging' to their own work. Bridging is an incidental activity that arises within a network of common interest and occurs in a number of ways, but is not always viewed as a positive act. The link, for example, into communities is not always a clean one. While network theory conceives intermediate ties as translators who aid the process of communication, it is also the case that such ties can misrepresent or filter conversations. Practically, this means that those bodies wishing to work effectively with communities need to establish an embedded link: one that allows them to work with many individuals and extend their reach into the broader community, thereby democratising a process that may occasionally be confined to only a handful of parish council members.

Some of the dangers of relying too much on parish councils, and on clerks, have been outlined in this chapter. More broadly, these councils are either loved or loathed, and every area in England has its own stories to tell in relation to the operation of parish councils. Some of these were alluded to in earlier chapters. Despite the reservations of some policy actors, others maintain that connection with parish councils is the only effective means of working with communities. Highways, for example, contrasted Ashford's urban areas with its rural ones:

> '[T]he urban areas don't have the parish councils ... and that sometimes is a bit of a stumbling [block] as you have to rely on the borough councillors being the voice of the people, whereas the parish councils [should] be there representing their parishioners.' (Highways)

Urban communities may consequently feel a "little bit neglected" and their members may feel that opportunities to express their views within the community, and to the community, are restricted. Their higher and denser populations may also mean that ward councillors struggle to represent the diversity of views and needs. It is in the rural areas that "things are working really well". In the urban areas, there have been experiments with unelected representatives – community networks or forums – but these suffer the drawback of limited accountability.

This chapter has sought to build on the overview of relationships at the community–policy interface presented in the previous chapter. The one-to-one relationships that are a feature of this interface are not always resilient to change or the best means of communication. Lobbying often has a focus on the short term and can be contrasted with the deeper relationships and interactions that support groups sometimes have with communities. These relationships, which give capacity to communities and bring them into the planning process, are dependent on adequate resourcing. Although wider evidence of effective bridging activities is perhaps weak, it seems likely that embedding communities, or neighbourhoods, into the future planning process in England will require additional investments, of both volunteer time and of the monies needed to mainstream some of the positive experiences observed in Ashford, particularly around independent support for community planning.

Finally, it is important to emphasise that the critical bridge with communities is provided by the parish councils themselves. These can be difficult bridges to navigate. A council is not the community – it does not always offer authentic representation of wider community ambition – and this is generally recognised by support groups whose first task when supporting community-based planning is to move into the community from what is often the point of entry – the parish council or more specifically the clerk. If democratic renewal is a genuine aim of the localism described in Chapter Four, and if neighbourhood planning is a tool for realising that renewal, then much more effort will be need to be dedicated to 'reaching into' communities from existing or new governance structures. Only then will there be movement towards the stated aim, highlighted at the beginning of Chapter Six, of building a 'collaborative democracy'.

Note

[1] Partly perhaps because they lacked the regulatory or enforcement role of planning officers.

TWELVE

Community-based plans

It is through the production of plans and statements that communities may seek to shape not only individual decisions but also the policies on which those decisions are built. Plans articulate a community's aspirations. Their production can be viewed as an exercise in channelling local energies, and as key to capacity building. But it can also be seen as an overt attempt to supply evidence to stakeholders in the hope that this evidence will influence the shape of policy. This chapter examines community and policy actor views on community-based plans, their value and role in the planning process, and lessons for future evolution. It begins by looking at the interest that these plans have generated and perceptions of the weight they have been given in policy development, before examining actual use and utility. It ends by teasing out lessons for future community-based planning, linking these lessons to neighbourhood development plans in England, introduced in Chapter Four.

The value and 'weight' of community-based plans

Parish plans

The weight given to community plans in policy development in England, and also their value *within* a community relative to their value beyond it, have been topics of major concern among commentators. It has also been suggested that community-based plans should not be viewed as 'planning' documents per se, but as markers for community aspiration and need; there to potentially inform the programmes and investments of multiple service providers. Communities themselves acknowledge the aspirational nature of their plans, their variable style and content and the limited data on which they are often constructed. They understand that these plans may not provide policy making with a strong foundation. However, a belief in the broader value of community-based plans generates great enthusiasm for their production. Many parish groups believe that by articulating what is important to the community, and what might potentially upset it, they are setting out a position that *politicians* will want to take note of. Three of the parishes – Great Chart with Singleton, Bilsington and Appledore –

noted that while the production of plans was encouraged by their ward members, planners were generally uninterested in the process. Plans helped in the forming of *political* agendas, but were viewed as less helpful for planning.

Image 12.1: The village hall at Appledore

It was the leader of Ashford Borough Council who gave most encouragement to producing new parish plans, a process kick-started by an invitation to draw up 'wish-lists' to inform ongoing development of the Council's Core Strategy. But there was not always consistent enthusiasm for parish plans amongst planning officers:

> '[Y]ou'd go to one meeting and they'd say, "yes, parish plans are a good idea, we want everybody to have one", and then six months later you'd go back and they'd say, "well, we don't actually think they're that important", so we had this yes, no, yes, no scenario.'

This generated uncertainty in the parishes and sparked the obvious question: was the drawing up of parish plans worth the time and effort? Although the politicians lauded the plans as a route to influence, the planners remained sceptical, and while officers supported their production 'in principle', they continually withdrew to the argument that they "had no vehicle for dealing with them". Indeed, much of the content of the plans appeared *ultra vires*: filtering the inactionable from the actionable, in planning terms, would mean an investment of resources that they did not have. Policy actors sometimes viewed parish plans as a mishmash of conservatism, discontent and diatribe from which it would be difficult to discern clear policy strands let alone align these strands with the principles of the Core Strategy or the detail of Development Plan Documents. They were simply not 'adoptable'. Parish groups frequently disputed this and also the claim of under-resourcing. Their plans were problematic, in normative planning terms, because the local authority failed to engage constructively with parish councils. Their dismissal of parish plans was contrasted with the more positive approach that many officers had taken to VDSs. This issue is picked up again below.

Staying with the parish plans: despite the political support they had received, officer reaction to the plans sometimes soured relations with the parish councils, which rather than seeing the plans as a point of positive engagement, came to view them as the point at which relationships broke down:

> '[T]hey didn't take it seriously, they never argued about anything, "oh, we're not going to do any of it, so we don't want to debate it". You think, "ok, thanks". If they had to do something they'd say, "hang on, just a minute, why do you want that, and how do you want that?" You'd have a more robust debate about it, but you could tell they weren't going to be really interested because they didn't really argue about any of it.' (PG3)

Officer reactions, ranging from 'vague' non-committal, through clear 'indifference', to stunned silence, seemed to confirm to the parish groups that plans were not for external consumption. They did not connect with the mindset of planning and, from the point of view of some parish groups, were never meant to. Rather, they were a way of focusing minds within the community, setting agendas where necessary and even just mobilising local energies. One parish expressed the role of their plan in the following terms: "we didn't see Ashford as being relevant. This was us ... we were an entity all to ourselves".

Disagreement over the role of parish plans in Ashford's communities – are they solely for communities (a focus for capacity building, expressing shared aspirations), are they lobbying agendas (lists of issues to take up with different service providers and the politicians) or are they 'supplementary planning documents' to be carried forward, at least in part, into the LDF? – is a disagreement that has been repeated across

England. It links back to the question of whether community action is an end itself (with a principal role in community development rather than in policy development), delivering by itself, or whether it needs to trigger a response across broader governance structures: self-help or a cry for help?

Village Design Statements

Views on this issue were coloured by the experience of drawing up VDSs. Those parishes that had produced a statement, and especially those that had seen their statements adopted as 'supplementary' planning guidance, had greater confidence in the process. Pluckley, for example, had established a number of working groups to take forward its statement. Around ten iterations went to the local authority, all being returned with detailed comment. Eventually, compromises were reached on key elements and the VDS was formally adopted into planning policy.

Some parishes believed that their broader parish plans would be treated by the planning process in much the same way as the VDS. Like other parishes, Bethersden put together a four-part plan, which included an historical preamble, a housing needs evidence base, a community plan element and an embedded VDS. The planning team extracted the VDS and discarded everything else. They then subjected it to the same level of scrutiny as the Pluckley statement and eventually adopted it. Two lessons emerge: first, planning professionals have needed to feel confident that the products of community planning are operable in a strict legal sense – this has resulted in a large measure of 'instrumental framing'; and second, broader, and perhaps more nebulous, parish plans have seldom commanded any confidence among planning professionals. A summary of the content and form of parish plans in the study area, and whether parish groups previously produced a VDS is provided in Table 12.1.

Because the welcome extended to VDSs was not extended to parish plans, groups actively seeking to influence planning policy sometimes looked enviously at those parishes that had won support for their design statements and regretted the time 'wasted' on producing broader plans (although PG6 appears to break this rule, and is now putting together a plan having never produced a design statement, possibly because it has its sights set on producing a neighbourhood development plan).

Table 12.1: Parish plan content

Parish group	Year of parish plan	Theme 1: Area background and history	Theme 2: Data analysis	Theme 3: Development aspirations and policies	Theme 4: Action plan	Year of last VDS
PG1	2003	X	X	X	X	2002
PG2	2005	X	X	X		2002
PG3	2007	X	X			2000
PG4	2011		X			2004
PG5	2009	X	X	X	X	2003
PG6	2011		X			n/a
PG7	2006	X	X	X		n/a
PG8	2005	X	X			n/a
PG9	2008	X	X			2002
PG10	2009	X	X			n/a

Note: PG4 and PG6 are both at an initial phase in plan preparation, and have recently undertaken preliminary surveys.

The case for clear guidance and support

But others did not accept that plans were destined for rejection. Their analysis was that parish plans were potentially complex documents, especially compared to the relatively simple design statements, but that connectivity to the local plan would be possible if community planning groups were issued with clear guidance. The Countryside Agency – before being separated into Natural England and the Commission for Rural Communities in 2006 – had issued some general guidance (see Chapter Four) but this had very rarely been seen by parish councils (at least the current membership), and was never sent to local authorities. The councils that had undertaken 'parish appraisals' contrasted that experience with the current plan process:

> '[W]ith the parish appraisal we got a software package and a ... more clear steer [on the] framework of questions. This time round, with the parish plan, there was nothing. You just got the request to do it. You were very much left alone to find your own way through and decide how you wanted to approach it and what you wanted to do, so I think it took us a while to get a feel for what it was.' (PG9)

Because there was no clear guidance on structure, the quality of plans was said to have suffered. Parish groups sought different data, in a wide variety of ways. Many groups felt that if the Borough Council had been serious about using parish evidence, it would have provided a template for gathering that evidence

> '[W]hat would be useful, if we were to do this again, is to have a more coordinated approach by the Council. It would have been good if they'd said, "well, here's your information pack on how to do it and here's an ideal example of what we'd like to see, here's a potential project plan for doing it", to save every single one of these parishes going and reinventing it. Reinventing the wheel every time because I don't see how they can coordinate our plan with somebody else's plan because it could cover totally different topics.' (PG3)

These views were shared by ACRK, which highlighted the quality of the evidence underpinning plans as a critical weakness, diminishing their potential to influence planning policy or meet the needs of service providers looking for a clear parish steer. Like the communities themselves, ACRK felt that guidance was important. But this could also be provided by the support groups, independent of the local authority, and therefore viewed as a neutral interface between community action and its policy implications: implications not only for planning, but also for the full range of services that communities received.

The use and utility of community-based plans

A view from the parishes

Few parish councils believed that the content of their plans had influenced the strategies or policies of the Borough Council. Consistency within the plans was one weakness: another was thought to be the danger of raising community expectation. There was a perception that officers played down the importance of parish plans and did not wish to be seen to engage in the plan process, lest they made a 'rod for their own backs', ultimately facing a backlash from disappointed parishes. Other parishes offered a more conventional explanation for limited influence: that significant policy change flows downwards, not upwards, rendering community input largely redundant:

'[T]he difficulty on the ground, for us peasants, is that you do all this work and, of course, you don't necessarily see that it is making much of a difference because it's apparent that there are factors that are more significant than what local people have said. I am seriously sceptical ... because unless you have a tier of professional officers who are at the face of activities, who are cognisant of what's going on, who are sympathetic to the message that a community should be participating; unless you've got people like that, then it can be very, very difficult and very, very frustrating.' (PG3)

It was not the case that Ashford's planning officers were evasive, but simply that they were part of a system that attached no significant value to community input. The encouragement given to draw up parish plans was viewed as an action without anticipated consequence: another tick in another box. After the plans were produced, the planning team was said to have never "showed the slightest interest in the work that was done", leaving the most cynical and frustrated parishes to conclude that they were "absolutely irrelevant":

'[W]hether anyone has looked at [the parish plan] is a complete mystery to me. I think that it's landed on the desk, they've ticked the box, "oh, yes, they've done one" ... I would have thought, having done a document like that, or any document from a parish since they instigate it, that we get someone come back and say, "ok, you've done that now, can we have a talk about this and go through and make sure we understand the views", but ... nothing. It just went into a black hole.' (PG9)

But still, parish groups returned constantly to the internal value of plans. The exercises leading to their production were reflective, leading the community to attach value to assets and community attributes that they felt were important. Great value was also attached to the 'social outcomes' that sprang from the activities linked to plan production, especially the way in which the parish councils often made new connections to residents. For many, the planning purpose of parish plans was not at all clear, but this contrasted to the seemingly obvious function of VDSs: to influence the process of development control and achieve clear design outcomes.

But the consistency of use made of the VDS appeared variable. PG1 were confident that their statement had shaped discussions with contractors and developers and that the community's presentation of key design attributes had been "taken reasonably seriously". But this was not the view of PG3, who felt that the statement had been routinely ignored, largely because of its weight relative to more significant planning documents and because of the general unresponsiveness of the system, and officers, to any form of community input. New developments, and changes to existing buildings, were clearly contrary to the framework established in the VDS. This may be explained by relative 'weighting', but the more cynical participants maintained that community-based plans, of all types, are not designed to challenge professional or political opinion, but merely to placate community interests in the face of irresistible change. Encouraging their production is part of a process of appeasement, addressing – in a superficial way – the frustrations that communities feel with local democracy, but accepting that expert input is more 'rational', offering the longer and the broader view, and ultimately delivering integrated solutions to future development needs.

A view from planning

The planning team, and other policy actors, expressed a general view that any evidence emerging from the parishes has a 'role to play' in communicating the aspirations of communities. Contrary to the views expressed in some parish groups, officers engaged in plan making appeared to attach some value to both plans and VDSs:

> 'I looked at the wish-lists and what the parish councils were saying round about 2003. I looked at whatever parish plans were out there and I've been talking to the relevant owners of those parish plans. The Village Design Statement process [is] very important as well, because that has an influence *and has a use*, and in fact in our plan we've referred to them as documents that should be taken account of if developments are coming forward in those areas.' (Planning Policy Officer; emphasis added)

But while the VDSs were considered to have 'some use', in planning terms, parish plans were viewed as being more nebulous, perhaps indicative of feelings but not useful in a 'straightforward' way. Colleagues in development control echoed this view, suggesting that parish plans often highlighted things that it was 'useful to know'. One story was relayed of an instance where the 'path of development' was smoothed by the retention of a piece of land for public use. Its value to the community was not appreciated until the parish plan appeared. At that point, pre-application discussions with the developer refocused on the cost of leaving the land open to public use. This did not adversely affect the viability of the development and so was ultimately agreed. In this instance, perusal of the plan provided an opportunity to understand how a particular arrangement might smooth the path to achieving an outcome wanted by the officers, by the community and by the landowner. The monitoring of plans could trigger further investigations or discussions that might ultimately create a win–win situation, for the Borough Council and for the community. But for others, including Ashford's Future (the 'special delivery vehicle' for the Growth Area), an assumption that any important messages contained in parish plans would inevitably filter upwards through the work of case officers in planning seemed nullified by the view that community-based plans were generally bereft of useable evidence and simply a focus for the political lobbying of a vocal minority.

Emerging from these and other discussions were two key perceptions of the use of community-based plans. First, they were a means of 'sensitising' actions to community concerns, and to aspirations. This meant that they formed part of a broader engagement strategy even if they did not directly inform local authority policy. Second, they were battle plans, detailing the grievances of a minority. Coalitions of pro-development interest edged towards the second perception, but planning officers tended towards the more generous view.

The support agency

A very different perception of utility, or potential utility, was offered by ACRK. It responded to the aspiration of some communities to influence the content of planning policy – and also the delivery of services – through the production of plans that connected directly to policy development, usually through the building of robust evidence bases that would be more difficult for officials and politicians to ignore. Communities with this aspiration tended to favour the production of VDSs over parish plans, as noted earlier, because of a history of adoption. This left ACRK in some difficulty as the organisation lacked staff with specific design skills. However, it was still able to offer advice on how "best to promote the idea of community-based planning within the parish" by sharing its views on how a good plan might be structured and helping communities understand the needs of service providers. There seemed to be no danger that ACRK would seek to manage expectation, by discouraging particular content or aspiration, but it did offer advice on what service providers, including planning, could realistically deliver and on the type of evidence needed to bring about changes in policy. ACRK has tried to bring a degree of focus to community-based planning in Kent.

Its basic remit, like similar bodies across the country, is simply to 'support' the activities of community groups looking to develop some sort of plan. The relationship it establishes to fulfil this remit – and to add capacity – was discussed in the last chapter. ACRK has tended to expand its *bridging* role, working with communities on the implementation of their plans and helping establish better connections with service providers and planners. This bridging is achieved in two principal ways. First, it is achieved by exposing service providers to all types of community-based plan, linking to the work of the South East Region's Rural Community Council (RCC), which has been constructing an internet database of all plans. This cross-references Ashford LSP and Kent Partnership themes to the contents of community-based plans, showing how these may be used to inform policy and tailor service delivery. Second, ACRK hopes to make the information contained in these plans more useful to service providers. Its objective is to get clear guidance from the providers as to the sorts of data they can use in making investment decisions, and then relay this to parish and community groups. Bridging is partly about managing expectation: the expectation of what service providers can do with the data reported in parish plans. The view of ACRK is very much that parish plan groups want to provide more robust information, which other stakeholders can act on; and that plans are often drawn up by residents who are seeking a 'proactive' influence over policy and change.

The 'evolution' of community-led plans

But this more positive judgement needs to be set against the view that community-based plans are indeed a reactive, lobbying tool. Officers in development control noted a "flurry of plans" after 2003 in response to the emerging Growth Area agenda. Community groups wished, reactively, either to get the best they could from what was considered inevitable change (in the form of developer contributions to community projects) or to express their opposition to growth. Future Neighbourhood Plans are likely to be triggered in the same way, drawn up by communities faced with the prospect of developments they support or, more likely, they oppose.

Although few policy actors were aware of the full extent of the neighbourhood planning agenda in early 2010, the subjects for this study were asked to comment on the prospects for more formal connection of community-based plans either to planning frameworks or to Sustainable Communities Strategies. The latter were thought to be relevant as Community Strategies were widely considered to be lacking the community 'building blocks' (Bishop, 2007) that would allow them to claim close correlation with grassroots aspiration or reflect the varied mosaic of community need. In reaction, the LSP respondent maintained that the link would still need to be through planning, with community-based plans transformed into local area action plans. This response did not answer Bishop's (2007) argument that parishes are not only concerned with planning and that by 'spatialising' the Community Strategy – by drawing in the evidence provided by parish plans – services could be better targeted. This whole debate, however, has now been lost in the push towards a neighbourhood *planning* agenda in which parish plans are perhaps the natural antecedents of neighbourhood development plans, and assumed therefore to have been mainly, if not totally, about land use. So what about planning's response to this potential evolution?

Unlike the coalition government a few months later, Ashford's planners in early 2010 saw considerable difficulty in bringing community-based plans into the local planning framework, seeing them instead as contextual pointers with little utility in the formal planning process:

> 'Parish plans give you a very good understanding of the direction or context of that particular settlement and parish, and also give you a good understanding of the age ranges, the associated economic side of things and where they intend to head in the next five or ten years, and that's very useful information. So, I think they both [parish plans and VDSs] have a role to play ... in the evolution of an approach.' (Planning Policy Officer)

The evolution referred to was not thought to be the eventual alignment of neighbourhood and local plans but rather a more systematic approach to 'taking note' of the 'action points coming from the parish plans'. The end point would possibly be some formal reporting back to the parish council on the 'planning issues', excluding of course those deemed *ultra vires*. This would not satisfy all parish councils, many of which were looking for concrete actions: but this was the reasonable, quiet evolution that officers were anticipating. If a union of plans was sought, then the experience of VDSs was thought to offer more useful lessons. In one example cited, the content of a VDS had helped the borough council develop the blueprint for a Conservation Area, setting parameters regarding materials and special features for retention. Following a careful dialogue with the group producing the statement, the borough council was able to connect this community-based plan with its own. But this had only been possible because the statement dealt only with issues regulated by planning and building control.

Do community groups, in general, really wish to become part of a formalised planning process, therefore, with the significant degree of 'instrumental framing' (perhaps manifest in the need for 'compliance' with broader policy) of their plans that this would entail? This point was picked up on several occasions. It is known now (in 2011) that neighbourhood development plans will need to conform to national and local planning policy, and that they will be unable to challenge plans for more housing (or for the siting of that housing) or for additional infrastructure. Integration, or rather compliance, with local plans will not necessarily give communities greater leverage over the principal changes that they are most concerned about. Around the issue of what a community-based plan is really designed to achieve, therefore, there was perhaps some meeting of minds.

Many community groups have long seen their parish plan as a multifunctional document, creating an opportunity to focus local energies around self-help projects. They should be locally owned. This understanding of parish plans was broadly shared by planning officers:

> 'It's not up to us, to my mind, to endorse it: it's up to them [the community] to say they're very happy with its contents, "who do I now contact in the relevant organisations to start delivering on some of the action points that we've addressed that are important?". So, you keep ownership of it; you don't pass ownership onto someone else and then play the blame game; you keep ownership of it; you keep talking it through; you keep proactively pushing your agenda and that's the way you should be doing it.'

ACRK, with all its experience of working with community groups, broadly concurred with this view. In any discussion of the utility of parish plans, the critical question is: utility for whom? Service providers appreciate the guidance that robust evidence offers; planning teams can act on issues relating to land use, or more easily navigate the planning process if they are sensitised to local concerns; but it is communities themselves who may be best placed to *deliver* against their own plans:

> '[A]round 40% to 50% of the actions in [a parish plan] are typically self-help things. There's often a perception that it's all about asking for help from other people, but actually I think they [the parishes] are starting to build some resilience and identifying things they can do for themselves and that may be at least as important, if not more so, than the "influencing role".'

It must be accepted that community-based plans have the primary intent of influencing strategy in order to see a case for modification aimed at bringing them into 'compliance' with other strategies. The counterview is that gaining influence over strategy is of less importance than the role these documents play in focusing the energies of people around agreed agendas. Capacity is built up and, by the time the plan is in place, the community is in a position to take the actions needed to deliver its goals directly, or engage the appropriate service providers. Development control officers, among others, acknowledged the "considerable value" of parish plans as a "way of pulling the community together to actually get some focus on where that community wants to go", adding that "that they are very valuable at the *community* level".

There was a concern that if community-based plans were to become miniature 'development plans', they might lose some of their broader ambition, and support for their production might ebb away:

> 'To my mind, informal is the way to go, purely because you want to try and engage these people: you want to try and encourage them to talk about issues that affect their settlement, not just planning related; as a whole, how do they feel their settlement is moving on? I think to limit to planning would be counterproductive and I think, if you were to go down that route, all you'll find is a lot of people becoming disillusioned with the [community] plan.'

But this appears to be the direction of travel. Although government seemed initially keen that neighbourhood development plans should be adopted in whatever form they might take – and continues to insist that there is scope for flexibility in their content (DCLG, 2011, p 17), the reality of compliance with local plans, achieved through a defined adoption process, means that they will be planning system led if not planner led. The transition from aspiration to pragmatism might not suit many community groups and awareness of the true, underlying, ambitions of communities may sometimes be lost. The price of new powers – to shape the detail of planning permissions for residential development that a community may not actually want – appears to be a loss of independence and a need to embrace a professional outlook, and this may result in some people turning away from the planning process.

Connectivity through dialogue

Despite such risks, and also despite fears that something intangible may be lost in the movement away from community-based plans in their current form, groups such as ACRK remain committed to assisting those communities wanting to produce their own plans. Few practical lessons in integrating plans at the neighbourhood-local level emerge from the recent history of parish planning in England, but a few can be gleaned from the VDS process. In order to achieve compliance between plans, there is often a need for intensive dialogue between local authorities and community groups. ACRK and other support groups have tended to lack the design skills, or indeed the specific planning knowledge, to help communities draw up 'compliant' plans. This will need to change. Either planning teams or support groups will need to provide more intensive support to 'neighbourhood' groups, not only to achieve that basic compliance, but also to make sure that communities are not overwhelmed by the requirements of the process or frustrated in their efforts to draw up operable plans.

There are many bigger questions concerning neighbourhood planning in England, and the few insights that this study can offer are saved for the final chapters. But the essential point emerging from this chapter is that the assumption that the transition from parish to neighbourhood plans is a like-for-like swap is entirely false. The former were only ever partly planning documents. Communities wished to influence not only planning policy through their community planning activities, but also a much broader array of service delivery. Neighbourhood plans will need to continue to connect to a range of providers. Moreover, parish plans have also performed a prized social role: bringing communities together, and harnessing local energies around shared concerns and ambitions. Neighbourhood plans need to retain broad appeal.

THIRTEEN

Planning's critical interface

All the chapters detailing the discussions that took place with community groups and service providers in Ashford are intended to offer an insight into the dynamics of relationships, and into outcomes, at planning's critical interface between policy producers and user communities. This interface looks set to become more critical in the years ahead as planners and community groups begin to navigate their way through the emergent neighbourhood planning agenda. It appears that much will have to change in the relationship between these key groups. Only a fundamental shift in the way that professionals think about their roles, and communities think about their responsibilities, will deliver the new culture of planning that practicable localism appears so dependent on. This chapter completes the task of drawing insights from the case study. It is retrospective, in the sense that it looks back on past experiences of community-based planning and interaction with policy makers. But it is also prospective in that it teases out challenges going forward.

Communities: participants or recipients?

In a world of top-down targets, all local actors were, in a sense, recipients of decisions beamed down either from the regions or from the centre. Local authorities appeared sometimes powerless in the face of many decisions and this reality played some part in the Labour Party's electoral defeat in 2010. However, when in government, Labour did much to promote community leadership and participative local governance. Yet, for many communities the reality was far removed from the rhetoric. Participation meant either 'blessing' decisions that had already been made or 'irritating' decision makers enough to make them, occasionally, stop and think. The description of parish councils as 'fleas on a chimpanzee', from Chapter Nine, neatly summed up how many parishes viewed their role.

Despite the rhetoric of the 2000s, parish groups in Ashford remained recipients of decisions made elsewhere: not only in London and in the regional assembly's office in Guildford, but also by the local council, citing many examples of policies and projects presented as fait accompli. Some parishes felt that they were given a serious hearing, that consultation was a task that the local authority undertook with real integrity, but that ultimately decisions were reached that rarely reflected parish concerns. The planning system was simply not geared up to accept much input from the bottom, being led fundamentally by a regional and national steer.

However, the role of parish councils as 'statutory' consultees gave many local groups a sense of duty within the wider system. It was important to feel that they had a formal part to play. But still, the rhetoric of 'participation' did not change the traditional role, or the perceived role, of parish councils. They continued to lobby, often through their ward members, and thought of themselves as part of a hierarchy of representative government. This also meant that some parish councils did not see any need to reach out to their wider community: they functioned with an electoral mandate, although sometimes a tenuous one, and simply 'got on with it'.

But even the traditional role of consultee seemed threatened in the 2000s. The Communities Plan (ODPM, 2003) 'set in stone' the will of national government to grow Ashford and other towns in Southern England. The targets that were set in the South East Plan left the Borough Council with little room to manoeuvre and in that context it could not, according to one parish respondent, 'even be bothered to maintain the pretence of consultation' . Consultation around the urban extension at Chilmington Green was viewed, essentially, as a 'notification' of what would subsequently transpire.

But could greater participation be achieved by drawing up a parish plan? These tended to emerge very slowly. Many communities wished to have greater input into the LDF process or in the content of specific DPDs but often felt that things moved so quickly at the borough level that they were constantly playing catch-up. At that level, the schedule of plan production was considered opaque, with communities never knowing the best time to feed in. For instance, some groups were frustrated with the insistence that detailed comments on local issues were not wanted during the Core Strategy consultation:

> '[Y]ou say something during the Core Strategy process, but it's too detailed. You can't comment on that because it's general, it's only an indicative line but then once that's gone through, that indicative line becomes a real line.' (PG7)

However, adoption of the Core Strategy, and the acceptance of key principles, often rendered specific local comments meaningless. As an example, many communities had fed into the Tenterden and Rural

Sites DPD. They had tried to raise very local issues during the Core Strategy stage but had been told that consultation was on issues of principle. So they waited until the Tenterden and Rural Sites DPD stage and articulated their detailed issues again. But at that stage, they were told that many of their detailed issues ran contrary to principles established in the Core Strategy and that it was now 'too late' to effect change in the wider framework. On the one hand, the problem is not in the planning system, but in communities' understanding of it, and specifically the interplay between broader principles and local detail. But the reality is of a planning system that seems difficult to input into and causes frustration. Some communities, however, learnt much from the early years of the LDF process, and believed that they would "get it right next time" (PG9), having acquired a better understanding of the system put in place in 2004.

Systems change, sometimes quite frequently, but the fundamental issue of how communities are engaged and the extent to which systems are input or output driven remain. The prevailing view in Ashford was that the parishes must content themselves with being 'hopeful bystanders' in the planning process. Views are expressed, often most cogently within parish plans, and communities then 'wait and see'. For many groups, this was the accepted state of play, but others had become increasingly disillusioned by the rhetoric of participation and local investment in consultation, which seemed to have no clear objective:

> '[T]hey keep asking us for our opinion, keep asking us to take part, and the whole feeling we get is [that] it says on their tick box we've got to consult with local parishes, tick, done it, but we don't have to pay any attention. It's using our time, their time, everybody's time and the other thing it's doing which, in a very insidious way, it's actually knocking democracy again. Everybody's worried about democracy in this country and why aren't people getting involved? People are not getting involved because, time and time again you hear it, "well, what's the point ... nobody listens to us".' (PG1)

While communities were undoubtedly viewed as the recipients of decisions, they were also being sucked into a process that failed, or did not even try, to empower them. Within some parishes, residents questioned the strategic ambitions of their community representatives. Effort to input into core strategies was viewed as a distraction from the proper business of community action. It was sometimes felt that the desire to participate in a bigger process amounted to certain individuals 'playing politics' when the right thing to be doing was sorting out the basic issues of dog fouling, littering and checking potholes.

Although such views were held by a minority (who felt that communities should look inwards, help themselves and mind their own business), it was generally agreed that the resources to fully participate at a more strategic level were simply not available to parish groups. This meant that the focus of parish councils remained firmly set on those things that they thought they might be able to control – the small incremental changes – rather than concerning themselves with the big principles. In practical terms, this meant that few parishes had scrutinised the Core Strategy when it was put out to consultation – but most had made representations to the Borough Council concerning the Tenterden and Rural Sites DPD, which appeared to be of more direct and obvious interest.

Image 13.1: The village of Wye

Finally, communities expected to 'receive' certain things. They expected, for example, to be the recipients of strategy and to be subject to it in some way. Their concern, however, in early 2010 was that SEEDA, as the source of this strategy, was 'locally insensitive' and wielded 'exclusive power'. In fact, much vitriol was reserved for the regional structures and this was balanced by a degree of sympathy for the local authority, and especially its officers, who were forced to look up for direction, and operate in a system that rarely looked down. There was some belief that local planners would be able to build a new relationship with communities if they were given new opportunities. In these rural and mixed parishes, all located in Southern England, the Conservative Party's emergent localism agenda had prompted some optimism.

A reciprocal relationship

Those who share power do so based on the assumption that those with whom they intend to share it will bring something to a prospective partnership, which will then improve the process of government. In the planning context, communities are engaged because greater legitimacy (to direct a process) is sought, or because knowledge will be acquired that eases the burden of regulation. This then raises a key question: do those who purport to share power seek an improvement in 'governmentality', that is, the art of government, for the benefit of all or only for those who govern? Are the relationships they form coercive, in the sense that they are designed to achieve more quickly the desired end of a particular actor? Such questions were introduced in Chapter Six.

Reciprocity is offered as a barometer of authentic partnership, often through 'agreements' that guarantee actions in certain circumstances. Ashford had its own Service Level Agreement (SLA) with the parishes. Aspects of how this had been formed were described by the LSP representative as evidence of a balanced partnership based around reciprocity. The parishes, for example, were brought by the Borough Council into a process of auditing local infrastructure. The parish councils supplied evidence, in particular outlining how current infrastructure provision matched or failed to match the shifting demographic in many villages and towns. This evidence was integrated with the local authority's own baselining exercise. The parishes were then told that the evidence could be used to support bids for one-off grants and that it would certainly, because of the SLA, form the basis of directing capital funding (when it became available) to specific locations. Officially, this was viewed as a strengthening of existing relationships, centred on evidence sharing. In a sense, the capability of the authority was enhanced through the process and there was a clear potential for the parishes to get something out of it as well.

This reciprocity enhanced a capability (to plan for infrastructure investments) and power was redirected, ostensibly to the Borough Council. Through the discussions, the study sought evidence of enhanced or expanded capabilities by examining the balance of gain in shared processes. However, there seemed to be 'more in it' for policy actors in terms of the immediate net gains from a more collaborative approach. Knowledge created an opportunity to target investments, or locally sensitise proposals for development. The gains for communities were dependent on their particular claim for resources or on the development they received. Their position in the process seemed fairly static: they gained some experience but few new capabilities.

Yet, in the vocabulary of local partnership, reciprocity was reflected in the sharing of information and in a culture of collaboration built on mutual understanding. This was not always measured in physical outcomes, although on those occasions when local ambition coincided with planning policy, it was possible to achieve specific local objectives:

> 'They [parish councils] have an in-depth knowledge of that local area that you do not have ... so we should be listening to them in relation to that, and there are certain things that we have responded to in our plan [LDF] that are very much based on the local perception, whether it be through the workshops or the parish plans or the Village Design Statements or the wish-lists or anything like that. If there's a case there that can be answered and the planner can do something about it, we have tried to react to those issues, and I think we've been relatively successful in doing that, so it's a two-way process and the Council could learn a lot from local people like they can learn from us and I think as long as you have an open and honest debate about it and say, "we can't guarantee the outcome will be x, y or z but we can go and look at the issue", and if there's the evidence to back that up as a position and it makes good planning sense, then the planning system could do something about it.' (Planning Policy Officer)

For this happy coincidence to occur, ambitions needed to align with 'good planning sense': they had to be compliant with it. Where this happened in the study area, parishes tended to enjoy improved relationships with the authority. Trust was in abundance, sometimes forestalling objections to later proposals. However, such coincidences concentrated in the more outlying parishes, away from the Growth Area. Knowledge partnerships of this kind worked best away from contested developments, where there was in fact far less development-led change.

Image 13.2: The Archbishop's Palace at the 'outlying' village of Charing

Much of the above supposes that the effectiveness of a partnership has to be read in all-party contentment with its outcomes. Returning to the questions set out at the beginning of this section, it seems certain that knowledge is often sought with a coercive objective in mind. Even generating trust is a means to an end. Likewise, the legitimacy that is thought to flow from dialogue or a participative process is not necessarily the cornerstone of a happy outcome. Even in a 'successful partnership', there may be frustrations with its results. Development control officers, who are witness to the brunt of objections, saw evidence of increased legitimacy (the benefit of working more closely with communities) in a reduction in the volume of representations to the Borough Council. 'Laying the facts on the table' at workshops was seen as a means of 'educating' and of persuading potential objectors, who might then decide not to object. The engagement itself *may* have a role in legitimising outcomes, but for some actors 'consensual planning' is simply boiled down to a lower level of apparent discontent. Engagements with residents may be viewed as inherently non-reciprocal, essentially as coercive, predicated on the simple goal of achieving development. Collaboration is transformed into an act of manipulation.

Work on the Tenterden and Rural Sites DPD – persistently referred to by policy actors – was viewed as a model of engagement and a means of building trust. But this was always 'trust' that the communities had in the leadership of the Borough Council, not trust *in* the communities.

The expectation was that trust would reduce the volume of rejection as the 'immediate response'. Parish councils felt that their position in the decision-making process had been clarified, and welcomed this, but still felt that most outcomes were predetermined. Referring to a project at Stanhope, a deprived urban neighbourhood within Ashford, housing officers reiterated the importance of achieving the right level of buy-in into the process:

> 'Once you got their initial buy-in to the proposal, they came with us. It was their solution, it was their design, it was their outcomes that they were looking for us to deliver and it gave them buy-in and now when the contract is actually up and away and most of the development works are now complete, they are very protective of their local community, of their bricks and mortar.... It is a good working example of how we involve a community in shaping their future. [Overall] I think it's about being honest and it's about making sure that they understand what the end-game is, managing their expectations and aspirations, and once you've got that then life is a lot easier and I think that could be adopted in terms of the work we do with the parish councils, so if they understood what the process is, and how they can be involved in the process, then I think you have better buy-in.'

Community groups need to believe in the 'end-game', have ownership of it, but also have their expectations and aspirations managed. Managing these things through a particular approach to community engagement is fundamental to achieving 'necessary compromises' and reaching what is deemed 'consensus'.

The importance of leadership is implicit in the expressed views of officers. The fractious relationship of *leader* and reluctant *follower* needs to be transformed into a more straightforward *leader–follower* arrangement (McNamara and Trumbull, 2007). This is achieved primarily through education and persuasion. But it is not a partnership. Communities clearly have things that policy actors want, but these things – knowledge and mandate – fuel a coercive relationship that has been central to the culture of planning at the critical interface between policy and communities.

Leaders and followers

Planners and other policy actors view their role as leaders as critical to the delivery of the right services in the right places. Compromises can be made, and inputs accepted, in order to achieve buy-in (and ease the path of regulation), but ultimately the power to decide – balancing social, economic and environmental objectives – must rest with a mandated authority. Leadership is important in stimulating debate (and even in firing controversy), getting communities to think about the path ahead, and to deliver a future public good. It is viewed as central to planning. 'Partnership' sits as a rhetorical poor relation to leadership, with the possibility of leadership incorporating authentic partnership often flatly rejected. Rather, inputs into the process should aid the task of leadership, but not run counter to the power of decision makers:

> 'At the end of the day, the Borough Council is the planning authority in relation to land-use planning in this area and that shouldn't change in my opinion, if they're doing the job right. I think the parish councils have a very important role to play in that, not just through the workshop processes, but *through dialogue* with the Borough Council.'

> 'You can consult to the Nth degree on something and it will take quite a long time to satisfy everyone, whereas if you take the lead and actually push something forward, then that concentrates minds and you end up getting a much better engagement by physically pushing it through, otherwise we just wouldn't get anything done realistically.'

The term 'partner' was often redefined for the purpose of explaining the relationship that policy actors shared with communities:

> 'I think they are a partner, but it's got to be caveated with "look, there's always a balance of needs and wants in any area" and to my mind it's the planning authority [that] needs to find the right balance ... based on sound planning judgement, but that won't please everyone: you'll never please everyone and you can't pretend, so it's a balance between the two partners and being "stakeholders" in the process.'

In the last quote, different groups are partners merely by virtue of having stakes in a process. The equality, or the reciprocity, that 'partnership' might infer is lost. But this looser language was subsequently tightened up by development control officers. The reality, in relation to planning's basic regulatory function, is that parish councils – far from being partners or even consultees (which is their statutory role) – are merely 'notified' of the receipt of planning applications. This presents the risk of objection, locking the parties into a simple action–response relationship. But like other officers, dialogue was viewed as a means of moving from the black and white of 'yes/no' responses. Dialogue was an opportunity to present subtle shades of grey and push big strategic decisions or projects through the planning system by turning communities into followers, or at least into less vocal objectors.

But still, followers need leaders and it is for mandated individuals – within a representative framework – to make the decisions. Actors articulated this view in different ways, but it remained a point of agreement, being considered central to good planning and to achieving broader social objectives. Inevitably, some big strategic decisions are challenged, but the local relationship between policy actors and communities requires the former to have the power to think and plan strategically. Community groups can then be 'brought in' when 'finer points are being agreed'. Power must remain the power to define principles: but if compromise features in the relationship between communities and policy actors, it must involve the former conceding principles to the latter, and the policy actors compromising on matters of detail. Different actors adhered to this view to different degrees. Some believed that anything more than cosmetic input was inherently a threat to 'good planning'. The planning team, however, saw clear value in taking into account the 'mountains of information' that consultation inevitably generates, which ultimately ensures that "outcomes are a better reflection of ... desires and aspirations". Leadership and good planning mean making an offer to communities and then working with communities to refine that offer.

The critical interface and framework reform

Debates over the role of leadership in the planning process feature in local and national discourse the world over. In the UK, there has been some talk of passing leadership responsibility from the local state to communities. Government publications have been heavily laced with such rhetoric. Labour intended to achieve community empowerment under the rubric of its broader strategic planning framework. The

Coalition Government since 2010 seemed at first to offer this type of empowerment through the elimination of regional structures together with the creation of a system of community-based development plans at the neighbourhood level. But ultimately, power to set principles has remained with planning authorities, which has provoked both relief and frustration. In the penultimate section of the chapter, we examine how recent national policy has affected relationships at the critical interface. It is split into two parts: Labour's local government and planning reforms; and early experience of 'localism', with initial lessons from this study.

Labour's reforms

Six years after the systemic changes brought about by the Planning and Compulsory Purchase Act 2004, it was generally felt that the planning process in England had become more complex, although the system was bestowed with considerable potential. DPDs could be reviewed separately from the Core Strategy, making the local planning framework potentially more flexible and responsive to local input. Still, complexity – and the pace of change in the system – had dented people's confidence in being able to engage with planning. As noted at several points earlier, the role of the Community Strategy in 'local visioning', and in relation to conventional planning frameworks, was poorly understood, adding to the sense that a complex system was becoming increasingly multi-layered and inaccessible.

There was a clear sense, among planning officers at least, that the complexity of the system could be transformed into a strength. Given the diversity of Ashford's neighbourhoods, complexity could in fact 'make sense', with generic issues covered in broader strategy documents and 'topic-based issues' dealt with in action plans or localised DPDs such as the much-cited Tenterden and Rural Sites DPD. Yet, the good sense that planning officers saw in the system was not always recognised by communities: as well as confusion over the status of the DPD relative to principles set out in the Core Strategy, parish groups often felt that the language of planning had become more obscure, adding to the sense that a professional group was 'marking its territory' and closing the door to external input: that planning was becoming internalised and focused on procedural integrity. Planners, at least in part, recognised this problem, conceding that "it's very difficult for people to get a true handle on the issues that we face as planners in the planning authority" due to the complexity of the "new system".

Communities turned out in strength during planning road-shows, and this was viewed by some as a measure of the 'openness' of the system and its capacity to "engage", as one officer put it, with "Uncle Tom Cobley and all". But although the road-shows and the need to produce a 'statement of community involvement' could be viewed as evidence of openness, the process of plan production was still thought to have remained opaque. Again, the case of the Tenterden and Rural Sites DPD was cited:

> 'I would say it [the planning system] is shrouded in mystery ... there really needs to be some kind of progress on mapping it out [...] to the parish councils and to the ward members [...] to actually explain the process to them because I don't think they fully understand, and the Core Strategy is the most important document that we can ever have, and then they're starting to argue down at Rural DPD level, they're not happy with things in the Core Strategy [which it is too late to change].' (Housing department)

The rhetoric of community leadership from the late 1990s onwards, and the focus on engagement that seemed so integral to planning and local government reform in the 2000s, raised the expectation of meaningful input into planning strategy at the neighbourhood level. Indeed, many more communities were encouraged to draw up their own plans. But, almost inevitably, planning's inability to grant all wishes led to disappointment. Labour drummed up a great deal of enthusiasm but hit the wall of strategic necessity (Davies, 2008), articulated most cogently in the 2007 planning White Paper:

> [A] purely local approach to planning cannot deliver the best outcomes for us as a society or nation, or for the environment. Sometimes, development may have national or regional benefits or impacts which go far beyond the immediate impact on local communities. Planning needs to reflect these wider regional and national factors. That is why we also have plan making at the regional level with Regional Spatial Strategies in each English region. (DCLG, 2007b, p 22)

This was perhaps too stark an admission for some, who viewed it as a signal that the apparatus of regional planning and infrastructure delivery were to be given new impetus. Indeed they were, through a review of subnational planning arrangements (DCLG and BERR, 2008) and the setting up of an Infrastructure Planning Commission. But the expectations of communities remained unaddressed, leaving the door open to promises of 'real' power and influence.

The coalition government's localism agenda

The prospect of a change of government grew as the discussions with Ashford's communities were drawing to a close. The shape of possible reform was unclear but there was an expectation of more power and associated responsibility. Parish council's tended to reflect on how existing responsibilities might grow and what the resource implications might be. The power to 'set agendas' was broadly welcomed but the fear of being 'overwhelmed' invariably entered discussions, and was usually introduced by parish clerks. Although parish councils expected to have a place in the hierarchy of local government (see earlier discussion), they were not well placed to become 'instrumental' parts of that hierarchy: delivery of services could never be part of their remit, simply because they lacked the support, the resources and the time. Hence, suspicions at the time that parishes or neighbourhoods in urban areas might have some formal role in project-managing development or in running devolved services were a source of some anxiety. The battle they had fought for decades was for a responsive planning system, not responsibility for the system:

> 'There have been some suggestions that work would be devolved from the Borough Council down to parishes under these new [arrangements] and I think parish councils would have a severe problem because of the amount of work involved.... I think it would be much better if Ashford Borough Council could act as the central point ... leave it with the expertise, and the professional people in planning and roads and all the rest of it there, but make the mechanism between the parish councils and them more responsive, that there's more respect for what the parishes want and the comments they make. I think that's what wants really strengthening.' (PG1)

A system that was supposed to serve the public good had lost its sensitivity, but that was not to say that the system could not recover its underlying values. For groups on the ground, trying to understand the politics of the 2010 General Election, localism was thought to be about rebuilding the link between communities and policy actors, re-establishing lost opportunities to input into the planning system, and ensuring that visions were genuinely shared.

But despite these reservations (that too much responsibility might be conceded to the parishes), the expectation of greater say in local planning matters – and especially control over residential and related development – was welcomed. It seemed clear that the Conservative Party (which many expected to achieve a clear parliamentary majority in May 2010) would give communities a 'seat at the high table', allowing them to challenge principles by fundamentally reforming the top-down approach to planning that had been continually strengthened under Labour.

Leadership or coercion?

> '[O]n the surface, it all sounds like it's going to be more in your favour but actually that's just the skin on the surface: underneath they're actually going to do whatever they like, regardless of the appearance of it.' (PG3)

This is a comment on the planning system in early 2010, but it also reflects a fear of what future reform might bring. At the critical interface between communities and policy actors, there is a lack of trust in the system of land-use regulation and in the language of planning. The emergent system of neighbourhood plans has not fundamentally altered the power relationship between community groups and policy actors. They remain locked in a conversation in which local authorities have the loudest voice. But it was never the intention of government to build spatial or land-use policy from the absolute bottom up. The Labour government's assertion that 'a purely local approach to planning cannot deliver the best outcomes for us as a society or nation or for the environment' (DCLG, 2007b, p 22) is echoed in the insistence that neighbourhood plans must conform to the strategic development proposals set out in the local plan. The unpopular strategic relationship between regional and local government has been reinstituted between local government and neighbourhoods, with the latter still subject to the 'targets' of the former. The key difference, as ministers pointed out during the Localism Bill's passage through Parliament, is that the 'unelected' regional bodies no longer set housing numbers. Power has been returned to locally elected representatives. This return of power to local politicians is central to a workable localism, rather than neighbourhood empowerment. The rhetoric of 'neighbourhood planning' seeks to achieve what all past governments have sought: greater acceptance of development at the point of receipt. In order to achieve this acceptance, there is a necessarily coercive relationship at planning's critical interface: one dependent on clear leadership, education and persuasion. Leadership is central to all of this, and to achieving the most basic of planning outcomes. Planning, even at the critical interface, is about big pictures, linkages and realising a broader public good. Some visions of localism attempt to obfuscate this fact, but it remains. Community input, even in a world of inflated rhetoric, will remain secondary to strategic necessity in the face of growth.

Part Four
Neighbourhood planning, leadership and democratic renewal

FOURTEEN

Responsibility and responsiveness: lessons from parish planning

The purpose of this and the next chapter is to reappraise some of the lessons arising from community-based *parish planning* in England, and to use these to illuminate the path of future local government reform and how networked community governance, of the type unpacked in the last 13 chapters, might realise its full potential in the years ahead. The narrative provided so far is distilled into a number of critical discussions around the mechanics of community-based planning, connectivity to strategic frameworks, and the responsibilities versus the responsiveness that communities seek through local action.

Lessons in community governance and support

The objective of neighbourhood or community-based planning is not solely to influence planning or even wider public policy. It has a crucial role in triggering collective interest, among residents, in local projects and in setting community priorities. Parish councils have been instrumental in this process, although how representative their views and priorities actually are is sometimes doubted. Councils, especially in areas popular with retiring households, may be dominated by older residents whose priorities differ from those of younger families. But this is not a universal pattern. Some parishes have a strong through-flow of participants, with the composition of their councils continually changing and mirroring shifts within communities themselves. Parish councils *may* form a discrete clique within a disengaged community, *but* the parish plan process may act to widen inputs and bring community benefits that outlast, and are often bigger than, the plan itself.

Community planning support groups have a critical part to play in this process. Alongside the important role they perform in connecting communities to service providers through a practical process of 'bridging', these groups also work with parish councils to widen inclusion in the participatory processes leading to plan production. As well as injecting additional skills and knowledge, support groups play a key part in 'democratising' the community planning process, broadening ownership of it. This is often their main function, although the desire of many communities to realise a more direct policy influence – through their plans – means that an increasing amount of effort is expended on plan implementation through 'bridging' activities.

But it is not always easy to broaden interest in neighbourhood plans, or increase participation among less visible groups. Little more than fleeting interest may be triggered by the showcasing events run by local authorities, and only a modest expansion may be achieved even by support groups. But it is the threat of unsettling change that really fires people into action and can popularise engagement in the planning process, directing it to those areas faced with major applications. Plan groups can form literally overnight and, in instances where contentious applications are received, communities may be able to mobilise rapidly. Parish councils are frequently instrumental in this mobilisation, bringing applications to the attention of residents and then co-opting interested parties. There is danger of course that the practice of co-opting will merely expand the clique without drawing in a broader range of opinion or priorities (potentially reinforcing opposition to change even in places where opinion is mixed or finely balanced, for and against). Effective mechanisms for popularising neighbourhood planning – ensuring that it is genuinely community based – will remain a priority in the years ahead.

But some communities will always have a greater tendency towards engagement around planning issues because they have stronger internal connectivity. The Ashford communities each comprised complex networks of local interests, with parish councils forming hubs at the centre. The spokes consisted of a range of specific interest groups centred on sports and leisure activities, a variety of pastimes, local conservation and heritage projects, youth groups and support for older people. In some cases, the parish councils used this connectivity as a means of popularising their planning processes, seeing group membership as indicative of the concerns that should be reflected in plans: hence leisure and conservation issues often figured prominently.

There is a dynamic in *some communities* that lends itself to 'successful' community action, measured in terms of the depth and breadth of resident engagement, although support groups can help establish aspects of this dynamic in communities that are less well connected. In instances where connectivity is strong, parish councils are able to harness an array of skills and energies in response to local challenges. Member diversity is important in mobilising community action: where councils are broadly representative of a community's social mix and age profile, they can find it easier to connect with a wider range of people. But leadership style is also crucial in this respect. Some council chairs are more autocratic, believing that they have a mandate to 'get on with things' – including the production of parish plans – while others develop hierarchical structures aimed at maintaining a flow of information from, and dialogue with, different parts of the community. Parish clerks also play a key role as gatekeepers to the community. The actions of parish chairs and clerks may result in councils becoming more 'closed' to wider participation, even rejecting external support. However, the presence of parish councils is important for neighbourhood planning. They act as a hub, often connecting to broader interests, are accountable to their communities through local elections, and are able to draw on support for their planning activities. Strong hubs and good support allow the neighbourhood planning process to become well rooted within communities.

Lessons in community connectivity to wider governance apparatus

A line of enquiry that was largely abandoned in the Ashford study concerned connectivity to policy actors through the LSP. Bishop (2007) had previously observed that a genuine 'community strategy' could only be developed with strong community input. Parish and other community-based plans could provide this input, becoming the building blocks of community strategies. These strategies were once considered the 'plan of plans' (Morphet, 2004b), providing an overarching framework for all other local plans and policies: strong community input into the community strategies, therefore, would mean clear community influence over health, highways, planning, housing and policing policies. But the line of enquiry was abandoned as it quickly became clear that the linkages on which such influence would be built were largely, if not entirely, absent. While the LSP and its community strategy might be conceived of as a potential bridge from communities to individual service providers – as a conduit for communication – this is in fact far from the truth.

The reality is that community groups place their faith in a few individuals working at the strategic level: they connect to wider governance apparatus via their parish clerks and onwards to local officials with specific responsibilities and remits. Communities react to issues arising, putting their trust in named planning, highways or housing officers, hoping that a telephone call will provoke a positive action. Personal relationships are critical at the interface between communities and policy actors. A parish council's entire experience of the principal authority is often boiled down to the relationship it shares with one or two named officers. If these officers have played a positive role in helping deliver a leisure services project or an affordable housing scheme, then the relationship is often a constructive one, built on a degree of personal trust. Conflicts arise most frequently in villages and neighbourhoods where the principal authority seems invisible. In such cases, even apparently innocuous development proposals may spark protest. Elsewhere, dialogue around proposals may forestall major conflict. Yet there seemed to be no clear pattern to the good and bad relationships between parishes and the principal authority. Fortune seemed to have played a big part in establishing trust and dialogue: it just so happened that there had been a positive experience in the past that had set the tone for future interaction. This suggests a case for more consistent investment in working with communities, not just around specific projects, but also around a community's broader aspirations. Investing officer time in neighbourhood planning is critical to building better relationships.

But working and interacting with communities is distinctly different from the culture of consultation, on which current planning practice is predicated. Both communities and policy actors claimed to value dialogue, but differing interpretations of, and expectations from, the process of dialogue were a source of friction. For communities, dialogue is continuous: it is a conversation that shapes outcomes, and occurs between parties who trust one another. Consultation does not amount to dialogue, but tends rather to be a hurdle that planners must cross to justify a decision already taken. But for policy actors, consultation *is* dialogue: it is an exercise in outreach, which aims to educate communities and manage expectation, thereby shortening the path to consensus around the *necessity of a decision*. Dialogue is a leadership tool, used to achieve buy-in to a particular vision. Planning is by its nature coercive, built on the conviction to plan in a way that delivers a wider public good that may not be entirely aligned with the aspirations of any specific community.

In thinking about the connectivity of communities to wider governance apparatus, it is important to emphasise the role of parish clerks, as 'gateways' or 'gatekeepers' to or from these communities. The clerks are generally regarded by policy actors as vital connectors. It is with clerks that dialogue regularly begins or continues after specific local projects have ended. They often act as powerful brokers between officials, the parish council and other residents. They can be viewed as a bridge to the parish council (and the council, thereafter, can be viewed as a bridge to the wider community), sometimes easy but occasionally difficult to traverse. In a sense, clerks can be viewed as *intermediaries*, or as bridges between the otherwise closed social network of the community and broader policy networks: a point at which useful interactions can start. But beyond these obvious links, an attempt was made in earlier chapters to identify other potential bridges between communities and traditional policy actors, with each being conceived as a separate entity divided by language and culture, but with a propensity to be brought together for mutual benefit. Using ideas from social network theory, it was suggested that certain individuals or agencies could play the role of 'weak' or 'incidental' ties, powerful by virtue of their position between groups, and able to create new capacities by bringing people together. But apart from very light evidence of parish councils reaching out to employees of the Borough Council who happened to live locally, encouraging them to bring community concerns to the attention of their colleagues, there was very little in the study to point to the *clear* existence of 'weak ties'. Rather, it is the support groups that act as the real bridges between communities and policy actors, and which are likely to continue to do so in the years ahead.

Lessons in 'bridging' to policy actors, and to communities

Building 'bridges' in order to overcome gaps within or between networks, and taking practical steps to ensure that communities and policy actors understand one another, consequently working together in appropriate and productive ways, are topics of concern in both conceptual analyses of collaborative planning and network building and in UK policy debate. In Ashford and elsewhere, it is the external mediators that tend to be the most conspicuous bridges. ACRK, through its one-to-one work with communities, was regarded by many as a genuine broker. It was ACRK itself that had identified a 'disconnect' between the evidence provided by communities to service providers, and what service providers actually needed to know as a basis for action. This was the only example of a positive, systematic process of bridging indentified in the study, and it was not hard to find. Support groups tend to label their own work 'bridging' and, alongside community capacity building and broadening community participation, this is a primary mission of such groups.

Other, less sturdy and less intentional bridges also featured in the Ashford study: some local authority officials, for example, felt that popular housing officers acted as vital bridges into parish affairs. They enjoyed the most positive relationships with the parishes. On numerous occasions, they had worked with parish groups to identify sites for local needs housing. Critically, they had regularly won the trust of parishes and gave the clearest indication of anyone in the Borough Council that the content of parish plans – especially those elements relating to housing need – were of value. For these reasons, housing officers tended to maintain good relations with clerks, chairs and co-opted plan working group members. And what they heard from the parishes, they communicated to other council departments. These departments acknowledged the possibility of 'linking through' housing, gaining some insight into emergent tensions and opportunities. But a key feature of a genuine bridge is its independence. Officers, whether they were from the planning or housing departments, acted to achieve policy outcomes: seen positively, their role was to sensitise plans to the concerns of residents; but a less generous analysis, and one that has been offered previously, is that coercion is an essential feature of planning's leadership function.

The view that some bridges limit network extension, rather than aiding it, is another clear reality of parish planning in England. The parish councils themselves, comprising their chairs, elected and co-opted members, and their clerks, are the most significant bridge in community-based planning networks. They are potentially the strong hub described earlier, but they do not always connect well to their spokes. Some parish councils represent a narrow set of interests; the planning activities they engage in are often mistakenly credited to the 'community' and 'community-based planning' is viewed as an inherently participative endeavour, when it may be undertaken by only a small clique. Getting beyond the council – into a wider community of diverse interests – can be difficult. This challenge will remain in the formalised, systematised world of neighbourhood plans. Despite the assertion that a collaborative approach to plan making can be essentially manufactured, through reform, it cannot be automatically assumed that a neighbourhood-based approach will be genuinely participative: parish councils or neighbourhood forums may simply seek a mandate to 'get on with it', lending support to the argument that participation is a threat to democracy, rather than an enhancement to it. Representative democracy has a mandate handed to it by a majority, whereas participative governance may rely on the input of a vocal and active minority.

Lessons in the use of community-based plans

Community-based plans have a part to play in sensitising traditional policy actors to neighbourhood concerns: they are used to articulate major issues and aspirations, often becoming a lobbying tool. Plans are not intended to speak to a single department or organisation; rather, their ambitions go beyond the remit of land-use planning and so it becomes the responsibility of communities themselves to own their plan and place elements of it with different stakeholders. This means that plans contain messages on policing for the police authority; on roads and traffic for the highways authority; on sports facilities for leisure; and on housing need for the housing department and its partners. The hope of the plan's authors is that one-off actions or investments will be triggered once the feeling of the community becomes known, and once this feeling is backed up by some evidence, although this evidence is not always robust, and this is where support groups can help. But some parish plans are reactive to current concerns or proposals, failing to anticipate change or look to the longer term. For this reason, planning policy may take limited interest in the plans, seeing them instead as a barometer of feeling towards impending change, and therefore of primary use to development control. Parish planning groups, however, frequently view their own plans as indicative of general ambition, which can be read as long term, and fail to understand why policy actors seem unable to take a collective view on what the community-based plans are telling them, and incorporate these messages into their strategies.

Attempts are sometimes made to place community-based plans in positions of influence, but an apparent lack of systematic consideration within the planning system leaves a question mark hanging over their value. The precise value of plans has been continually questioned over the last decade. It has been periodically suggested that a clearer focus on land-use matters would allow plans to be *integrated* more effectively into broader strategies and policy (Countryside Agency, 2003; SQW Consulting, 2007), thus giving communities a louder voice. Integration is distinctly different from the bridging that others have suggested, which involves a more mixed and varied use of community-based plans, bridging into land-use decisions by seeking influence over the policies of health, police and housing authorities (and thereafter into the land-use decisions needed to support broader investments). In Bishop's (2007) reckoning, keying into the work of the LSP might be an effective means of influencing broader spatial policy, although community linkages to these structures appear weak, as noted above.

However connections are achieved, it is important to recognise that parish plans are never solely land-use planning documents. They convey a much broader set of concerns within, and aspirations for, their area. Unconstrained by planning orthodoxy, parish plans might be described as being genuinely spatial, although from a narrow land-use policy standpoint, their content often appears whimsical and undeliverable. The desire to constrain plans, and focus on clearly demarcated land-use concerns, is apparent in recent policy debate. Neighbourhood plans are in fact 'development' plans. It would be unfortunate if future community-based plans were prevented from conveying the full range of concerns and interests that had a traditional home within parish plans. This might act to limit community buy-in and stifle interest in the neighbourhood planning process (past plans were broad because communities wanted them to be broad). Parish plans in the study were often found to have their greatest value *within* a community rather than in the narrower world of land use-policy. For communities themselves, the process of plan production is often more important than the product, focusing local energies, bringing groups together and building new ties.

Reflections

Communities and policy actors occupy different parts of a potentially shared network, but are cut off by difficult lines of communication. Models of collaborative governance point to the possibility of building, restoring or improving these lines, bringing mutual benefit to all actors. Indeed, an association is often drawn between good governance and genuinely interactive processes, which are likely to deliver strategic outcomes that have broader ownership and that will command a greater degree of multi-level support. This view has now taken stronger root in national planning policy in England, which now implies a belief that systematised community ownership of the planning process will generate acceptance of a broader range of development outcomes, including additional housing in many instances. We have not taken a view on whether enhanced democracy delivers a greater propensity to accept decisions that are still taken elsewhere, now primarily within local authorities. However, the study of community-based planning in and around Ashford shows that having a community-based planning process in place does not offer any guarantee of more equitable, consensual or democratic outcomes. The parish planning process was hampered in this respect firstly by local organisational shortcomings (ie, the extent to which such planning is genuinely undertaken by the 'community') and secondly by weaknesses and uncertainties at the interface between communities and policy actors. The first difficulty is left unaddressed by the transition to Neighbourhood Development Plans, being attributable to community dynamics and to existing mechanisms for broadening inclusion. These mechanisms remain largely unchanged and the work of support groups remains critical. The second seems to be addressed by the legal compliance required between neighbourhood and local plans, but this compliance is no substitute for the trust that accumulates when professional silos are vacated and officials begin to build lasting relationships with communities.

However, the most recent reforms of the English system suggest some movement towards a more input-orientated, *responsive* approach to planning. This is combined with some devolution of decision making (eg, through the 'neighbourhood development orders' described in Chapter Four). There has, in the recent past, been considerable frustration with an output-orientated system that involved local authorities receiving direction from above, leaving them with little choice but to ignore inputs from below. The revocation of regional strategies in 2010[1] created an opportunity to work in different ways with those neighbourhood structures, including the parish councils, which already existed. But government's broader approach has been to formalise community-based planning, steering it towards a land-use focus, and to hand new responsibilities to parish councils and neighbourhood forums. Yet, the rhetoric of a more input-orientated system cannot disguise the reality of a system that remains output driven. Good planning, as previously argued, needs to be underpinned by leadership and by the pursuit of a broader public good: reform has not challenged that reality. Devolved responsibility is achieved within a framework of command and control, with communities accepting principles and being bound by them. Many of the controversial planning objectives – often concerned with housing and infrastructure – that were once rooted in Regional Spatial Strategies now begin in local plans. This has left some communities feeling frustrated, on this occasion by reforms that they believe were miss-sold (Bishop, 2011). People have been brought into a process of decision making in which decisions have already been made.

Reform, in itself, has not solved any of the underlying problems at the interface between communities and policy actors. The more subtle challenges of connectivity and trust remain. The responsiveness craved by many is not delivered under the umbrella of localism. But by sleight of hand, new responsibilities have been created, which communities did not covet. Like the hierarchical relationship between parish and principal authorities, these responsibilities – to take some planning decisions and decide some priorities – are designed to make communities feel part of a broader system, to give partial ownership of a process. But from the point of view of Ashford's communities at the beginning of 2010, when the direction of reform was first becoming clear, real 'localism' should be about rebuilding links between communities and policy actors, re-establishing lost opportunities to input into the planning system and ensuring that visions are widely shared, even if consensus remains elusive. That planning has a role in leading change was not disputed in the study, although leaders should also listen. Greater local freedom from principles determined upstream creates the opportunity to renegotiate the relationship with communities, and policy actors agreed (with the parish councils) that their 'offer' to these communities may change if they are less constrained by strategic priorities over which they have no control.

Note

[1] This removal was actually intermittent during 2010 and 2011. An ongoing legal battle between government and a house builder, CALA Homes, resulted ultimately (in June 2011) in an uneasy stalemate: local plans still needed to be in conformity with Regional Spatial Strategies, but the intention to revoke these strategies through the Localism Act was accepted as a material consideration in planning decisions.

FIFTEEN

Conclusions

Tensions between communities and policy actors are ever-present in representative democracies, with strategic decisions at all levels often bringing local consequences that communities find it difficult if not impossible to live with. Over time, a build-up of pressure for greater bottom-up input into decision making is inevitable, but even when greater input is achieved the frustrations that communities feel rarely disappear. Rather, they become increasingly personalised, focusing around divisions within communities themselves or around the narrowness of dominant interests. Residents seldom speak with a single voice, but policy actors are often drawn to the most articulate or to those who shout loudest. The apparent 'empowerment' of communities can *presentation* bring as much conflict as it does contentment, although this is often not immediately visible. It causes a brooding unease within villages and neighbourhoods, manifest in dissatisfaction with parish councils or forums, and in a belief that power is too regularly hijacked by cliques and busybodies. And frustration with what is actually achieved through community-based action also remains, because such action is still framed, necessarily in most cases, by a broader and higher process of meta-governance. Despite recent concerns in England that strategic planning would be consigned to history and too many decisions would be delegated to neighbourhoods, the reality is that politicians continue to pursue a greater public good, with planners directed to coordinate the provision of new housing and new infrastructure across entire boroughs, districts and unitary authorities, being charged also to cooperate with their neighbours. Mandated power has not been removed, or even diluted, by the recent attempts of government in England to reinvent itself and 'reconnect' with civil society.

However, the change of government in 2010 brought us to a new chapter in the continuing evolution of a more participative approach to local planning. The meta-governance arrangements shifted markedly with the effective removal of regional structures, creating the opportunity to renegotiate the relationship between principal authorities and urban and rural communities. The pressure for this new relationship had grown in the 2000s.

A legacy of frustration

The previous government had placed great emphasis on strategic planning, especially at the regional level, but also through its promotion of new national structures. But as set out in the opening chapters, this emphasis sat uneasily with the accompanying rhetoric of community leadership. Like modernising democracies everywhere, it wished to strike an auspicious balance between the right level of input and what it viewed as the best outputs. And yet the propensity for tension, for delay in the planning system and for frustration with both processes and products was underplayed. In the run-up to key legislation in 2004, a vision of the planning system working in harmony, for both communities and businesses, was offered but this lacked any clear view of how conflicting interests might be realigned. The plan was simply to create more opportunities for engagement, presumably to bring a wider spectrum of groups into a process that would thereafter be more broadly owned. An unremitting programme of local government reform was set in train aimed, ostensibly, at strengthening community input into local decision making. However, this programme sat uneasily with sometimes scathing, and always sustained, attacks on the alleged 'parochialism' of local planning, the narrowness of its interest and the weight it appeared to give to vexatious local objection to necessary development. In the context of unprecedented growth, such parochialism posed a clear and present danger to meeting the nation's housing and broader economic needs. The picture painted was one of a broadly sound planning system being prevented from facilitating development at the point of implementation.

Dozens of examples of planning failure were lined up, demonstrating the costs of delay. It was often the slow gestation of major infrastructure projects that provided points of reference for attacks on the planning system, including the 525 days at inquiry before Heathrow Terminal 5 was finally given the go-ahead. But the country was also dotted, north to south, with examples of stalled residential developments that were seen to be contributing to declining housing supply and diminishing affordability. It was within this context that two Treasury Reviews of housing supply and land-use planning in 2004 and 2006 were able to push for greater strategic steer in planning for housing and a leaner and faster process of decision making for major infrastructure.

A market-led approach, at the subregional level, to planning for housing (set within the context of regional planning's housing targets, which were generally regarded as undemocratic), alongside a national framework for infrastructure, were always bound to be contested.

Government was quick to concede this reality: 'national infrastructure is *by its nature* controversial and it is unlikely that complete agreement or consensus will be achieved through consultation; however stakeholders, communities and individual members of the public must have the opportunity to participate' (DCLG, 2007b, p 51; emphasis added). The subtext is that some things need to be done, however unpopular they might be. There is an undeniable case for a clear strategic steer (to push through the changes that are rejected by a parochial outlook, but which are essential for sustained economic wellbeing or to support future populations), yet the planning reforms of the mid to late 2000s and the parallel local government reforms (lending support to the concepts of 'community leadership' and 'empowerment') were rooted in two seemingly irreconcilable paradigms: a highly professionalised conception of power being wielded *over* people and *over* communities, in pursuit of a predetermined end, versus an 'emancipatory' sharing of that power (Clegg, 1989), in pursuit of less certain and more fluid goals. Two highly desirable objectives – the mobilisation of community interest through an awakening of civil society, and the creation of a planning system that delivers when it needs to deliver – were arguably mishandled in Labour's package of reforms, although no government has ever handled them without considerable difficulty.

But during its final years in power, Labour seemed to push on relentlessly: the regional housing targets framing local development plans (and directing growth in Ashford) were in 2010 to be placed with the regional development agencies. These targets had been formalised within Regional Spatial Strategies since 2004, and owned by the regional assemblies. Because of local political representation on the assemblies, the targets seemed to have slight legitimacy. But the transfer to the development agencies eliminated even this element of local input. The move was unpopular and seemed symptomatic of government's failure to deliver on its rhetoric of community leadership.

Meta-governance and the public good

Central to these 'failures', or what many view as inevitable centre–local tensions, is the idea of meta-governance (see Jessop, 2003). At different levels, actions are constrained by broader framing actions. Ambition at the lowest levels may be frustrated, leaving individuals and communities feeling powerless, and in the shadow of distant bureaucratic structures. presentation And even where responsibilities are locally delegated, this delegation occurs within strict limits. Throughout this book, we have focused on the relationship between community groups and local bureaucrats, implying that they may be brought together within networks where information flows freely and new capacities to act are generated. Such collaborative power structures drive a growth in social capital, and in capacity, and may allow communities to challenge established ways of working and to insist on, or influence, the trajectory of local change. Yet, these networks have existed (and flourished in some instances) under a dominant paradigm that seeks to avoid the costs of parochialism. This is the 'output-orientated' or representative democracy that planning reform in England sought to strengthen in the 2000s, and it can be contrasted with the popular notion of an 'input-orientated' participative democracy in which communities become the biggest stakeholders (Scharpf, 1999, pp 2-3). The offer to the electorate at the UK General Election in 2010 was of a move to a new input-orientated politics: a 'Big Society' and a commensurately 'small state'. Like others before them (but this time with reference to Labour's centralising tendency), the Conservatives offered a democratisation of government, arguing that the state had hitherto been *closed* to sufficient public input: that the capabilities of local government, in particular, had been too heavily circumscribed and disciplined by national objectives (see also Corry et al, 2004). Apart from returning power to local authorities (thereby bringing decision making closer to those potentially affected by decisions), it was not immediately clear how government would become more open. Scharpf (1999) notes that openness can be achieved in one of two simple ways: either through a complete and unfettered devolution of *power* to a lower level (to community groups, for instance) or by devolving *responsibility* for delivering against objectives agreed elsewhere. Combined with the return of power to local authorities, implementation of the latter scheme would mean a re-instatement of meta-governance arrangements at the local level once a Conservative administration, if elected to power, had delivered on its promise to dismantle regional structures and revoke the top-down targets contained in spatial strategies.

Meta-governance is, in part, the leadership alluded to in earlier chapters: it sets the ground rules and provides the big vision, and the regulatory order, needed to ensure that the actions of local actors add up to something coherent (Jessop, 2003, p 20). It is an expression of the view that these actors cannot be freed from the collective good: that there must be some bigger logic guiding their actions. Scharpf (1999, p 41) argues that state power is increasingly expressed through the workings of more localised governance structures, but that these structures are themselves forged in the ever-present 'shadow of hierarchical authority'. In England, the election of a new government in 2010 and the fulfilment of the pledge to abolish regional planning, appears to have delivered this more localised governance structure, with meta-governance (in the planning system) achieved through legal compliance between neighbourhood development plans and local plans, with the latter taking precedence. This is not the empowerment that some communities had hoped for (Bishop, 2011, p 73) as it simply localises many of the conflicts that were previously regional in scope. The authority of the local state appears strengthened (although its own capacity to act has been curtailed by swingeing spending cuts) at the expense of the regional structures, but gains for communities are less easy to calculate. Moreover, whereas community groups, local politicians and bureaucrats may once have been unified by their frustration with regional decisions, local authorities now look to be sole masters of local planning, and a new focal point for discontent over 'strategic' decisions, which run contrary to community aspiration.

From the vagaries of parish planning to the clarity of 'neighbourhood plans'?

Critics of past arrangements rightly pointed out that it was national and regional government that gave the local state its 'output' orientation, limiting its capacity to gather meaningful input from below. But to what extent will the emergent neighbourhood planning arrangements in England deliver new opportunities for this meaningful input, transferring real power rather than just responsibility? And what will the arrangements mean, also, for the local relationships that are so vital when building a degree of consensus, or at least understanding, around the case for development? Once all the complexities are waived aside, it is the ownership of decisions, and understanding of those decisions, that the new politics of planning seeks to achieve at the neighbourhood level. If greater connectivity between politicians, professionals and communities can be achieved, then the new neighbourhood planning will have made great strides towards a less combative politics of local development.

But early evidence, some gathered during the course of this study and some from other analyses, is not entirely positive. There is insufficient focus, within the architecture of neighbourhood plans, on everyday connectivity between community groups and planning professionals. Despite inferences to a more open system in which officials engage more readily with residents (DBIS, 2010), it is not clear how this will happen, or whether it will simply be a matter of communities continuing to form chance relationships with a few sympathetic and proactive officers. True to the model of meta-governance, neighbourhood planning groups have been handed new responsibilities in a context of strictly defined principles. Their plans must be compliant with those of the principal authority. In a legal, regulatory sense, neighbourhood plans will be integrated into a hierarchy of frameworks (neighbourhood, local and national) in a way that was perhaps unimaginable a few years ago. But the process of neighbourhood planning will not necessarily bring communities closer to professionals. There is no new partnership, but rather continuing subservience to political and planning interest: the leader–follower relationship will in many cases be as grudging or as unwilling as ever, especially where communities are handed the power – or rather, the responsibility – to 'sanction' significant levels of house building by incorporating it into their own plans. Their 'choices' will frequently be limited to accepting developments that, in the past, would have been flatly rejected and then concentrating on negotiating changes in detail. Of course, this rejection will still be apparent in the probable failure of many areas to agree a neighbourhood plan. Residents simply will not wish to be complicit in making decisions they do not support. Rather than bringing a belief in local ownership of the planning system, the move to neighbourhood plans is likely to expose – in many communities – a frustrated desire to set principles, and to plan, rather than to simply colour in the detail. Is this frustration inevitable? In some places, it probably is, but elsewhere a greater investment of time in working with communities, at planning's 'critical interface', may have a chance of forestalling some of these problems. Planning is certainly about leadership, but leadership is not simply about establishing principles and frameworks, and thereafter enforcing compliance. It is also about working closely with communities towards a common understanding – this means good communication.

When a system of neighbourhood planning was being debated in Parliament, it was viewed by many as a cost-saving exercise, bringing an army of volunteers onto the front line of planning practice. But good neighbourhood planning is expensive, although this expense is not necessarily incurred within neighbourhoods themselves. Considerable investment of time and resources is needed within local government. One of the lessons of parish planning is that the closed, inaccessible local authority can become a focus of mistrust. And when mistrust is allowed to spread, even apparently innocuous development decisions may spark an adverse reaction. Dialogue is essential, and good neighbourhood planning is absolutely dependent on it.

What of the plans themselves? There was some early concern that their restricted land-use focus would limit community interest (Bishop, 2011, p 73; Woodin, 2011, p 78). A clear reality of parish plans was

presentation

that they were not really plans at all, in a land-use sense. They were closer in form to community strategies, although their links to these strategies were either weak or more usually non-existent. The broadness of their focus was often reflected in the broadness of interest in them. Despite some plans being produced by only a few individuals, with little wider community buy-in, many more were the products of extensive participation, often facilitated by support groups and through extensive village appraisals) Early advice on the form of neighbourhood plans (DCLG, 2011, pp 17-18) gave them a role in setting planning objectives, understanding the planning context, promoting projects and infrastructure priorities, development management, setting site-specific policies for housing, economic development and environmental issues, and sometimes changing the coverage of planning designations. The accent was placed very much on land use, but with some connectivity to context. On the one hand, the narrower field of vision of neighbourhood plans may be a demotivating factor for some potential participants, but the key-in to projects and infrastructure, means that the door remains open to a range of community issues that previously had a home in older plans. But parish and neighbourhood plans are miles apart in other respects: the former were primarily a catalyst and focus for community action. Few people expected a clear programme of action to follow the publication of a parish plan. They were seldom adopted into planning frameworks, and the small trickle that were, dried up completely after 2004 when all 'supplementary' planning documents became subject to protracted sustainability appraisal. But still, communities continued to bring forward parish plans, to use them as a basis for lobbying authorities and service providers, and as internal documents with a pivotal role in auditing local capacity and marshalling voluntary effort around those projects the community considered important. Neighbourhood plans will be judged against different measures of success. There is an expectation of influence, even if principles and real 'planning objectives' are)beyond a community's control Government has stepped in to say what is and what is not permissible. A silent contract has been drawn up, and expectations have been raised. Few people expect these plans themselves to trigger significant rethinks of strategy – although some decisions will continue to be challenged and changed by the weight of local feeling – but there is an expectation of influence over the quality of development and the way in which new funding, including monies generated through an 'infrastructure levy' and a 'homes bonus', are spent. Whether the impact of the plans is slight or locally significant, there is a clear expectation of impact that was absent with many parish plans.

Finally, neighbourhood plans must be viewed in the context of the democratic renewal sought by government. They form part of the present government's pledge to emphasise participation and move from 'state action to social action' (Conservative Party, 2010b, p viii), partly by rolling back the state, but also by establishing new forms of community governance. The study in Ashford focused wholly on rural and urban-edge 'parished' communities, although some references were made to non-parished urban neighbourhoods with their residents' associations and networks. During the passage of the Localism Bill through Parliament in 2011, many groups praised parish councils as an accountable and democratic form of community governance, contrasting these credentials with the limitations of 'neighbourhood forums' set up by a minimum of three people.[1] But the seemingly narrow interests that are able, in theory, to establish a forum are also found in some parish councils. Turnout at parish elections is notoriously low, with more members sometimes being co-opted onto councils than are actually elected. These structures do not provide a solid base on which to build any democratic renewal – a point on which the vast majority of commentators on this subject now agree. The neighbourhood planning agenda is flawed in many respects, but it may at least prompt new interest in public engagement. If this happens, then having the right community structures in place becomes critical. These must be inclusive structures, constituted to expand participation in the planning process, delivering genuine community leadership (ie, a *legitimacy* to lead). There will need to be investment in this process, from support groups and from local authorities. The support groups must be seen to bring an independent perspective to the process, being on no-one's 'side'. The interests of planning professionals will be assumed from the start but if experience with parish plans provides any lessons, it demonstrates that the communicative authority – which invests officer time in working with community groups rather than viewing engagement as a burden – is more likely to gain trust, and its officers and politicians will be better placed to perform their leadership roles. Planning's role in leading change must not be understated or obscured behind vague references to community ownership. Communities must acquire a stake in a much broader public good, accepting that the right policies and the right decisions do not always accord with narrow vested interest. Only then will the apparatus of neighbourhood planning, in whatever form it takes in the short to long term, be judged a success.

Note

[1] This figure was increased to 21 during the passage of the Localism Bill through Parliament.

References

ABC (Ashford Borough Council) (2008) *Local Development Framework: Adopted Core Strategy*, Ashford: ABC.

ABC (2010) *Tenterden and Rural Sites Development Plan Document*, Ashford: ABC.

ABC (no date) *Consultation Portal*, http://ashford-consult.limehouse. co.uk/portal/, accessed 19 November 2009.

Aldridge, M. (1979) *The British New Towns: A Programme Without a Policy*, London: Routledge.

Allmendinger, P. and Tewdwr-Jones, M. (2002) 'The communicative turn in urban planning: unravelling pragmatic, imperialistic and moralistic dimensions', *Space and Polity*, 6, 1, pp 5-24.

Ansell, C. and Gash, A. (2007) 'Collaborative governance in theory and in practice', *Journal of Public Administration Research and Theory*, 18, pp 543-71.

Bailey, N. (2003) 'Local strategic partnerships in England: the continuing search for collaborative advantage, leadership and strategy in urban governance', *Planning Theory and Practice*, 3, pp 443-57.

Baker, M. (1998) 'Planning for the English regions: a review of the Secretary of State's regional planning guidance, *Planning Practice and Research*, 13, 2, pp 153-69.

Banner, G. (2002) 'Community governance and the new central–local relationship', *International Social Science Journal*, 54, pp 217-31.

Barker, K. (2004) *Review of Housing Supply – Securing Stability: Delivering our Future Housing Needs*, London: HM Treasury.

Barlow, Sir M. (1940) *Report of the Royal Commission on the Distribution of Industrial Population*, London: HMSO.

Barnes, J. (1954) 'Class and committees in a Norwegian island parish', *Human Relations*, 7, pp 39-58.

Baumann, G. (1996) *Contesting Culture: Discourses of Identity in Multi-Ethnic London*, Cambridge: Cambridge University Press.

BDOR (2006) *An Exciting Future for Community Plans*, A report by BDOR Limited for MCTA and SWAN, Bristol: BDOR Ltd.

BDOR (no date) *Parish Plan Case Studies*, Bristol: BDOR Ltd.

Beck, U. (1994) 'The reinvention of politics: towards a theory of reflexive modernization, in Beck, U., Giddens, A. and Lash, S. (eds) *Reflexive Modernization: Politics, Tradition and Aesthetics in Modern Social Order*, Cambridge: Polity Press.

Beem, C. (1999) *The Necessity of Politics: Reclaiming American Public Life*, Chicago, IL: University of Chicago Press.

Bishop, J. (2007) 'Plans without planners?', *Town and Country Planning*, 76, pp 340-4.

Bishop, J. (2010) 'Localism, collaborative planning and open source', *Town and Country Planning*, 79, 9, pp 376-81.

Bishop, J. (2011) 'What chance for neighbourhood plans?', *Town and Country Planning*, 80, 2, pp 72-6.

Boissenvain, J. (1979) 'Network analysis: a reappraisal', *Current Anthropology*, 20, 2, pp 392-4.

Booher, D. and Innes, J. (2002) 'Network power in collaborative planning', *Journal of Planning Education and Research*, 21, pp 221-36.

Bott, E. (1955) 'Urban families: the norms of conjugal roles', *Human Relations*, 8, pp 345-85.

Bott, E. (1957) *Family and Social Networks*, London: Tavistock Publications.

Burt, R.S. (1992) *Structural Holes: The Social Structure of Competition*, Cambridge, MA: Harvard University Press.

Burt, R.S. (2000) 'The network structure of social capital', *Research in Organizational Behaviour*, 22, pp 345-423.

Cabinet Office (2010a) *The Coalition: Our Programme for Government*, London: The Stationery Office.

Cabinet Office (2010b) *The Big Society Programme*, www.cabinetoffice. gov.uk/ sites/default/files/resources/building-big-society.pdf, accessed 23 February 2011.

Cameron, D. (2009) *Speech: The Big Society*, www.conservatives.com / News/Speeches/2009/11/David_Cameron_The_Big_Society.aspx, accessed 10 January 2011.

Carley, M., Chapman, M., Hastings, A., Kirk, K. and Young, R. (2000) *Urban Regeneration through Partnership: A Study in Nine Urban Regions in England, Scotland and Wales*, Bristol: Policy Press.

Carter, J. (2004) 'Capitalism in the raw (or how the death of socialism made anti-capitalists of us all)', in Morland, D. and Cowling, M. (eds) *Political Issues for the Twenty-First Century* (pp 47-70), Aldershot: Ashgate.

Castells, M. (2000) *The Rise of the Network Society: Volume 1 – The Information Age: Economy, Society and Culture* (2nd edition), Oxford: Blackwell.

Chaskin, R.J., Brown, P., Venkatesh, S. and Vidal, A. (2001) *Building Community Capacity*, New York, NY: Aldine De Gruyter.

Clark, D., Southern, R. and Beer, J. (2007) 'Rural governance, community empowerment and the new institutionalism: a case study of the Isle of Wight', *Journal of Rural Studies*, 23, 2, pp 254-66.

Clegg, S. (1989) *Frameworks of Power*, London: Sage Publications.

Cloke, P., Milbourne, P. and Widdowfield, R. (2000) 'Partnership and policy networks in rural local governance: homelessness in Taunton', *Public Administration*, 78, 1, pp 111-33.

Coaffee, J. (2005) 'New localism and the management of regeneration', *International Journal of Public Sector Management*, 18, 2, pp 108-13.

Coaffee, J. and Headlam, N. (2008) 'Pragmatic localism uncovered: the search for locally contingent solutions to national reform agendas', *Geoforum*, 39, 4, pp 1585-99.

Cohen, A.P. (1985) *The Symbolic Construction of Community*, London: Routledge.

Coleman, J.S. (1990) *Foundations of Social Theory*, Cambridge, MA: Harvard University Press.

Coleman, J.S. (1994) 'A vision for sociology', *Society*, 32, pp 29-34.

Conservative Party (2008) *A Stronger Society: Voluntary Action in the 21st Century*, London: Conservative Party.

Conservative Party (2009) *Control Shift: Returning Power to Local Communities*, London: Conservative Party.

Conservative Party (2010a) *Open Source Planning: The Conservative Planning Green Paper*, London: Conservative Party.

Conservative Party (2010b) *Invitation to Join the Government of Britain: The Conservative Manifesto 2010*, Uckfield: Pureprint Group.

Corry, D. and Stoker, G. (2002) *New Localism: Refashioning the Centre–Local Relationship*, London: NLGN.

Corry, D., Hatter, W., Parker, I., Randle, A. and Stoker, G. (2004) *Joining-Up Local Democracy: Governance Systems for the New Localism*, London: NLGN.

Countryside Agency (2003) *Parish Plans and the Planning System: Guidance and Advice for Local Planning Authorities*, Cheltenham: Countryside Agency.

Countryside Agency (2004) *What Makes a Good Parish Plan?*, Cheltenham: Countryside Agency.

CPRE (Campaign to Protect Rural England) (2007) 'Will the South East Plan deliver sustainable development?', Press Release, 16 August, www.cpre.org.uk/news/view/425, accessed 18 October 2009.

Dahl, R.A. (1989) *Democracy and its Critics*, New Haven, CT: Yale University Press.

Davies, J.S. (2008) 'Double-devolution or double-dealing? The local government White Paper and the Lyons Review', *Local Government Studies*, 34, 1, pp 3-22.

DBIS (Department for Business, Innovation and Skills) (2010) *Local Growth: Realising Every Place's Potential*, London: DBIS.

DCLG (Department for Communities and Local Government (2004) *Community Involvement in Planning: The Government's Objectives*, London: DCLG

DCLG (2006) *Strong and Prosperous Communities: Local Government White Paper*, London: DCLG.

DCLG (2007a) *Homes for the Future: More Affordable, More Sustainable*, London: The Stationery Office.

DCLG (2007b) *Planning for a Sustainable Future*, London: The Stationery Office.

DCLG (2008a) *Communities in Control: Real People, Real Power*, London: DCLG.

DCLG (2008b) *Community Power Pack: Real People, Real Power*, London: DCLG.

DCLG (2009a) *Communities in Control: Real People, Real Power – Government Response to the Improving Local Accountability Consultation*, London: DCLG.

DCLG (2009b) *Communities Progress Report*, London: DCLG.

DCLG (2010) *Press Notice: Planning Power from Town Hall and Whitehall to Local People*, London: DCLG.

DCLG (2011) *Supporting Communities and Neighbourhoods in Planning: Prospectus*, London: DCLG.

DCLG and BERR (Department for Business, Enterprise and Regulatory Reform) (2008) *Prosperous Places: Taking Forward the Review of Sub National Economic Development and Regeneration*, London: DCLG and BERR.

Dennis, N. (1972) *Public Participation and Planners' Blight*, London: Faber and Faber.

DETR and MAFF (Department for the Environment, Transport and the Regions and Ministry for Agriculture, Food and Fisheries) (2000) *Our Countryside: The Future: A Fair Deal for Rural England*, London: DETR and MAFF.

Doak, J. and Parker, G. (2005) 'Meaningful space? The challenge and meaning of participation and new spatial planning in England', *Planning Practice and Research*, 20, 1, pp 23-40.

DoE (Department of the Environment) (1971) *Memorandum on Part I of the Town and Country Planning Act 1968, Circular 44/71*, London: HMSO.

DoE (1989) *The Future of Development Plans: White Paper*, London: HMSO.

DoE (1992) *PPG12 Development Plans and Regional Planning Guidance*, London: HMSO.

DoE (1994) *RPG9: Regional Planning Guidance for the South East*, London: HMSO.

DTLR (Department for Transport, Local Government and the Regions) (1998) *Modern Local Government: In Touch with the People*, London: HMSO.

Ellis, H. (2011) 'Questions of far-reaching reform', *Town and Country Planning*, 80, 1, pp 15-20.

Falk, I. and Kilpatrick, S. (2000) 'What is social capital? A study of interaction in a rural community', *Sociologia Ruralis*, 40, 1, pp 87-110.

Featherstone, M. (1990) 'Global culture: an introduction', *Theory, Culture & Society*, 7, 2, pp 1-14.

Field, J. (2003) *Social Capital*, London: Routledge.

Flyvberg, B. (1998) *Rationality and Power: Democracy in Practice*, Chicago, IL: University of Chicago Press.

Forester, J. (1989) *Planning in the Face of Power*, Berkeley, CA: University of California Press.

Forester, J. (1999) *The Deliberative Practitioner: Encouraging Participatory Planning Processes*, Cambridge, MA: MIT Press.

Foucault, M. (1980) 'The confession of the flesh, in Gordon, C. (ed) *Power/Knowledge*, New York, NY: Pantheon Books.

Foucault, M. (1982) 'The subject and power', *Critical Inquiry*, 8, 4, pp 777-95.

Friedkin, N.E. (1980) 'A test of structural features of Granovetter's Strength of Weak Ties theory', *Social Networks*, 2, pp 411-22.

Fung, A. and Wright, E. (eds) (2003) *Deepening Democracy: Institutional Innovations in Empowered Participatory Governance*, London: Verso.

Futrell, R. (2003) 'Framing processes, cognitive liberation, and NIMBY protest in the U.S: chemical-weapon disposal conflict', *Sociological Inquiry*, 73, pp 359-86.

Gallent, N., Hamiduddin, I. and Madeddu, M. (2011) 'Selecting and allocating sites for housing development: politics, expedient sites, regional planning and localism, in *FiBRE Series*, London: RICS Education Trust.

Gallent, N., Morphet, J. and Tewdwr-Jones, M. (2008) 'Parish plans and the spatial planning approach in England', *Town Planning Review*, 79, 1, pp 1-27.

Giddens, A. (1998) *The Third Way: The Renewal of Social Democracy*, Cambridge: Polity Press.

Giddens, A. (2000) *The Third Way and its Critics*, Cambridge: Polity Press.

Gilg, A.W. (2005) *Planning in Britain: Understanding and Evaluating the Post-War System*, London: Sage Publications.

GOSE (Government Office for the South East) (2009) *The South East Plan (South East Regional Spatial Strategy)*, Guildford: GOSE.

Granovetter, M. (1973) 'The strength of weak ties', *American Journal of Sociology*, 78, pp 1360-80.

Habermas, J. (1984) *The Theory of Communicative Action: Part 1: Reason and the Rationalization of Society*, Boston, MA: Beacon.

Halcrow/ABC (Ashford Borough Council) (2002) *Ashford's Future: Ashford's Capacity – A Handbook for Change*, Ashford: ABC.

Hall, P. (1999) 'The regional dimension, in Cullingworth, J.B. (ed) *British Planning: 50 Years of Urban and Regional Policy*, London: Athelone Press.

Haughton, G. and Counsell, D. (2004) *Regions, Spatial Strategies and Sustainable Development*, London: Routledge.

Healey, P. (1997) *Collaborative Planning: Shaping Places in Fragmented Societies*, Basingstoke: Macmillan.

Healey, P. (1999) 'Deconstructing communicative planning theory: a reply to Allmendinger and Tewdwr-Jones', *Environment and Planning A: Environment and Planning*, 31, pp 1129-35.

Held, D. (2003) 'Cosmopolitanism: globalization tamed?', *Review of International Studies*, 29, 4, pp 465-80.

Hewson, D. (2007) *Saved: How an English Village Fought for its Survival, and Won*, Leicester: Troubador Publishing.

Holman, N. (2008) 'Community participation: using social network analysis to improve developmental benefits', *Environment and Planning C: Government and Policy*, 26, 3, pp 525-43.

Innes, J. (1995) 'Planning theory's emerging paradigm: communicative action and interactive practice', *Journal of Planning Education and Research*, 14, pp 183-9.

Innes, J. (2004) 'Consensus building: clarifications for the critics', *Planning Theory*, 3, 1, pp 5-20.

Innes, J. and Booher, D. (1999) 'Consensus building and complex adaptive systems: a framework for evaluating collaborative planning', *Journal of the American Planning Association*, 65, 4, pp 412-23.

Innes, J. and Booher, D. (2000) *Collaborative Dialogue as a Policy-Making Strategy*, Berkeley, CA: Institute of Urban and Regional Development, University of California.

Innes, J. and Booher, D. (2003) *The Impact of Collaborative Planning on Governance Capacity*, Berkeley, CA: Institute of Urban and Regional Development, University of California.

Innes, J. and Booher, D. (2004) 'Reframing public participation: strategies for the 21st century', *Planning Theory and Practice*, 5, 4, pp 419-36.

Innes, J. and Gruber, M. (2001) *Planning Styles in Conflict at the San Francisco Bay Area's Metropolitan Transport Commission*, Berkeley, CA: Institute of Urban and Regional Development, University of California.

Jacobsson, B. and Sundström, G. (2007) *Governing State Agencies: Transformations in the Swedish Administrative Model*, Stockholm: Stockholms centrum för forskning om offentlig sektor.

Jessop, B. (2003) 'Governance and metagovernance: on reflexivity, requisite variety, and requisite irony', in Bang, H. (ed) *Governance, as Social and Political Communication*, Manchester: Manchester University Press.

John, P. (1990) '*Recent Trends in Central–Local Government Relations*, London: PSI.

Jones, A. (2007) 'New wine in old bottles? England's parish and town councils and New Labour's neighbourhood experiment', *Local Economy*, 22, pp 227-42.

Kent Online (2006) 'Heavyweight protagonists clash over future of Ashford', *Kent Online*, 3 October, www.kentonline.co.uk/kentonline/newsarchive.aspx?articleid=28705, accessed 20 November 2009.

Lowe, P. and Ward, N. (2007) 'Rural futures: a socio-graphical approach to scenario analysis', Paper presented at the Institute for Advanced Studies Annual Research Programme, Lancaster University, UK, 9-10 January.

Lowndes, V. (2001) 'Rescuing Aunt Sally: taking institutional theory seriously in urban politics', *Urban Studies*, 38, 11, pp 1953-71.

Lukes, S. (1974) *Power: A Radical View*, Basingstoke: Macmillan.

Lyons, M. (2007) *Place-Shaping: A Shared Ambition for the Future of Local Government: Executive Summary*, London: The Stationery Office.

McEvily, B. and Zaheer, A. (1999) 'Bridging ties: a source of firm heterogeneity in competitive capabilities', *Strategic Management Journal*, 20, 12, pp 1133-56.

McNamara, P. and Trumbull, D. (2007) *An Evolutionary Psychology of Leader–Follower Relations*, New York, NY: Nova.

Manor, J. (1999) *The Political Economy of Democratic Decentralisation*, Washington, DC: World Bank.

Marsh, D. and Rhodes, R. (1992) 'Policy networks in British government: a critique of existing approaches', in Marsh, D. and Rhodes, R. (eds) *Policy Networks in British Government*, Oxford: Clarendon Press.

Marsh, D., Toke, D., Belfrage, C., Tepe, D. and McGough, S. (2009) 'Policy networks and the distinction between insider and outsider groups: the case of the Countryside Alliance', *Public Administration*, 87, 3, pp 621-38.

Mersham with Sevington Parish Council (2006) *Mersham with Sevington Parish Council's Comments Made In Response To Core Strategy Submission Document*, www.mershamwithsevingtonpc.kentparishes.gov.uk/userfiles/File/corestrategynotes.doc, accessed 18 November 2009.

Ministry of Justice (2007) *The Governance of Britain Green Paper*, London: The Stationery Office.

Misztal, B.A. (1996) *Trust in Modern Societies: The Search for the Bases of Social Order*, Cambridge: Polity Press.

Mitchell, G.D. (1951) 'The parish council and the rural community', *Public Administration*, 29, 4, pp 393-401.

Moreno, J. (1934) *Who Shall Survive? Nervous and Mental Disease*, New York, NY: Beacon Press.

Morphet, J. (2004a) 'The new localism', *Town and Country Planning*, 73, 10, pp 291-3.

Morphet, J. (2004b) *RTPI: Scoping Paper on Integrated Planning*, London: Royal Town Planning Institute.

Morphet, J., Tewdwr-Jones, M., Gallent, N., Spry, M., Hall, B. and Howard, R. (2007) *Shaping and Delivering Tomorrow's Places: Report, Findings and Recommendations*, London: Royal Town Planning Institute.

Moseley, M. (1997) 'Parish appraisals as a tool of rural community development: an assessment of the British experience', *Planning Practice and Research*, 12, 3, pp 197-212.

Moseley, M. (2000a) 'Innovation and rural development: some lessons from Britain and Western Europe', *Planning Practice and Research*, 15, 1-2, pp 95-115.

Moseley, M. (2000b) 'England's village services in the late 1990s: entrepreneurialism, community involvement and the state, *Town Planning Review*, 71, 4, pp 415-33.

Moseley, M. (2002) 'Bottom-up village action plans: some experience in rural England', *Planning Practice and Research*, 17, 4, pp 387-405.

Mulgan, G. and Bury, F. (2006) *Double Devolution: The Renewal of Local Government*, London: Smith Institute.

Nadin, V. (2007) 'The emergence of the spatial planning approach in England', *Planning Practice and Research*, 22, pp 43-62.

Newby, H. (1979) *Green and Pleasant Land? Social Change in Rural England*, London: Hutchinson.

Newman, J. (2007) 'Rethinking "the public" in troubled times: unsettling state, nation and the liberal public sphere', *Public Policy and Administration*, 22, pp 27-47.

NHF (National Housing Federation) (2009) *Home Truths 2009: How the Recession has Increased Housing Need – South East*, Bristol: NHF.

ODPM (Office of the Deputy Prime Minister) (2001a) *Planning Green Paper – Planning: Delivering a Fundamental Change*, London: The Stationery Office.

ODPM (2001b) *Strong Local Leadership – Quality Public Services*, London: The Stationery Office.

ODPM (2003) *Sustainable Communities: Building for the Future*, London: The Stationery Office.

ONS (Office for National Statistics) (2001) *Neighbourhood Statistics*, Cardiff: ONS, www.neighbourhood.statistics.gov.uk/dissemination/, accessed 19 November 2009.

ONS (2007) *Indices of Deprivation 2007: Local Authority Summaries*, Cardiff: ONS, www.neighbourhood.statistics.gov.uk/dissemination/, accessed 19 November 2009.

ONS (2008) *Regional Gross Value Added (GVA)*, Cardiff: ONS, www.statistics.gov.uk/downloads/theme_economy/NUTS1-2-3.pdf, accessed 7 September 2009.

ONS (2009) *Worklessness: Summary Statistics Neighbourhood Statistics*, Cardiff: ONS, www.neighbourhood.statistics.gov.uk/dissemination/, accessed 19 November 2009.

Oppenheim, C., Cox, E. and Platt, R. (2010) *Regeneration through Co-operation: Creating a Framework for Communities to Act Together*, Manchester: Co-operatives UK.

Owen, S. (1998) 'The role of village design statements in fostering a locally-distinctive approach to village planning and design in the UK', *Journal of Urban Design*, 3, pp 359-80.

Owen, S. (1999) 'Village design statements: some aspects of the evolution of a planning tool in the UK', *Town Planning Review*, 70, pp 41-59.

Owen, S. (2002a) 'From village design statements to parish plans: some pointers towards community decision-making in the planning system in England', *Planning Practice and Research*, 17, pp 81-9.

Owen, S. (2002b) 'Locality and community: towards a vehicle for community-based decision-making in rural localities in England', *Town Planning Review*, 73, 1, pp 41-61.

Owen, S. and Moseley, M. (2003) 'Putting parish plans in their place: relationships between community based initiatives and development planning in English villages', *Town Planning Review*, 74, 4, pp 445-71.

Owen, S., Moseley, M. and Courtney, P. (2007) 'Bridging the gap: an attempt to reconcile strategic planning and very local community-based planning in rural England', *Local Government Studies*, 33, pp 49-76.

Pahl, R. (1975) *Whose City? And Further Essays on Urban Society*, London: Penguin Books.

Panelli, R. (2006) 'Rural society, in Cloke, P., Marsden, T. and Mooney, P. (eds) *Handbook of Rural Studies* (pp 63-90), London: Sage Publications.

Parsons, T. (1963) 'On the concept of political power', *Proceedings of the American Philosophical Society*, 107, 3, pp 232-62.

Pollitt, C. (1990) *Managerialism and the Public Services: The Anglo-American Experience*, Oxford: Blackwell.

Pollitt, C., Talbot, C., Caulfield, J. and Smullen, A. (2004) *Agencies: How Governments do Things through Semi-Autonomous Organizations*, Basingstoke: Palgrave.

Putnam, R. (2000) *Bowling Alone: The Collapse and Revival of American Community*, New York: Simon & Schuster.

Raco, M. (2007) *Building Sustainable Communities: Spatial Policy and Labour Mobility in Post-War Britain*, Bristol: The Policy Press.

Raco, M., Parker, G. and Doak, J. (2006) 'Reshaping spaces of local governance? Community strategies and the modernisation of local government in England', *Environment and Planning C: Government and Policy*, 24, pp 475-96.

Rhodes, R.A.W. (1997) 'Governing without government: order and change in British politics', in Rhodes, R.A.W. (ed) *Understanding Governance, Reflexivity and Accountability* (pp 3-25), Buckingham: Open University Press.

RTPI (Royal Town Planning Institute) (2001) *A New Vision for Planning*, London: RTPI.

Rushkoff, D. (2009) *Open Source Democracy*, London: Demos.

Scharpf, F. (1999) *Governing in Europe: Effective and Democratic?*, Oxford: Oxford University Press.

SEEDA (South East England Development Agency) (2006) *Regional Economic Strategy*, Guildford: SEEDA.

Skeffington Report (1969) *Report of the Committee on Public Participation in Planning: People and Planning*, London: HMSO.

Smith, A. (2008) 'Flint sticks to 240,000 homes target', *Building*, 17 June.

Somerville, P. (2005) 'Community governance and democracy', *Policy & Politics*, 33, 1, pp 117-44.

Sørensen, E. and Torfing, J. (2008) 'Theoretical approaches to democratic network governance', in Sørensen, E. and Torfing, J. (eds) *Theories of Democratic Network Governance* (pp 233-46), Basingstoke: Palgrave Macmillan.

SQW Consulting (2007) *Integration of Parish Plans into the Wider Systems of Government*, London: DEFRA.

Stoker, G. (1998) 'Governance as theory: five propositions', *International Social Science Journal*, 50, 155, pp 17-28.

Stoker, G. (2002) 'Life is a lottery: New Labour's strategy for the reform of devolved governance', *Public Administration*, 80, pp 417-34.

Stoker, G. (2004) *Transforming Local Governance: From Thatcherism to New Labour*, Basingstoke: Palgrave.

Stoker, G. (2007) *New Localism, Participation and Networked Community Governance*, Manchester: University of Manchester/Institute for Political and Economic Governance.

Tewdwr-Jones, M. (2002) *The Planning Polity: Planning, Government and the Policy Process*, London: Routledge.

Tewdwr-Jones, M. (2004) 'Spatial planning: principles, practices and cultures', *Journal of Planning Law*, 16, 1, pp 204-16.

Tewdwr-Jones, M. and Allmendinger, P. (2007) 'Regional institutions, governance and the planning system', in Dimitriou, H.T. and Thompson, R. (eds) *Strategic Planning for Regional Development in the UK*, London: Routledge.

Tewdwr-Jones, M., Morphet, J. and Allmendinger, P. (2006) 'The contested strategies of local governance: community strategies, development plans and local government modernisation', *Environment and Planning A: Environment and Planning*, 38, pp 533-51.

Thatcher, M. (1987) 'Interview', *Woman's Own*, 31 October.

Thornley, A. (1993) *Urban Planning under Thatcherism: The Challenge of the Market*, London: Routledge.

Tönnies, F. (1887) *Gemeinschaft und Gesellschaft*, Leipzig: Fues's Verlag (translated as [1988] *Community and Society*, Washington, DC: Library of Congress Publications.)

Urban Initiatives with DTZ Pieda Consulting, Alan Baxter and Associates, Turner and Townsend and Studio Engleback (2005) *Greater Ashford Development Framework, Final Masterplan Report, April 2005*, London: Urban Initiatives.

UTF (Urban Task Force) (1999) *Towards an Urban Renaissance*, London: UTF.

Warner, W. and Lunt, P. (1941) *The Social Life of a Modern Community*, New Haven, CT: Yale University Press.

Whitehead, C. (2009) 'Land supply and the planning system, in CABE (ed) *Who Should Build Our Homes? Six Experts Challenge the Status Quo* (pp 8-31), London: Commission for Architecture and the Built Environment.

Williamson, O.E. (1995) 'Transaction cost economics and organization theory', in Williamson, O.E. (ed) *Organization Theory: From Chester Barnard to the Present and Beyond* (pp 207-56), New York, NY: Oxford University Press.

Woodin, S. (2011) 'The building blocks of neighbourhood', *Town and Country Planning*, 80, 2, pp 77-81.

Woolcock, M. (1998) 'Social capital and economic development: towards a theoretical synthesis and policy framework', *Theory and Society*, 27, pp 151-208.

Wye with Hinxhill Parish Council (2009) *Re: Cheeseman's Green and Waterbrook Area Action Plan Issues and Options Report*, http://ashford. limehouse.co.uk/portal/ cplanning/tenterden_issues_and_options? pointId=181856#document-181856, accessed 18 November 2009.

Index

A

Action with Communities in Rural Kent (ACRK) 98–9, 101–2, 142–3, 154, 157–8, 160–1, 162, 185
agencification 11, 24, 25
Aldington parish 103
alliances, between parishes 103–5
Allmendinger, P. 69
AONB (Area of Outstanding Natural Beauty) 116
Appledore parish 149–50
Ashford borough 58–61
Ashford Community Network 138
Ashford Growth Area 61
  aims of study 4–6
  community-based plans 158–62
    motivating 86–90, 158
  critical interface
    impact of policy 173–6
    leaders and followers 171–2
    reciprocal relationship 167–70
    status of parishes 163–7
  direct community–local government links 123–5
    connectivity 132–3
    local authority perspective 131–2
    parish perspective 125–30
    parochialism 133–5
  intermediaries 185–6
    communication 145
    council officers 139–41, 185–6
    LSPs 138–9
    parish clerks 143–5
    support groups 141–3, 147, 185
  networked governance 77–8
  parish alliances 103–5
  parish plans
    content and form 152, 153–4
    production 90–3, 155, 164
    support and guidance 98–103, 141–3, 147, 153–4
    use and utility 154–8
  value and weight 149–52
  parishes studied 79–81
  role of parish clerks 97–8
  role of parish councils 95–6
  strategic planning context 55–7, 67
authenticity 71, 76, 167

B

Barlow Report (1940) 53
Barnes, J. 75
BDOR study 117–18
Bethersden parish 101, 103, 152
Big Society 29–31, 46
Bilsington parish 80–1, 96, 101, 103, 149–50
Bishop, J. 38, 39
bonding 111–12, 114, 118–19
Booher, D. 71
borough councillors 124, 146
Bott, E. 75
bottom-only approach 49
bottom-up planning 49
bridging 109–11, 121–2, 146–7, 181–2, 184–6
  and plan making 117–18
  practicalities of 114–15
  role in capacity building 110, 111–12
  to reconcile tensions 112–13
  unintended 123
  see also intermediaries
brokers see intermediaries
Burt, R.S. 110

C

Campaign to Protect Rural England (CPRE) 101
capacity 71–3
  role of bridging 110, 111–12

see also alliances; parish clerks;
  support and guidance
Charing parish 80, 103, 169
Cheeseman's Green 64, 65, 66
Chilmington Green 63–4
co-option 91, 92, 182
coercion 76, 167, 169, 186
Coleman, J.S. 75
collaborative democracy 31
collaborative governance 13, 69
collaborative planning 69–71
  critiques of 75–7
communication, types of 144–5
communicative action 69–70
communities
  motivation for action 79–80, 86–90,
    158, 182
  as participants or recipients 163–7
  participation in parish councils
    84–6
  place of parish councils in 83, 85–6,
    95–6, 134–5, 136, 147, 182–3, 186
  relationship with policy
    professionals *see* community–
    policy interface
  role in policy making 3–4, 13–14,
    30, 172–6, 189
    community-based plans 45,
      112–13
    legislation 14–16
    spatial planning 16–19
  see also Ashford Growth Area;
    interest groups; sociodemographic
    profiles
Communities in Control (White Paper)
  33
Communities Plan 56, 164
community dynamics 79
  see also parish councils; parishes
community governance 14–15, 198
  networked community governance
    28–9, 77–8
  and strategic planning 3–4, 21
  see also parish councils
community groups, variety of 82–3
Community Strategies 15, 118, 138,
  139, 159, 173, 183
community-based planning
  aims and benefits of 14, 181, 186–7
  definition viii
  evolution of 40–4
  and local policy 48–9
  motivating and mobilising 86–90,
    135, 158, 182
  rhetoric and reality 34–5

and strategic planning 45, 112–13,
  117–18, 120
support for *see* support and guidance
see also neighbourhood planning;
  parish planning
community-based plans
  evolution of 158–62
  see also neighbourhood development
    plans; parish plans; village design
    statements
community–policy interface 11–12,
  49, 77–8
  direct links 114, 121, 123–5, 135–6
  connectivity 132–3, 183–4
  local authority views 131–2
  parish views 67, 125–30
  parochialism 133–5
  framework reform 26, 172–6
  intermediaries *see* bridging;
    intermediaries
  leaders and followers 170, 171–2
  in neighbourhood planning 176–7,
    195–6
  participants or recipients 163–7
  plan making 115–21
  reciprocal relationship 167–70
  tension 112–13, 119, 191
commuter areas 59, 87
connectivity 37, 132–3, 182, 183–5,
  195–6
  see also networks; support and
    guidance
consensual power 73, 76, 109
consultation 126, 129–30, 140,
  164–5, 184
Control Shift (Green Paper) 31
Core Strategy 61–4, 67, 126, 133,
  164–5, 166, 173, 174
council officers
  community relations with 127, 128,
    130, 131–2, 139–41, 183–4, 185–6
  personal contacts 124–5
  views of local plans 140–1, 150–1
  see also development control officers
councillors *see* borough councillors;
  parish councillors
Countryside Agency 42–3, 115–16,
  153
CPRE (Campaign to Protect Rural
  England) 101
critical interface *see* community–
  policy interface

D

Davies, J.S. 26
democracy, and governance 113
democratic renewal 12, 13, 14–16, 198
development agencies 34, 54, 55, 56, 144–5, 166, 193
development control officers 123, 131, 133, 134, 161, 169
Development Plan Documents see DPDs
dialogue 70–1, 77, 129–30, 184
disaggregation 10, 11, 12–13
diversity
  in networks 70–1
  in society 10–11
double devolution 9, 33
DPDs (Development Plan Documents) 126, 133, 164–5, 166, 169, 173, 174

E

eco-towns 57
egocentric network analysis 75
empowerment 15, 72–3, 172–3, 195
English Heritage 101
English Rural Housing Association 142
environmental services 126
expectations 88, 125, 154, 158, 170, 174
expertise (in community-based planning) 92–3, 116, 117–18, 133–4
  see also support and guidance

F

Flyvberg, B. 76
followers 170, 171–2
Foucault, M. 73
funding bids 43, 89, 91, 126, 167
Fung, A. 13

G

gatekeepers 97, 137, 143–5, 183, 184
Giddens, A. 69
globalisation 10
governance
  and democracy 113
  see also community governance
government policy 192–5

centre-local relations 24–6, 30, 32–3
changes in 3–4, 9, 11, 21, 188–90, 191
growth agenda 19–20, 55–7
impact on 'critical interface' 172–6
local government reform 9, 10–12, 14–19, 192
on strategic planning 53–5
  see also localism
Granovetter, M. 110
Great Chart with Singleton parish 80, 81, 89, 90, 96, 127, 149–50
Greater Ashford Development Framework (GADF) 61
group dynamics, and parish councils 82–6
growth agenda 19–20, 55–7
Growth Areas 19, 56, 61
  see also Ashford Growth Area
Growth Points 57
guidance see support and guidance

H

Habermas, J. 69–70
Highways Authority 145
Holman, N. 76–7
Homes Bonus 32
house prices 55, 87
housing density and types 66
housing officers 123, 127, 132, 140, 185–6
housing supply 57, 61, 63, 64

I

individualisation 10–11
Infrastructure Planning Commission 21, 33, 175
Innes, J. 71
integrated spatial planning 16–19
integration of plans 45, 117–18, 120, 187, 196
interdependence, in networks 71
interest groups 12, 82–3
  see also communities
intermediaries 109, 121–2, 123, 137
  communication 145
  council officers as 139–41, 185–6
  local strategic partnerships (LSPs) 137, 138–9
  parish clerks as 137, 143–5, 183, 184–5

support groups as 141–3, 147, 158, 185
see also bridging
interpersonal relationships 124–5, 127, 128, 130, 132, 133–4, 139–41, 145, 183–4

K

Kent Association of Local Councils (KALC) 98, 101, 142

L

land-use planning 16–17, 187, 196–7
LDFs *see* local development frameworks
leadership 76, 170, 171–2, 182–3, 196
legislation 14–16, 17–18, 20, 54, 55
legitimacy 167, 169
leisure services 126
liberal democratic view of state 24
lobbying 123–5
  local authority perspective 131–2
  parish perspective 125–31
  and 'special relationships' 139–41
Local Area Agreements 15
Local Democracy, Economic Development and Construction Act (2009) 55
local development frameworks (LDFs) 17, 18, 20, 54, 88–9, 104, 116
local government
  planning, localism and 31–4
  reform of 9, 10–12, 14–19, 192
  relationship with central state 24–6, 30, 32–3
  see also council officers; policy professionals
Local Government Act (2000) 15
Local Government and Public Involvement in Health Act (2007) 15
Local Government and Rating Act (1997) 37
local plans 46, 47, 48–9, 53
  relationship with parish plans 45, 117–19, 120
local strategic partnerships (LSPs) 15, 16, 118, 132–3, 137, 138–9, 144, 183
localism 3, 4, 20, 23, 175–7
  and Big Society 29–31

local government, planning and 31–4
networked community governance 28–9
origins of 23–6
purpose of 26–7
and strategic planning 26, 27–8, 32, 33–4, 47
Localism Bill (2010) 32, 46
Lowe, P. 59
Lunt, P. 75

M

McEvily, B. 111
Mersham with Sevington parish 65, 66, 80, 81, 101, 103, 127
meta-governance 193–5
Modern Local Government: In Touch with the People (White Paper) 14–15
Moreno, J. 75
Moseley, M. 40

N

neighbourhood development orders 46–7
neighbourhood development plans 34, 35, 46–8
  compared with parish plans 196–7
  and local context 32, 48–9, 119, 120
  move toward 4, 158–62
  support for producing 162
neighbourhood forums 47, 186, 189, 198
neighbourhood planning 176–7, 195–8
  conditions for 34
  definition viii
  see also community-based planning; parish planning
neoliberal approach 25
network power 71–7
network-based planning 74–5
networked community governance 28–9, 77–8
networks 12, 71, 79, 194
  and parish councils 96, 100, 182
  role of parish clerks 97–8
  social networks 74–5
New Public Management 25
New Towns programme 53

O

open source approach 31
Open Source Planning (Green Paper)
 31
Opportunity Areas 57
Our Countryside (White Paper) 41
Owen, S. 40, 43–4, 113, 139

P

parish appraisals 40–1, 153
parish clerks 97–8, 124, 134, 136,
 137, 143–5, 183, 184–5
parish councillors 82, 83–4, 89, 100,
 133
parish councils 37–8, 82–6
 and community governance 14–15,
  198
 composition 83–4, 100, 133, 181
 contact between 99–100, 102, 105
 local government view of 131
 reactions to Growth Area proposals
  65
 role of 42, 47, 89–91, 146, 164, 172,
  175, 183
 support for 98–9, 101–2, 181
 views of local government 126, 127
 and wider community 83, 85–6,
  95–6, 134–5, 136, 147, 182–3, 186
parish forums 99, 128–9
parish planning 37–9, 77
 guidance and support 98–103,
  141–3, 147, 153–4, 181
parish plans
 compared with neighbourhood
  plans 196–7
 content and form 152, 153–4
 evolution of 40–4
 motivation 88–90, 187
 production of 90–3, 115–21, 155,
  164
 relationship with local plans 45,
  117–19, 120
 role of parish clerks 97–8
 use and utility of 126, 154–8
 value and weight of 149–52, 187–8
 see also village design statements
parishes 37
 alliances between 103–5
 case studies 79–81
 isolation and parochialism 102, 105,
  106, 133–5
 local government view of 131–2

 view of community-based plans
  154–6
 view of local government 67,
  125–30
 view of LSPs 138–9, 144
 see also Ashford Growth Area;
  communities
parochialism 96, 100, 102, 105,
 133–5, 192
Parsons, T. 173
participative democracy 44, 45, 70,
 194
partnership
 and leadership 171–2
 see also local strategic partnerships;
  reciprocity
personal contacts 124–5
 see also interpersonal relationships
placing 123
*Planning: Delivering a Fundamental
 Change* (Green Paper) 17
Planning Act (2008) 20, 33
Planning Aid 116
planning applications 103–4, 125–6,
 131–2, 172
Planning and Compulsory Purchase
 Act (2004) 17–18, 39, 54
planning reform
 integrated spatial planning 16–19
 localism 31–4
 reflections on 188–90
plans *see* community-based plans;
 local plans; neighbourhood
 development plans; parish plans;
 strategic planning
Pluckley parish 80, 81, 95–6, 103,
 152
policy making
 impact of societal diversity on
  10–11
 role of community in 3–4, 13–14,
  30, 172–6, 189
 community-based plans 45
 legislation 14–16
 spatial planning 16–19
policy professionals 12
 and community-based planning
  48–9, 156–7
 relationship with communities *see*
  policy–community interface
policy–community interface 11–12,
 49, 77–8
 communities as participants or
  recipients 163–7
 direct links 114, 121, 123–5, 135–6

connectivity 132–3, 183–4
local authority views 131–2
parish views 67, 125–30
parochialism 133–5
framework reform 26, 172–6
intermediaries *see* bridging;
intermediaries
leaders and followers 170, 171–2
in neighbourhood planning 176–7,
195–6
plan making 115–21
reciprocal relationship 167–70
tension 112–13, 119, 191
population *see* sociodemographic
profiles
power 9–10, 193, 194
concepts of 72–3, 76–7, 109
network power 71–7
see also empowerment; gatekeepers
privatisation 25
professionalism 92–4, 114
Putnam, R. 72, 111–12

R

reactive communities 135–6
reactive plans 158, 187
reciprocity 71, 76–7, 167–70
regional development agencies 34,
54, 55, 56, 144–5, 166, 193
Regional Development Agencies Act
(1998) 54
regional planning 31–2, 195
see also strategic planning
regional planning guidance (RPG)
17, 19, 54, 56
Regional Spatial Strategies 17–18,
20, 54, 56, 189, 193
representative democracy 44, 45, 194
responsibility 29–30, 175, 189, 194,
196
Rural Community Councils 116,
117
rural fringe 65
rural governance *see* parish councils
Rural Round Table 140

S

Scharpf, F. 194
SEEDA (South East England
Development Agency) 56, 166
Service Level Agreement (SLA) 167
Shadoxhurst 80
'smart' growth 56

social capital 27, 70, 71–4, 75,
111–12
social democratic model of state 24
social network analysis 74–5, 109,
110–11, 146
sociodemographic profiles
of borough 58–60
of parish councils 83–4, 133, 181
of parishes 80–1
South Ashford Parish Partnership
104–5
South East England Development
Agency (SEEDA) 56, 166
spatial planning 16–19, 39–40, 69,
88–9, 159, 187–8
see also Regional Spatial Strategies
'special relationships' 139–41
see also council officers
SQW Consulting 118–19
see also government policy; meta-
governance
Statement of Community
Involvement 18, 131, 133
Stoker, G. 26–7, 29
strategic planning 191–3
Ashford Growth Area proposals
61–7
and critical interface 174–5, 176
evolution of 53–5
growth agenda 19–20, 55–7
and localism 26, 27–8, 32, 33–4, 47
reconciliation with community-
based planning 45, 112–13,
117–18, 120
relationship with community
governance 3–4, 21
see also meta-governance; Regional
Spatial Strategies
*Strong Local Leadership, Quality Public
Services* (White Paper) 33
Strong and Prosperous Communities
(White Paper) 15, 33, 38–9
A Stronger Society (Green Paper) 30
structure plans 53, 54
support groups 98–9, 101–2, 141–3,
154, 157–8, 162, 181, 185
support and guidance 92–3, 98–103,
116–18, 153–4
Sustainable Communities Act (2007)
18, 33
Sustainable Community Strategies
18, 33, 118, 159

T

*Tenterden and Rural Sites Development
    Plan Document* (DPD) 126, 133,
    164–5, 166, 169, 174
Tewdwr-Jones, M. 69
traditional authority 10
transport infrastructure 65, 87
trust 128, 130, 168, 169–70
'tunnelling in' strategy 124

U

urban areas, representation of 146–7
urban extensions 61–7

V

village design statements (VDSs) 38,
    89, 152, 155–6, 160, 162
Vital Villages initiative 42

W

Ward, N. 59
Warner, W. 75
Waterbrook development 64
Weald of Kent Preservation Society
    (WKPS) 101
welfare programmes 24
wildlife habitats 65–6
Woodchurch parish 80, 96, 97
Woolcock, M. 71
Wright, E. 13
Wye College 67
Wye with Hinxhill parish 67, 80,
    95–6, 166

Z

Zaheer, A. 111